Hooked on Growth

Hooked on Growth

Economic Addictions and the Environment

Douglas E. Booth

ROWMAN & LITTLEFIELD PUBLISHERS, INC.
Lanham • Boulder • New York • Toronto • Oxford

ROWMAN & LITTLEFIELD PUBLISHERS, INC.

Published in the United States of America
by Rowman & Littlefield Publishers, Inc.
A wholly owned subsidiary of The Rowman & Littlefield Publishing Group, Inc.
4501 Forbes Boulevard, Suite 200, Lanham, Maryland 20706
www.rowmanlittlefield.com

PO Box 317, Oxford OX2 9RU, UK

British Library Cataloguing in Publication Information Available

Library of Congress Cataloging-in-Publication Data

Booth, Douglas E.
   Hooked on growth : economic addictions and the environment / Douglas E.
Booth.
      p. cm.
Includes bibliographical references and index.
   ISBN 0-7425-2717-4 (cloth : alk. paper)—ISBN 0-7425-2718-2 (pbk. : alk. paper)
   1. Economic development—Environmental aspects. 2. Consumption
(Economics)—Environmental aspects. 3. Sustainable development. 4.
Environmental responsibility. I. Title.

 HD75.6.B663 2004
 338.9'27—dc22

                                                                2003026055

Printed in the United States of America

⊗™ The paper used in this publication meets the minimum requirements of
American National Standard for Information Sciences—Permanence of Paper
for Printed Library Materials, ANSI/NISO Z39.48-1992.

To my sons, Edward and Jeremy.
May they find interesting
and joyous paths through life.

Contents

Preface

I have never been much of a shopper. If retailers had to depend on the likes of me for expanding sales, they would be in deep trouble. Whenever my computer conks out and I need a new one, the big-box retailers get a bit more business from me than usual. On my visits to these establishments, I am always struck by the frenetic pace of customer activity as well as how overly serious and almost unhappy everyone seems to be. There is a certain compulsiveness in the air. The world of shopping doesn't appear to me to be a very pleasant place. People seem to be there not so much for pleasure but because of some inner drive or need. It's almost as if shopping and buying are addictive. It is not something we want to do, but something we have to do.

In my role as an academic economist, I know that economic growth is largely driven by the consumer. Without growth in consumption, economic stagnation is the result. I also know that without growth, unemployment is bound to rise. When I put on my ecological economist hat, things look a little different. I see an ever-expanding economy operating within the confines of a stable global ecosystem. This to me spells trouble. The pressure of economic expansion within fixed ecological constraints is bound to result in significant environmental harm.

Compartmentalizing parts of our life is a strategy we all employ to navigate a complicated world. To understand larger relationships in the world we do sometimes need to make connections between areas of our life that on the surface appear to be distinct. The world of consumption and shopping is one compartment; employment and the macroeconomy is another; a third is the natural environment. Linking up these three compartments allows us to address what I think are some really interesting questions. Is an addiction to economic growth the cause of environmental decline? Can we get unhooked from growth? If we can, why would we want to? My goal in this book is to use ideas from economics, ecology, and environmental ethics to address these questions and to try to do so in terms understandable to readers who have not been previously exposed to these disciplines.

This book rides on the shoulders of truly creative thinkers such as Thorstein Veblen, Joseph Schumpeter, Aldo Leopold, and Herman Daly. To them I owe my greatest thanks. My mistakes of course can't be their fault. I also owe a debt of gratitude to an anonymous reviewer who opened my eyes to the works of certain contemporary economists who are beginning to look at the world in a new way. Finally, I want to thank my book club, The Guys Who Read Books, for taking the time to look at an earlier version of this book and for their penetrating and trenchant remarks. I especially want to thank Kate Renchin for going through the manuscript with a fine-tooth comb in search of errors and for suggesting improvements in wording.

1

Hooked on Growth:
Introduction

A n addiction to something suggests that we have to have it, yet in our more reflective moments we know we really don't want it at all, or at least we don't want to be in the position of having to have it. Can something like this be claimed for the economy as a whole? Is the economy hooked on growth? Growth is widely seen by modern society as essential to fully employ everyone and forestall economic decline. Economic expansion is popularly viewed as a birthright, a fundamental means for solving all social problems. We must have growth for social peace and progress. But does growth indeed make everyone better off, or does growth create more problems than it solves? More specifically, does economic growth damage the environment and threaten the ecological underpinnings of life itself? This is a serious issue. Are affluent societies hooked on environmentally damaging growth, and, if so, how can they be freed of this addiction? This question forms the core of this book.

THE NATURE OF ADDICTION

An individual human addiction involves a craving for something. Those who get their object of addiction experience pleasure and euphoria, but if they don't get it, they suffer discomfort at best and serious withdrawal symptoms at worst.[1] Some addictions are debilitating, and some are not. For most people, alcoholism would create serious problems. Under the influence of alcohol, most suffer from a reduction in both physical and social capacities. Drunkenness in others, from the perspective of sobriety, is unpleasant if not comic. Drunkenness is dangerous for those who insist on conducting certain ordinary functions of life, such as driving. Alcoholics generally face great difficulty leading normal lives. Debilitating addictions of the sort represented by alcoholism carry with them serious personal and social costs.[2]

Not all addictions are necessarily debilitating. Many people are addicted to caffeine in coffee or other drinks, and yet their lives suffer few if any negative consequences. For most, caffeinated coffee poses little harm. Those who don't get their coffee regularly, however, may experience withdrawal symptoms such as irritability or a headache. Nonetheless, if coffee is a part of people's daily routines, they don't suffer for it, and most find the habit quite enjoyable. There is nothing like the aroma and taste of a good cup of coffee or espresso. So some addictions are not really much of a problem.[3]

While the standard position on the phenomenon of addiction—a craving, euphoria, withdrawal, and debilitation—is widely accepted, the range of substances and behaviors that are potentially addictive is subject to debate.[4] At one end of the spectrum, addiction is treated as a strictly biochemical phenomenon induced by a drug.[5] Addiction is chemically induced and likely has a strong genetic component, according to this view. At the other end of the spectrum, the object of addiction can be "any potent experience" and involves compulsive and destructive behaviors of all kinds.[6] Such behaviors include drug addiction but extend to other activities such as overeating or compulsive gambling.[7] Addiction does not have to be chemical or physical but can extend to experiences that are strictly psychological.

In most instances, moderate indulgence in such activities as gambling or eating a good meal can bring pleasure and is not necessarily addictive. Addiction appears to be an extreme form of normal consumer behavior. In Tibor Scitovsky's view, consumption is undertaken for the purpose of moving from a state of material or social discomfort to one of comfort.[8] In the process of doing so, feelings of pleasure are experienced. Pleasure is a dynamic phenomenon associated with an act of consumption that alleviates a sense of discomfort and is not any different in kind than that experienced by the addict. Seen in this way, an addiction is an obsessive and excessive form of normal consumer behavior, and where the line between normal consumption and addiction should be drawn is unclear.[9] At some point on a behavioral spectrum the simple desire for pleasure by the consumer is transformed into the compulsive need of the addict.

SOCIAL ADDICTION AND ECONOMIC GROWTH

The process of an individual addiction is fairly easy to understand. Using addiction as an analogy in a social context is another matter. What can it mean for a society to be addicted to something? To be of any interest, a social addiction would have to have two features. First, the object of social addiction would have to be something that brings with it some kind of individual or social benefit or "euphoria" if it is consumed and some sort of individual or social withdrawal pain if it isn't. Second, some form of long-term individual or social debilitation would have to result from the addiction. The euphoria created by an addictive substance is usually immediate, while the resulting debilitation from the addiction occurs or accumulates over a longer time span.

The analogy of addiction can apply to society as a whole in various ways. The simplest would be if some phenomenon were experienced by all collectively and simultaneously and if that phenomenon were, in itself, individually addictive in the normal sense of the term for a significant portion of the population. For instance, if the acquisition of consumer goods brought forth substantial euphoria among a large number of individuals, and if the absence of such acquisition caused measurable discomfort, additions to consumption would have at least two key features of an addiction. To maintain a given level of pleasure and to avoid discomfort would require periodic additions to consumption. In the absence of long-run debilitating effects, growth in consumption would lack any adverse consequences. For consumption growth that feeds an addiction to be of any real interest, damaging effects of some sort would be necessary.

A more serious form of social addiction to consumption growth occurs if its absence results in some kind of severe social disruption. If, for example, economic growth were required to prevent the social pain of unemployment, growth would be essential for social tranquility. Society as a whole would be hooked on growth irrespective of individual addictions to growth in consumption goods purchases. This would be a more dangerous form of addiction. Without growth, people would lose their livelihoods as opposed to merely forgoing the pleasure of more consumer goods or having to experience the discomfort of unrealized consumption expectations.

For an addiction to truly matter, it must have long-term destructive consequences. If economic growth were required to either maintain the pleasure of increases in consumption or prevent the pain of unemployment, growth, like "mom and apple pie," would be universally desired. What could ever be wrong with increasing consumption and reducing unemployment? This can hardly be called an addiction. But what if growth has problems of its own? Then the addiction analogy makes some sense. Growth offers the euphoria of more consumption and avoids the withdrawal pains of higher unemployment. But if growth in itself causes problems for society over the long haul, growth can be looked at as addictive.

THE TROUBLE WITH GROWTH

The debilitating effects of growth are less immediate and more controversial than its benefits. Some argue that growth puts people on an economic treadmill that provides ever-increasing material abundance but places increased demands on the time needed to enjoy the "immaterial" pleasures of life.[10] While the economic growth treadmill may indeed cause people to miss out on much that is worthwhile, this will not be the central concern here. Instead, the key problem is this: Economic growth brings with it a significant transformation of the natural environment that is incredibly damaging to both human individuals and nonhuman species. Embedded in this statement are a number of critical issues. First, does economic growth result in environmental decline? A body of research on something called "environmental Kuznets curves" suggests otherwise.[11] Economic growth is in fact needed to bring about improvements in environmental quality, according to some researchers. As per capita income rises for a country, at first environmental quality deteriorates because of industrialization and economic development, but beyond a threshold income level environmental quality begins to improve. This occurs because of rising political demands for improvements in environmental quality by an emerging middle class and shifts in economic activity toward cleaner, more environmentally friendly industries. In the very early stages of industrial development, cities become dirtier and smokier, but later on, as industrialization brings forth affluence and a middle class that wants a cleaner environment, pollution control measures are instituted. Unfortunately, this phenomenon tends to be confined only to the most visible environmental problems, and the Kuznets curve analysis cannot be generalized to the environment as a whole.

The reasons why the Kuznets curves approach is fundamentally flawed need to be explained in detail in order to demonstrate the truth of the linkage between economic growth and environmental change. Otherwise, being hooked on growth would in fact be good for the natural environment and there would be no need for this book. Chapters 4 and 5 will be devoted to the task of demonstrating the connection between growth and environmental decline and refuting the conclusions of the Kuznets curves approach. Chapter 4 will consider the linkage between the environment and economy historically, while chapter 5 will focus on key contemporary environmental issues and how everyday economic activity alters the environment. Chapter 5 will offer evidence that global warming, the loss of natural habitat, and exotic "weedy" species are serious contemporary environmental threats driven by current patterns of consumption and economic growth.

THE NEED FOR GROWTH

If indeed economic growth is environmentally damaging, being hooked on growth matters. To be hooked on growth in the full sense of the term requires an underlying drive for economic expansion, the existence of serious withdrawal effects if growth is absent, and long-run debilitation from growth in the form of environmental decline. The underlying drive for economic growth is best understood with the help of Thorstein Veblen and Joseph Schumpeter. Veblen helps in understanding growth on the demand side of the economy, while Schumpeter helps out on the supply side, as will be shown in chapter 2.

Veblen coined the phrase "conspicuous consumption" in his classic work, *The Theory of the Leisure Class*, and described the behavior patterns underlying the desire for ever-expanding consumption.[12] While the book is over a hundred years old, it offers an analysis of consumer behavior that continues to ring true. Add to Veblen's conspicuous consumption Tibor Scitovsky's analysis of comfort and pleasure seeking in *The Joyless Economy*, and a relatively complete and compelling theory of consumer behavior emerges.[13] According to Scitovsky, as already noted, pleasure is a fleeting phenomenon attached to the movement from discomfort to comfort. To experience pleasure in the realm of consumption requires goods that provide various kinds of comforts. In the modern world, however, boredom with existing comforts is widespread, leading to the pursuit of new kinds of comforts. The result is a quest for ever-rising levels of consumer purchases. To the existing stable of comforts, people often desire to add new kinds in order to prevent their experience of pleasure from diminishing.

In his classic, *Capitalism, Socialism, and Democracy*, Joseph Schumpeter summarized the underlying driving force of growth in a capitalist economy in his phrase "creative destruction."[14] For Schumpeter, the constant entrepreneurial quest for the new and the novel keeps the capitalist engine advancing and the pleasure-seeking consumer satisfied. Schumpeter and Veblen together offer a compelling picture of the functioning of the modern capitalist economy. Add a little macroeconomics to the mix, and a convincing story can be told as to why a modern capitalist macroeconomy requires growth. Without growth or with growth below the economy's potential, as chapter 3 will demonstrate, capitalism will have difficulty creating jobs for everyone who wants to work and people will lose their livelihoods. The potential of the economy to produce expands for two basic reasons: growth in the labor force and growth in output per hour worked (labor productivity). With more potential working hours from more workers, more goods can be produced. The same is true if the output per hour worked goes up because of new technologies. Recently, the potential of the economy to produce has grown in the 3 to 4 percent range annually. If economic growth is not up to potential, fewer workers are needed and unemployment results. In short, withdrawal from growth will bring on the pain of unemployment but continuation of growth will in the long run bring on the pain of a declining natural environment. In the context of existing economic arrangements, the dilemma is this: a diminished pace of growth will bring forth fewer additions to consumption and rising unemployment, but continued rapid economic growth will perpetuate historical trends in environmental decline and the damage that goes with it. It's either the economic frying pan or the environmental fire.

GETTING UNHOOKED FROM GROWTH

This dilemma brings with it a host of additional questions. If avoiding environmental decline requires less economic growth, do citizens in modern societies desire to address the dilemma, or are they content to let the economy and the environment continue along their existing pathways? Is the public willing to put up with fewer additions to its market basket of consumer goods for the sake of limiting damage to the natural environment?

Two strategies are possible for addressing the problem of environmental deterioration. The approach of conventional environmental economics is to adjust the environment to the economy. The approach of ecological economics is, conversely, to adjust the economy to the environment. Adjusting the environment to the economy gives the economy priority; adjusting the economy to the environment gives the environment priority. Chapter 6 sets out the two approaches and the likely consequences of each for the economy and everyday life. The conventional view in standard environmental economics is to adjust the environment to the economy. Pollution emissions will be cleaned up under conventional arrangements only if the addition to social benefits from another unit of pollution control exceeds the addition to costs. Ozone smog causing pollutants will be cleaned up only to the degree that the added benefits from improved human health and well-being exceed the added costs of purchasing and operating pollution control equipment. This approach uses economic standards to choose the extent of environmental regulation. To put it differently, the environment is adjusted to the economy using economic criteria.

The approach of ecological economics is to take the protection of the environment as a given and adjust the economy to the environment. Ecological criteria and environmental health standards are fixed and pollution emissions are restricted so as to meet those standards. If the maximum concentration of ozone consistent with decent human health is .08 parts per million, then caps ensuring that the health standard is met would be set on the amount of ozone-causing pollutants. Businesses and consumers would then have to meet emission limits set by the caps irrespective of costs.

The approach of ecological economics is potentially more restrictive than the approach of conventional environmental economics. Under ecological economics, the productivity of environmental resource use will establish the amount of economic growth that is possible. If, for instance, an absolute limit on energy consumption results because of the need to use scarce renewable energy resources (such as solar) in order to avoid the problem of global warming, then the economy can be expanded only to the degree that the amount of economic output per unit of energy use can be increased. This would result in an environmentally determined speed limit on economic growth that is likely below the rate of growth needed to prevent rising unemployment. If this is the case, how can the problem of unemployment be addressed in an environmentally friendly, slow-growth economy? To get unhooked from growth, the withdrawal pains of unemployment somehow need to be avoided. This will require a new kind of macroeconomic policy and, perhaps, even reforms in the motivations and structure of business institutions. Briefly, as the labor force expands and as each worker becomes more productive, the work of producing output that is limited by environmental constraints will somehow have to be spread over more people to avoid layoffs. One way of accomplishing this is to shorten the length of the workweek for all. All this will be given detailed treatment in chapter 6, as will the question of what life would be like in everyday terms in a world where the economy is adjusted to the needs of the natural environment instead of the reverse.

Whether societies choose to get unhooked from environmentally damaging economic growth ultimately depends on the values and commitments of their citizens. Different levels of commitment to preservation of the natural environment imply different approaches. If individuals see the environment in strictly instrumental terms as valuable for what it can do for them personally, then they will most likely be interested in adjusting the environment to the economy. The environment in this view would be simply a means to the attainment of economic ends. If individuals see nature as valuable for its own sake, then they will most likely be interested in adjusting the economy to the environment. The natural environment in this view would be more than just a means to an end; it would be an end in itself. Values are important in determining what is to be done.

Establishing the philosophical underpinnings of environmental values and assessing the reality of public attitudes toward the natural environment will be the task of chapter 7. Most environmental philosophers look to Aldo Leopold's "land ethic" as the inaugurating work of their discipline.[15] Leopold saw ethics in both historical and social terms. Historically, ethical standards evolve and alter their coverage. Socially, ethics rest upon membership in the community. Just as ethics evolved historically to include Odysseus's slave girls, it can evolve to include the land. "The land ethic simply enlarges the boundaries of the community to include soils, waters, plants, and animals, or collectively the land." Moreover, according to Leopold, "a land ethic changes the role of *Homo sapiens* from conqueror of the land-community to plain member and citizen of it." To admit the world of nature to a widening circle of ethical concern suggests a human capacity for empathy with nonhuman life and the scientific recognition that human beings are the product of evolutionary processes along with all other species. What is valued by a society depends on both human passions and understandings, and both of these are altered and shaped by the path of history.

The concerns of the land ethic are of little importance if they are not a part of the public discourse. Survey research indeed suggests that individuals express ethical concern for the natural environment and often do so on the grounds that nature is valuable for its own sake. Respondents to surveys frequently accept the notion that all species have a right to exist irrespective of any material benefit to human beings. While the path by which members of the public have acquired such attitudes is difficult to establish with any finality, public exposure to environmental issues and ideas is undoubtedly an important part of the story. This is apparent from the profound impact on the public consciousness of the controversy surrounding the publication of Rachel Carson's *Silent Spring*. Public discourse matters.[16]

While environmental values necessarily play a role in determining whether society is willing to unhook itself from excessive economic growth, they are not sufficient for the task. Even if most people favor environmental protection, whether it occurs depends on the political decision-making process. The natural environment is truly a public good; it affects everyone and everyone's actions affect it. Public goods must necessarily be decided on politically. Under political democracy as experienced in the United States, powerful economic interests exercise significant influence over economic decision making, and these same interests benefit substantially from continuing, unfettered economic expansion. Even if the public favors significant environmental protection that imposes an environmental speed limit on the economy, public desires may not be strong enough to overcome the power of vested interests. Surprisingly, a relatively influential environmental movement exists in this country even though large, voluntary interest groups are hard to organize, because gains from the activities of such groups benefit individuals irrespective of their contribution to group efforts. Explaining the forces behind the growth of the environmental movement offers insight into whether getting unhooked from growth is a reasonable possibility. If such forces have the potential for further expansion, then the serious protection of the natural environment is a distinct possibility. Unquestionably, environmentalism is an issue that affects each of us, regardless of our particular vision of the good life. If in a pluralistic world the environmental problem is an issue that affects everyone in all walks of life, then there is at least a chance that the environmental movement can overcome the economic interests arrayed against it. To establish the significance of the environmental problem and the likelihood that it will be adequately addressed in a democratic political system is the task of the final chapter.

NOTES

1. Jon Elster, *Strong Feelings: Emotion, Addiction, and Human Behavior* (Cambridge, Mass.: MIT Press, 1999), 60–65; Stanton Peele, *The Meaning of Addiction: Compulsive Experience and Its Interpretation* (Lexington, Mass.: Lexington Books, 1985), 1.

2. Avram Goldstein, *Addiction: From Biology to Drug Policy* (New York: W. H. Freeman, 1994), 119–35; Peele, *The Meaning of Addiction*, 27–37; Jim Orford, *Excessive Appetites: A Psychological View of Addictions* (Chichester: John Wiley & Sons, 1985), 9–28.

3. Goldstein, *Addiction*, 179–89.

4. Elster, *Strong Feelings*, 57.

5. Goldstein, *Addiction*, 1–29.

6. Peele *The Meaning of Addiction*, 2, 25.

7. Orford, *Excessive Appetites*, 7–106.

8. Tibor Scitovsky, *The Joyless Economy: An Inquiry into Human Satisfaction and Consumer Dissatisfaction* (New York: Oxford University Press, 1976), 59–79.

9. Scitovsky, *The Joyless Economy*, 127–31.

10. Juliet B. Schor, *The Overworked American: The Unexpected Decline of Leisure* (New York: Basic Books, 1991), 107–38.

11. Gene M. Grossman and Alan B. Krueger, "Economic Growth and the Environment," *Quarterly Journal of Economics* 110 (1995): 353–77; Dale S. Rothman and

Sander M. de Bruyn, "Probing into the Environmental Kuznets Curve Hypothesis," *Ecological Economics* 25 (1998): 143–45.

12. Thorstein Veblen, *The Theory of the Leisure Class: An Economic Study of Institutions* (New York: The New American Library, 1953).

13. Scitovsky, *The Joyless Economy.*

14. Joseph A. Schumpeter, *Capitalism, Socialism, and Democracy,* 3rd ed. (New York: Harper and Brothers Publishers, 1950).

15. Aldo Leopold, *A Sand County Almanac* (New York: Ballantine Books, 1970).

16. Rachel Carson, *Silent Spring* (Boston: Houghton Mifflin, 1962).

2

Conspicuous Consumption, Novelty, and Creative Destruction

To understand how a society can be hooked on growth requires knowledge of what motivates growth in the first place. In order for growth to occur, in a market-dominated economy consumers must be willing to purchase the additional goods created by growth and businesses must be willing to produce them. Or, as economists would put it, there must be growth in both demand and supply. According to the arguments to follow, conspicuous consumption and the desire for novelty drive growth in demand, while the entrepreneurial quest for the novel technology and the new market drives growth in supply. In short, the forces behind growth involve a blending of Thorstein Veblen's "conspicuous consumption" and Joseph Schumpeter's "creative destruction."

CONSPICUOUS CONSUMPTION

Thorstein Veblen's *Theory of the Leisure Class* is one of the classic works in economics and is the first to address in any detail the motivations of consumption.[1] Veblen coined the widely used phrase, "conspicuous consumption." While the book is over a century old, it still offers insights into modern consumer behavior. Veblen's central theme is that leisure and conspicuous consumption have always been the key means by which individuals demonstrate their social status and economic accomplishments. While leisure as a symbol of status is perhaps more appropriate to a Victorian-era aristocracy, certainly consumption remains a primary means by which individuals communicate who they are and where they stand in the economic pecking order. Although in an earlier era mainly the wealthy engaged in conspicuous leisure and consumption, in a modern industrial society conspicuous consumption extends to all classes. According to Veblen,

> The basis on which good repute in any highly organized industrial community ultimately rests is pecuniary strength; and the means of showing pecuniary strength, and so of gaining or retaining a good name, are leisure and a conspicuous consumption of goods. . . . No class of society, not even the most abjectly poor, forgoes all customary conspicuous consumption. The last items of this category of consumption are not given up except under stress of the direst necessity. Very much squalor and discomfort will be endured before the last trinket or the last pretense of pecuniary decency is put away.[2]

The power to generate income has little outward social significance in many societies unless it is demonstrated through acts of consumption. Conspicuous consumption takes on a special importance in a world of where it is impossible to be personally acquainted with more than a very small portion of the total populace. Since neighbors in large urban communities seldom know much about one another, the anonymity of modern society increases the need for physical manifestations of wealth.[3] Conspicuous consumption, as described by Veblen, is a central feature of a modern urban and industrial society.

Most important for the macroeconomics of consumption is Veblen's insight into the interdependence of consumer behavior. The consumption of one individual depends on that of others.[4] Individuals want to keep up with their peers. Most don't want to suffer a loss of status by allowing their standard of consumption to fall behind those around them. While maintaining a consumption standard equal to that of their peers takes first priority, the temptation is strong for individuals to look beyond their current circumstances and to emulate the next class above them in the economic pecking order.[5] The first order of business for individuals is to keep up with their peers; the second order of business is to try to obtain a standard of consumption enjoyed by those just above them in the economic and social hierarchy. This occurs whenever an increase in income allows it.[6] As income rises, consumption inevitably does as well. Conspicuous consumption puts everyone on a treadmill. As all become more productive and as everyone's income rises, no one can relax and work less. Otherwise, others will increase their standard of consumption and status and move ahead of those who opt for less work and disposable income. This phenomenon is familiar in the modern world of work,[7] but Veblen recognized it as well.[8] A kind of "arms race" results where an increase in consumption by one, permitted by increased productivity and income, causes others to increase their consumption as well so as to not fall behind the prevailing standard.

So as Veblen suggests, a critical social reason for consumption is the demonstration of status. Individuals wear certain clothes, drive a certain car, and live in a house with a certain style located in a particular neighborhood to demonstrate their economic position in the social pecking order. The status demonstrated with a particular commodity depends on its rarity. If BMW automobiles are expensive and rare, they will convincingly communicate the status of their owner. If almost everyone can afford them, they lose their effectiveness as a means for demonstrating status. If suburban subdivisions with large lots, winding roads, and three-car garages are relatively rare, then they persuasively illustrate the status of their residents. If suburban living becomes available to all, then it begins to lose its luster as a means to demonstrate status, and a move to trophy houses in the countryside beyond the suburban boundary becomes necessary for a proper expression of wealth.

The consumption of status goods leads to the problem of "keeping up with the Joneses." If some in society get ahead of others in terms of the costliness of their consumer purchases, then the goods consumed by those falling behind begin to lose their relative luster. If the neighbor of someone driving a Jeep Grand Cherokee gets a promotion and buys a more expensive Land Rover, the Jeep owner may well experience a loss of satisfaction with his own car. The utility a person gets from a given bundle of goods diminishes even though nothing about those goods has changed. Rather, the context has changed. Others have altered their pattern of consumption.

MACROECONOMICS AND CONSPICUOUS CONSUMPTION: SAVINGS BY RICH AND POOR

The critical role of the conspicuous consumption "arms race" for the economy as a whole is to keep consumption rising as income grows. Otherwise, stagnation in total demand for goods in the economy is a distinct possibility if no other form of spending is able to fill the gap between rising income and stagnating consumption. Disposable income can either be consumed or saved. There are no other alternatives. Understanding why consumption in fact keeps up with income and why savings as a proportion of disposable income fails to rise is critical. If savings did rise relative to income, then some other form of spending—investment (plant and equipment), government, or export—would have to fill the gap in order to avoid a slump on the demand side of the economy.

The rich tend to save a bigger share of their income than the poor. A seemingly logical extension of this observation is that as a society as a whole gets wealthier its share of income saved should rise. If this occurred, then the share of income consumed would necessarily decline. If no other form of spending fills the gap left by the lower share of consumption, then economic expansion would slow, and too little consumption would foster economic stagnation. With the rising share of U.S. income devoted to consumption in recent years, the problem of stagnating consumption has not yet occurred here. So why doesn't the share of income saved rise as income increases for society as a whole? Veblen's notion of "conspicuous consumption" offers an answer to this question.[9]

Suppose everyone's income rises. Perhaps some individuals don't have a desire to increase their consumption, but their friends start moving to newer, more luxurious subdivisions farther away from the central city, opening up housing for lower-class families in older suburbs. Those who remain behind see the status of their neighborhood declining, even though nothing physical has changed. They may decide to also move to a new subdivision, not because of its intrinsic merits but just because they don't want to see their own status decline. Keeping up with the Joneses keeps consumption rising and helps prevent an increase in the proportion of income saved.

So why do the rich save a bigger share of their income than the poor? This may seem puzzling in light of what has been said so far. Why don't the rich seek additional status through increased consumption expenditures just like everyone else as they move up the income ladder? The answer is that they do. To increase status, however, all that is necessary for the rich is some increased expenditure on status goods. This can be done while at the same time increasing the share of income saved. So as incomes for some go up relative to everyone else, those who are getting relatively richer can increase spending in comparison to others and still increase the proportion of income they save. Both are possible. If Bill Gates makes an extra billion, all he has to do to demonstrate rising status is to throw a few more fancy dinner parties each year or add another wing to his mansion, all costing maybe a few million.

While it is true that the rich save relatively more than the poor, as everyone's income increases over time, rich and poor alike will add consumer goods if conspicuous consumption prevails. Rich and poor will purchase new symbols of status to keep up with the Joneses. No one is exempt from the consumption arms race. Because the rich have much greater absolute incomes, they can both purchase more goods that demonstrate status and spend a lower proportion of their income than the poor. In sum, as the income of others increases, all will spend more to maintain their relative position in the status hierarchy. As incomes rise, to keep up with the Joneses, consumption rises in proportion to income. The savings rate is stable. The rich, just like the poor, increase their consumption in proportion to their income. Conspicuous consumption provides insurance against economic stagnation caused by insufficient demand for goods. This is the virtue of conspicuous consumption.

THE JOYLESS ECONOMY

Compelling as it may be, Veblen's conspicuous consumption doesn't offer a very psychologically sophisticated theory of consumer behavior. Another work, Tibor Scitovsky's *The Joyless Economy*, fills the gap rather nicely. Scitovsky's work relies on the simple and intuitive idea of psychic arousal.[10]

Simply put, arousal is the amount of the brain's activity manifested physically in the form of electrical impulses. The level of arousal depends on a variety of stimuli from the outside, including the internal organs and the senses, and from within the brain itself. The average degree of arousal sinks to its low during sleep and rises to a peak during waking hours, declining again as sleep is approached. The level of arousal is expressed in different feeling states. In a state of high arousal individuals feel alert, attentive, excited, tense, emotional, and anxious, while in a state of low arousal they feel groggy, relaxed, and slow. The level of arousal is critical to the efficient performance of the tasks of everyday life. Individuals perform poorly at more complex physical and mental tasks if they are insufficiently alert. Conversely, too much stimulus and arousal can be inimical to individual efficiency and even the ability to function. Excessive stimulus from chaotic situations can result in paralysis and inaction.[11]

The level of arousal is a critical element in human behavior. The extent of stimulus and arousal influences human actions. Too much stimulus manifests itself in stress, anxiety, and discomfort; too little stimulus and arousal leads to the pain of profound boredom. A middle ground of stimulus and arousal is sought that gives rise to feelings of "comfort and well-being."[12] Desired arousal levels in practice are more dynamic and complex than this. After a period of extreme stimulus and arousal, for instance, a period of relaxation and low arousal may be desired. The idea of a middle ground of stimulus is perhaps best viewed as an average over time, taking into account the ups and downs of our stimulus needs.

The notion of arousal is especially important in explaining consumer behavior. At a basic biological level, excessive arousal and discomfort caused by hunger motivates us to seek out and consume the food we need for physical sustenance. In our sophisticated modern culture, merely thinking about a future need, whether physical or social, arouses us to action. In planning for a Saturday night dinner party, our level of arousal rises, to be alleviated only by a visit to, for instance, the liquor store to procure the wine needed for the meal. The desire to reduce the discomfort of excessive arousal explains a wide range of human behavior, consumer or otherwise.[13] Unsatisfied needs or wants stimulate arousal, causing the individual to seek satisfaction of those needs or wants.

Discomfort also occurs as a consequence of too little arousal and too much boredom. Boredom is relieved through physical or mental stimulus. Physical stimulation can come from manual labor, exercise, and participation in athletic activity. Mental stimulation is often mixed with physical but also can come with more physically passive activities, such as various forms of entertainment, spectator sports, games, art, reading, philosophy, and scientific inquiry. Even these activities can become boring, however, if they amount to simple repetition. The human organism requires novelty. Novelty may well spark arousal for reasons of evolutionary adaptation. Novel circumstances often pose threats that require a response. A new set of circumstances often breeds fear in both humans and animals. Repeating the circumstances, however, breeds familiarity and reduces arousal. Too much novelty and unfamiliarity can be stressful and result in unpleasant arousal. Flight rather than curiosity can be the reaction, although exposure to a limited danger can be exciting. Novelty, to be enjoyable, must have the familiar as its point of departure. It has to have a context. Sensory overload, stress, and tension can be the product of too much novelty. In a symphony, we depend on repeated themes to bring coherence to the piece, but our enjoyment is heightened by unexpected turns and twists the thematic material takes. We would not normally enjoy highly dissonant disorganized noise in a musical work, unless it were somehow connected to something familiar. Similarly, a little uncertainty can be exciting, as at the race track or in the gambling casino, but too much uncertainty can be highly unsettling, such as the stress associated with not knowing where the next terrorist attack will take place.[14]

What in life do we desire to achieve? What has been said so far suggests that individuals desire to achieve just the right level of arousal that offers comfort and avoids discomfort and pain. But what of pleasure? Pleasure, according to Scitovsky, is a fleeting phenomenon, one experienced in the movement from discomfort to comfort. Comfort and discomfort have to do with the level of arousal, whether it is too little, too much, or in the optimal range, while pleasure has to do with a change in arousal, a movement from an uncomfortable level of arousal that is either too great or too little, to a level of arousal that offers comfort. Pleasure is, roughly speaking, a dynamic phenomenon generated in the movement from discomfort to comfort.[15] The attraction of pleasure is perhaps best modeled by eating. Pleasure flows from the removal of the pangs of hunger through the act of eating. The act of eating is often so pleasurable that we want it continue as long as possible. This often results in the delights of the palate being indulged in well beyond biological need. The pleasure gotten from eating causes an ingestion of food beyond that necessary to remove the discomfort of hunger. This is amply demonstrated by the common practice of infrequent but periodic feasting, even among the poor who more than likely can ill afford the expense.[16] While eating is an innate biological desire, many wants are acquired. Even so, the process of arousal and generating of pleasure in moving from discomfort to comfort operates in the same way for learned wants as it does for the innate.[17]

Pleasure comes not only from reducing arousal caused by discomfort, but also from increasing arousal from a state of lethargy and boredom. The pleasure generated from such moves can itself become mildly addictive. Arousal from a lethargic state results from participation in a game of Monopoly or chess, but, once involved in the game, participants may have trouble bringing it to an end. The pleasure of the game becomes a goal in itself long after the level of arousal has reached its optimum. The same can be said of other forms of activity, such as eating, reading a good book, drinking socially at a party, or watching television. In retrospect, individuals sometimes wish they had not engaged in an activity as much as they did. The pursuit of pleasure can be seductive, and at times can go too far.[18]

Pleasure and comfort, ironically, are at odds. In a perpetual state of comfort, the pleasure associated with moving from either too little or too much arousal to the optimum state is forgone. The pleasure of eating can't be experienced without the discomfort of being hungry. Tension and discomfort must be built up before the pleasure of resolving the tension can be experienced. Comfort is a desired state, but too much comfort can come at the expense of pleasure. Disturbance to comfort, according to the framework laid out by Scitovsky, is essential to a life with pleasure.[19]

Material goods offer comforts and pleasures, and they frequently do so in the social arena. The human being is out of necessity social in nature. We cannot survive without each other. Once true of primitive hunter-gatherer societies, it is even more so today in a complex global, information-based industrial society. Belonging to the group is important, and to feel a sense of belonging is critical to achieving social comfort. Some portion of the modern consumer's purchases will be directed at solidifying group ties. We want to demonstrate that we are indeed an integral part of the group, and we do this in part through forms of visible consumption that communicate our level of status in society. Our minimum desire is to have the same standard of consumption as our peers in order to demonstrate our membership in society. Some of us will want to go beyond simple membership to a particular achievement of social rank, and we will want the satisfaction of the status that goes with our accomplishment. For some, simple public recognition of their good work and skill in their profession or their avocation, such as a sport or a hobby, will be enough. Some, who measure their accomplishments by their income, will want to communicate their status, and the only way they can do that is through excelling in their standard of consumption. Such a measure will by its nature be relative to the consumption of others and will require an ever-increasing amount of spending if consumption standards are rising generally.[20]

All this, of course, differs little from Veblen's conspicuous consumption and is no doubt inspired by it. It is not only the goods themselves that result in arousal and pleasure; it is what they represent as well. Social comfort in consumption can be disturbed and tension created if friends, for example, are observed adding something new to their mix of consumption goods. Feelings of deprivation are experienced and resulting stresses and tensions are resolved by going out and buying similar goods. Keeping up with the Joneses is required to maintain social comfort levels. Some become dissatisfied with the comfort of the status quo and become agents of change themselves, going beyond what their friends consume in order to enjoy the pleasure of increasing their own status. In such circumstances goods are consumed not just for their intrinsically useful qualities, but for what they represent. Scitovsky and Veblen agree on conspicuous consumption.

Apart from the pursuit of status, in an affluent society what explains the continual rise in consumption? Why do some in society always want more? One obvious answer is the boredom of comfort. In an affluent economy, material comfort is easily achieved. The pleasure of satisfying the simple wants, so difficult to do in a poor society, are removed. Everyday is feast day. Tensions are aroused by only the new and the novel. In an otherwise boring world, stimulation and arousal are sought through new and novel consumption experiences. Once incorporated into daily routines, the novelty of new consumer items wears off and the pleasure of acquiring and making use of them diminishes. Playing a new computer game sparks arousal and creates tension; learning to play the game and succeeding at it brings the pleasure of tension reduction. As the experience is repeated, the level of arousal diminishes, and so does pleasure.

Scitovsky suggests that this pattern of consumption behavior is not unlike an addiction. New kinds of consumption become a matter of habit and essential to the maintenance of comfort levels. The daily use of a computer for many has become a habit pattern. When computers malfunction, individuals often become very upset and remain in a high state of discomfort until a repair is completed. Such a disruption of normal consumption patterns creates discomfort not unlike the pain of withdrawal from a chemically addictive substance. While the novelty of something new arouses and brings forth the pleasure of change, repeated use results in diminishing pleasure. The special enjoyment of a new, faster computer or shiny new automobile eventually disappears. Such goods sustain a sense of comfort and would be sorely missed if taken away, but their repeated use brings diminishing pleasure. This pattern is not too different from the behavior of the drug addict or alcoholic. Habituation to a drug results in diminishing pleasure and euphoria from successive doses taken, but serious withdrawal pains occur without it. Habituation also brings attempts to restore diminished pleasure through increasing the frequency or amount of ingestion. A similar pattern is possible in more ordinary kinds of consumption. If the novelty of adding something new to habitual patterns of consumption is what brings pleasure, then to maintain pleasure, increasing levels of consumption are required.[21]

The virtue of Scitovosky's analysis of consumer behavior is that it takes us beyond Veblen's concept of "conspicuous consumption" by offering a more sophisticated view of consumer psychology. The desire for the social comfort of belonging explains the propensity to "keep up with the Joneses," while the stimulus and pleasure that go with the achievement of higher status propel increased levels of consumption of those kinds of goods capable of publicly communicating relative position in the economic pecking order. In addition to conspicuous consumption driving the demand for goods ever upward, Scitovsky notes that the desire for novelty and the fleeting nature of pleasure interact to a similar end. The maintenance of pleasure and the avoidance of boredom interact to encourage increasing levels of consumption much in the same way an addict requires increasing amounts of an addictive substance.

STATUS, NOVELTY, AND ADDICTIVE CONSUMPTION

The key human goals behind consumption, if Scitovsky is right, are physical and social comfort, an optimal level of psychic stimulus, and the enjoyment of pleasure. These goals take concrete form as the pursuit of novelty and status. The pursuit of both novelty and status has the qualities of an addictive form of behavior, although at the individual level it may well lack the dysfunctional consequences normally associated with addiction. Boredom with an existing bundle of goods leads to desiring, even craving, something new and exciting. A higher level of stimulus and the pleasure that goes with the acquisition or use of something new and novel is wanted in much the same way an addictive drug user desires an initial sense of euphoria from another dose. Similarly, we feel a sense of unease

and discomfort if others move ahead of us in the consumption pecking order, and we experience a craving to catch up. Habituation to an exhibited
level of status in society is the norm; a relative decline in status causes distress and pain, much as an addict suffers withdrawal symptoms from going without addictive drugs. There is, of course, a major difference between the "normal" pursuit of novelty and status and a destructive
addiction. Increasing consumption in and of itself doesn't necessarily have
destructive consequences at the individual level. The pursuit of novelty
and status through consumption is a perfectly normal form of behavior,
even though it may well have the same behavioral basis as an addiction.

The whole notion of addiction as a "normal" form of behavior may
seem odd and needs to be explored further. Compulsive or addictive consumption has been recognized in recent years as a form of dysfunctional
behavior akin to other kinds of addictions. Those who suffer from addictive buying tend to have certain psychological problems such as low self-
esteem, depression, difficulty establishing intimate social relationships,
excessive needs for social approval, an overly active fantasy life, or an
overly powerful drive for sensation seeking. The addictive consumer
through buying seeks to alleviate anxiety associated with insufficient social approval or intimacy or to increase arousal to offset feelings of boredom or depression. Consumer purchases are not normally destructive in
the same way as an addiction to drugs or alcohol can be, but if carried to
excess, buying can manifest itself in such injurious phenomena as credit
card abuse and conflicts in marital relationships. Although the act of buying can increase the level of arousal and pleasure or relieve feelings of
anxiety in the short run, it can have ruinous financial or social consequences in the long run. Even so, the addicted consumer feels compelled
to repeat the behavior as an immediate solution to emotional problems.
Once the immediate euphoria of the purchase has worn off, the consumer
often feels a sense of guilt about the long-term consequences of the act.
Ironically, the addicted consumer frequently has little use for the product
purchased and achieves an emotional lift mainly from the act of purchase
and the social interaction with the sales person. In some instances, however, the good itself is important because its possession demonstrates a
certain expertise in shopping that may induce a perception of social approval from friends or family members. This could be true for those who
believe themselves to be experts in, say, computer or photography equipment. Compulsive consumers do perceive a link between buying and social status to a greater degree than others.[22]

Compulsive consumption and ordinary consumer activity have some
clear differences. As already noted, the orientation of the compulsive consumer appears to be more to the act of buying than to the use of the product itself, although in instances where the desire to exhibit consumer ex-

pertise is strong, ownership of the good is important. Unlike ordinary shoppers, the compulsive consumer lacks normal self-control over purchasing behavior and engages in it to the point where it has destructive consequences. Still, the goals of both the ordinary and compulsive consumer are to experience increases in arousal and pleasure and relieve feelings of anxiety. The main difference is the intensity of the drive or desire for an altered arousal level. For the compulsive consumer, the intensity of the drive may be unbearable, whereas for the ordinary consumer the drive is subject to some degree of control. From an economic perspective, a key difference between the compulsive and normal consumer is that the latter can live within the constraint of disposable income while the former has difficulty doing so. Although those who can be diagnosed as compulsive consumers constitute only 1 to 6 percent of the consuming population, consumption behavior seems to occur along a continuum, suggesting that a strong urge to consume plays a significant role for much normal consumption as well as abnormal consumer behavior.[23] The normal urge to consume for many is probably sufficient to keep consumption expanding as disposable income increases. This possibility is consistent with U.S. data on consumption.

In the United States., consumption grows roughly in proportion to disposable personal income, suggesting that satiety in consumption is not a part of the American experience. Consumption in the 1990s averaged about 94 percent of disposable income, and this figure is up from the average of the last four decades, about 92 percent.[24] As income rises, more is consumed and the share of income devoted to consumption fails to decline. The urge to buy offers a simple but compelling explanation for this phenomenon. Satisfying such an urge could easily use up increases in income. The psychic arousal and pleasure experienced with the purchase of the new and novel consumer item serves to keep consumption growing among truly addicted consumers and probably to a lesser degree among many others who enjoy the pleasures of consumption but are not compulsively addicted to it.

EVIDENCE FOR STATUS CONSUMPTION

Consumption beyond strict biological need is fundamental to the human experience. This is clear from both Veblen's and Scitovsky's descriptions of consumer behavior. We are object-loving, object-using beings. Our sense of self and powers in the world are partly defined by the goods we possess and use. Goods are exosomatic extensions of our physical, social, and psychological existence. In the economic realm such extensions account for much of our incredible productivity. In the social and psychological realm, they serve as markers of our status and are part of our extended sense of self and identity. In many ways we exhibit who we are through what we consume.[25] We do this not just for demonstrating status, but to communicate to others the nature of our personal being. Exosomatic extensions of ourselves are essential to accomplish those things that make life a joy. Lovers need the privacy of the bedroom; gourmet cooks need stoves; preachers need churches; families need a home; artists need paints, brushes, and canvas; soccer players need cleated shoes and soccer balls; computer code writers need computers. In all these cases, consumption is a means or an instrument for the carrying out of some other activity. The focus of attention is not on the good as such, but on the activity or end being sought. While it is entirely possible that consumption will continue to rise to provide the means for participating in activities that bring human pleasures and joys, rising consumption is not a necessity. One can imagine that steady-state consumption levels provide sufficient means for desired human activities. A soccer player will need new shoes periodically and a writer will need to replace a worn-out computer from time to time, but the frequency of consumption of such items need not necessarily increase.[26] If consumer goods are desired to demonstrate status and if status is a relative phenomenon, then steady-state consumption levels are ruled out. As incomes grow, increases in status consumption will be pursued and consumption will grow as well. Is status consumption more than just a theoretical possibility?

Can the more specific notion of status consumption be confirmed in empirical research as well? While the belief that status consumption exists is widespread outside the discipline of economics, economic research on the subject is fairly limited. Researchers in consumer behavior have found that reference groups do matter in consumer decisions. Reference groups include those we want to be like as well as those whose opinions we care about. Such groups can include people close to us, such as family members, close friends, and coworkers, but also can include individuals we identify with, such as sports figures or movie stars.[27] Survey research indicates that for some individuals reference groups matter in their product and brand selections, especially for publicly displayed luxury goods.[28] Consumption is at least partly oriented to communicating a certain identity and to impressing others.

Although economists have largely ignored consumer interdependence, at least two studies of demand patterns have found interactions of the type described by Veblen. An increase in the consumption of conspicuous goods by one consumer tends to increase consumption by others.[29] The most interesting economic study of status consumption, undertaken by Angela Chao and Juliet Schor, investigates purchasing patterns for women's cosmetics. Some cosmetics, such as face cream, are privately consumed and are unlikely to be consumed for status purposes, and some, such as lipstick, are publicly consumed and are prone to evaluation in terms of status. Face cream is used in the privacy of the home, while lipstick is often applied in a visible public setting. Chao and Schor find that the correlation between price and intrinsic quality is less for publicly as opposed to privately consumed cosmetics. In product selection the quality of privately consumed face cream matters relative to its cost, not to the prestige of the brand. But for publicly displayed lipstick, the prestige of the brand, as measured in part by its price, is essential in product selection. Chao and Schor find that the likelihood of purchasing expensive brands increases with the social visibility of the product and that status consumption is positively related to education, income, and a more anonymous urban location. In an urban setting, signaling of status is more likely to be necessary than in a rural setting where everyone is likely to know everyone else and their economic circumstances. As Chao and Schor point out, the benefits of status signaling may well increase with education and professional position. Status signaling may be necessary to signal economic success and competencies. A real estate agent with a ten-year-old economy sedan is unlikely to inspire much confidence for a homeowner seeking a broker. As one's income rises relative to others, it is easier to play the status game, and within limits the incremental gains to status may well increase. On the other hand, the poor may well have to forgo the status game for lack of the necessary funds. In the language of economists, status seeking is income elastic. If this is the case, then the share of income devoted to status seeking rises as income increases.[30]

HAPPINESS, POSITION, AND CONSUMPTION

While many mainstream economists are prone to ignore theories offered by the likes of Veblen and Scitovsky, economists who have done work on the role of consumption and economic position in the determination of expressed happiness have found evidence to support the importance of novelty and status in economic behavior. Researchers measure happiness, or subjective well-being, by asking survey respondents how satisfied they are with their lives.[31] While such evaluations are inherently subjective, they do tend to be consistent with other measures of well-being. In judging social welfare, what makes more sense than to ask individuals how they feel about the life they are leading?

The rather surprising discovery of this research is that beyond a certain point economic growth fails to bring forth overall increases in human happiness. Perhaps less surprising is the importance of the noneconomic dimensions of life in the determination of happiness. While

economic circumstances play a role, other factors are often more important in explaining expressions of happiness, including marital status,
enjoyment of leisure, membership in a church, friendships, sexual activity, contact with the outdoors, and personal health.[32] It is true that
within a society happiness tends to be associated with higher income.[33]
As one person's income increases relative to others, that person is more
likely to express a higher level of happiness. It is also true that across
countries with less than $10,000 in per capita income (in 1995) average
subjective well-being increases as per capita income increases, but for
countries above $10,000 in per capita income a significant correlation
between income and well-being is absent.[34] As the average income for a
society rises, well-being increases, but only up to a threshold level.[35] Finally, aggregate economic growth in affluent countries fails to bring
forth increases in average happiness. Between 1946 and 1991 U.S. per
capita income (defined in terms of purchasing power) more than doubled while average happiness decreased slightly. Between 1958 and
1986, purchasing power for the average Japanese increased fivefold, an
astounding amount, but mean satisfaction remained unchanged.[36] In
the relatively affluent countries of the world, economic growth has
done nothing for expressed happiness. Oddly, individuals can increase
their own subjective well-being by increasing their income, but a society as a whole cannot improve the average subjective well-being of its
citizens through economic advance once a certain threshold of average
income is attained.

How can the positive relationship between individual income and happiness be reconciled with the absence of a relationship between society-
wide average income and happiness? First, it is relative income, not absolute income, that fosters increased happiness. Increased happiness flows
from one's income rising relative to everyone else's. When given a choice,
survey respondents often prefer a higher relative amount of some good to
a higher absolute amount. Many would prefer to live in a world where
they earn $50,000 a year and others earn $25,000 than in a world where
they earn $100,000 and others earn $200,000.[37] Position relative to others is
more highly valued than the actual amount of material wealth. People care
about where they stand in comparison to others (as Veblen also tells us).
One sister in a family, for example, will be more inclined to enter the labor
force to raise her family's income and relative economic position if the
other sister is in the labor force.[38] Psychic arousal is apparently stimulated
in individuals when they are interacting with others having higher social
status.[39] Evidence of this kind clearly suggests that relative economic position is of critical importance to most human individuals.[40]

Second, subjective well-being is at least partly transitory in response to
the consumption of new and novel consumer goods. Pleasure has a stable

component dependent on the accustomed consumption flows, but it also has a component that is dependent on change (as noted by Scitovsky). Once the change occurs and the new consumer item becomes a part of the daily consumption bundle, the pleasure of novelty disappears and overall satisfaction returns to the original amount.[41] A new kind of cereal at breakfast will temporarily add to our pleasure, but eventually our enjoyment of breakfast will return to its normal level.[42] Also, as our incomes and material standards rise, so do our expected achievements. The purchase of a second automobile made possible by rising income increases our subjective well-being, but at the same time our aspirations rise and a second car becomes a part of our consumption expectations.[43] The shrinkage in the gap between our expectations and realizations returns our subjective well-being to its normal amount.

The reason higher income for all doesn't necessarily lead to increased average satisfaction is now apparent. Relative income cannot be increased for all, and increases in the pleasure of additional consumption quickly dissipate. In short, many experience economic life as a treadmill. As the economic treadmill speeds up, everyone advances in tandem, and if anyone gains relatively it is necessarily at the expense of others. Speeding up the treadmill cannot increase happiness associated with relative position. Also, as the standard of living advances, the pleasures of new consumer items quickly dissipate. We either tire of the new and the novel or adjust our expectations upward and subjective well-being returns to original levels.

According to the research on happiness, economic progress beyond a basic threshold is a questionable means for increasing society-wide subjective well-being, but for the individual there are two clear economic paths to greater satisfaction. One is to increase income and consumption in comparison to others. The second is to seek out new kinds of consumption experiences. Success at either or both will increase subjective well-being. The individual pursuit of happiness thus underlies a powerful propensity for consumption to grow in the modern affluent economies of the world today. How does this propensity play into the growth of the aggregate economy? To answer this question will require a vision of how exactly economic growth occurs.

CREATIVE DESTRUCTION AND ECONOMIC EXPANSION

Conventional theories of growth point to savings and investment as the driving forces for economic expansion. The bigger the share of income devoted to savings and investment, the higher the rate of growth in the aggregate economy. The economy is like a balloon. Pump some savings and investment air into it, and it will expand in a balanced, uniform fashion.

Joseph Schumpeter, historically one of the intellectual giants in the economics profession, suggests otherwise. He argues that the fundamental impulse for growth comes from new consumer goods, new methods of production, new markets, and new forms of industrial organization. New forms of economic activity drive economic expansion. The economy is not like a balloon uniformly expanding. New high-growth sectors are the engines of economic expansion. Schumpeter puts this as follows:

> The fundamental impulse that sets and keeps the capitalist engine in motion comes from the new consumers' good, the new methods of production or transportation, the new markets, the new forms of industrial organization that capitalist enterprise creates.[44]

New forms of economy activity are created and the old decline and sometimes even disappear. To describe this process, Schumpeter coined the term "creative destruction."[45] The analogy in evolutionary biology is the creation of new species through genetic mutation and evolution and the destruction (extinction) of species unable to adapt to changing conditions. New firms and industries are constantly appearing, while old ones are declining and disappearing. New businesses with new products will take away markets from the old. New firms with new products or technologies will attain quasi-monopoly positions, only to see their market eroded away by still newer firms with newer products and technologies.[46]

Schumpeter goes on to suggest that price competition as taught by economists is of little real importance and instead it is competition from a new product or technology that really matters. The price competition that economists idolize is a fairly minor sideshow.[47] The usual view is that firms compete with one another for markets by offering their customers price reductions. As a consequence, price is driven down to the minimum possible to the benefit of the consumer. The reality is that businesses compete for market niches by offering something that their rivals lack to consumers. In this way, a business can dominate a product niche in the market place and avoid profit-draining price competition. Businesses seek to avoid competition through technological innovation.

In view of this theory, innovations in products, production technologies, markets, and methods of organization are likely to come in waves or clusters. Entrepreneurs are attracted to the latest new products or technologies. These become the engines of economic growth driving the economy forward through market expansion. During the high-growth phase, capital and entrepreneurs are attracted to the growth engines and ignore other possibilities. Often a pioneer enterprise initiates a new technology and fosters a number of spinoff enterprises that fill related product niches or emulate the pioneer.[48]

Schumpeter's theory of creative destruction suggests that industries have life-cycle patterns of development characterized by initial rapid growth, a subsequent slowing of growth, and, in some instances, decline. An industry grows rapidly until it reaches market saturation; all those at a given income who desire the product are consuming it. This part of the growth process involves diffusion of information about the new industry's product or technology, including advertising to convince the public of the product's importance. Once this period has ended, growth in demand for the product is related to income and population growth and the rate at which competing new products and technologies enter the market and attract consumer attention. With a slowing of growth in new industries because of saturated markets, growth in economic activity as a whole necessarily slows. Eventually, entrepreneurs begin to search for other new products and technologies, but this takes time.

CREATIVE DESTRUCTION AND COMPUTER SOFTWARE

The emergence of the personal computer software industry and its dominant producer, the Microsoft Corporation, is a perfect example of creative destruction in action. The key features of creative destruction include the pursuit of monopoly through the development of unique new technologies and products, the unimportance of price competition as opposed to competition in the form of product features, and economic expansion through the creation of entirely new industries. These features are all central to Microsoft as an enterprise and the industry it dominates, personal computer software.[49]

Computer software is subject to two economic phenomena that predominate in the information age: the network effect and high fixed costs combined with very low marginal costs of production. According to the network effect, the advantages of consuming a product increase with the number of users. The telephone offers a simple example. The greater the number of individuals hooked up to a telephone system, the greater the ability of any single user to contact other individuals. For this rather obvious reason, telephones are in practice linked through a single system of interconnecting networks.

A similar advantage holds for computer software.[50] For example, computer users who wish to share files and make use of them in common must be utilizing compatible software programs. As the number of users with compatible software increases, the advantages of the ability to share files expands. If MS Word is used by more computer users than any other word processing program, then it pays for someone who wants to exchange files with others to purchase MS Word as opposed to competing programs such as WordPerfect.[51] All the users of MS Word constitute a network, and the bigger the network the greater the advantage of using MS Word. The computer program that is able to attract the most users will exercise a clear marketplace advantage. This will be true not only because of file compatibility across users, but also because more users will be familiar with a particular program, reducing training costs for businesses and increasing the availability of informal sources of assistance for learning how to use a program for both business and home users.

The network issue is even more important for operating system software.[52] The operating system program essentially directs traffic on a computer, allowing the user to store and move files, call up programs for the work of computing such as word processing, and communicate with other computers through networks or Internet connections. Applications software that does the work of computing—word processing, spreadsheets, statistical packages, accounting software—must be written for specific operating systems in order to function. Software businesses will find it to their advantage to write software packages for the most popular operating system. This will ensure access to the largest market for software applications and allow the spreading of the fixed costs of software development over a larger number of customers, increasing profit margins and reducing the price needed to cover the per-unit total costs of production (including the fixed costs of development). The network effect for applications will be synergistic. The greater the availability of applications software for a particular operating system, the greater its appeal to new users.[53] The operating system with the most users will have an obvious and dominant advantage that will be difficult for other operating systems to overcome. The other key economic feature for computer software is the relatively high costs of developing a program and the near zero cost of making another copy.[54] Once the program is developed, the cost of supplying another customer a copy is insignificant. The software supplier that is initially successful in attracting a large base of users will have a distinct cost advantage. Either the price can be lowered to fend off competition, or the revenue generated from sales above costs can be used to invest in new features that increase the appeal of the program relative to the competition.

Microsoft, through a combination of luck, cunning, and technological skill, became the dominant supplier of operating systems software for personal computers.[55] Once it gained the dominant position in operating systems, Microsoft enjoyed the advantage of a very low marginal cost for supplying additional users and the monopoly power that comes with the network effect. As a consequence the company has been able to sustain a relatively high price and profit margin for its most important product, the Windows operating system.[56] Microsoft achieved a virtual monopoly in operating systems, controlling well over 80 percent of the market.[57] Asserting that the Microsoft Corporation represents the rule rather than the exception in the structure of the modern economy would be over-reaching. Still, in the information age, networks are of critical importance and high fixed costs are common. Both help explain Microsoft's market dominance. Because technology is always changing, there is no guarantee that a monopoly like Microsoft's will be permanent. The possibility of online computing or the use of "middleware," software that connects to the computer through a Web browser program or some other intermediate step, could diminish the Microsoft operating systems monopoly. As Schumpeter suggests, it is competition in product characteristics that matters, not competition in the form of price.[58]

The final issue is whether Microsoft and the computer software and hardware industries fulfill the "engine of growth role" played by newly emergent sectors in a Schumpeterian-style economy. If this is the case, then the concept of creative destruction fits as a reasonable description of the computer industry. The personal computer enters the economic arena in two ways, first as a consumer good and second as a capital good for business. The personal computer is a new and novel kind of consumer good capable of serving as an indicator of status (households at the upper end of the income stream are more likely to have personal computers) and able to provide new forms of sensual stimulus (i.e., computer games, music on CDs, and movies on DVDs).[59] The personal computer fits both Veblen's theory of conspicuous consumption and Scitovsky's theory of psychic arousal. Having the latest in computer technology communicates affluence as well as expertise as a consumer. Between 1990 and 1997, the percentage of households owning computers increased from 15 percent to 35 percent, indicating a substantial rise in demand for computers as a consumer good. Much of this demand growth was confined to the upper 40 percent of the income distribution. Close to two-thirds of households in the top 20 percent of the income distribution and around half of all households in the next lower 20 percent own computers. Conversely, in the bottom 40 percent of the income distribution, less than one in five households owns computers.[60] A personal computer is a consumer good that appeals to the relatively affluent and well-educated segments of society.

The second entry point into the economy for the personal computer is as a business tool for improving economic efficiency and productivity. Computers stimulate business investment spending on the demand side and ultimately increase productivity and expand the supply side of the economy as well. Computers are an engine of growth because they add to total product demand, but they are also important because they can increase the productivity of the economy as well. Spending by businesses on information processing equipment and software increased from around 20 percent of private fixed investment in the 1980s to around 26 percent in the 1990s.[61]

Whether the computer revolution has actually increased productivity is a topic of considerable debate. Only in the latter half of the 1990s has the rate of productivity growth accelerated. If this is indeed the consequence of applying computer technology, the delay in productivity improvement can be attributed in part to a fairly long learning curve for effectively using the computer. Most users have doubtlessly experienced the frustrations of screen freeze-ups and disconcerting "fatal error" messages. To learn to deal with such frustrations and to learn how to apply computers to increase work efficiency takes time, and software writers are only just beginning to create software packages that are truly user-friendly.[62] Mounting evidence for individual firms does suggest that investment in computers and software is indeed paying off in terms of growth in productivity.[63] The computer and software industries apparently served as significant engines of economic progress in the 1990s, fulfilling the Schumpeterian vision of creative destruction.

CREATIVE DESTRUCTION, CONSPICUOUS CONSUMPTION, AND NOVELTY

Creative destruction and conspicuous consumption need one another. We just saw how they interact in the personal computer industry. The personal computer and the software that runs it together constitute a new and novel consumer product as well as a status good, and the computer and software industries are clearly major engines of economic expansion. Businesses with hot new product ideas need consumers looking for something novel that brings with it a new form of pleasure, a new kind of comfort, or a new means for exhibiting status. Businesses need markets for new products that embody advances in technology, and consumers need new kinds of goods to stave off boredom or demonstrate status. Novelty is at the root of both consumer desire and the modern business economy. Without novelty both would stagnate. Consumers would look elsewhere for sensual and mental stimulation, and that part of the business economy that's rooted in innovation would shrink in scope.

Conspicuous consumption requires a periodic infusion of new kinds of status goods. Productivity improvements, declining costs, and increased per capita consumption render status goods more widely available and less functional in demonstrating position in the economic pecking order. At one time, owning one car was unusual and demonstrated a higher level of status than the norm. But soon a second car was required in the driveway, and now maybe even a third—probably a sport utility vehicle.

At one time a three-bedroom ranch house in the suburbs suggested that one was rising in the economic arena, but to demonstrate increasing status today one needs a five-thousand-square-foot trophy home on the suburban fringe filled with the latest electronic technology. For the very rich, rooms filled with big-screen TVs, garages filled with fancy cars, and perhaps even ownership of an executive jet are needed to effectively advertise their economic position. Conspicuous consumption blends with creative destruction. Entrepreneurs create new kinds of goods that can be new ways to demonstrate status. The wealthy are usually the leaders in adopting new goods that embody new technologies.

Newness and novelty are important to the materialistically oriented consumer not solely because they communicate relative status. The quest for self-identity through consumption also frequently relies on new purchases. To be "fashionable" requires a frequent upgrading of one's wardrobe or a periodic redecorating of one's house. The collector who embodies some piece of his identity in the objects collected always wants something not yet owned. The same is true for the experiences of the senses. The latest technology in entertainment systems reduces the appeal of the old. After watching a movie on a big-screen, high-definition TV, to go back to the old nineteen-inch screen is not easy. The phone booth is rather unattractive in comparison to the convenience of the cell phone. One gets bored with going to the same old restaurants and is always on the lookout for new gastronomic experiences. The squeaks and rattles of the old car get tiresome after a while and one longs for the smell, the power, and the quiet ride of a new one. The spaciousness, improved driver visibility, and the protective bulk of the new sport utility vehicle is certainly more appealing than an economy car that is several years old.

CONCLUSION

The central proposition set forth in this chapter is that the modern economy can be described by essentially two phenomena: "the consumption of novelty" and "creative destruction." Creative destruction is a metaphor for a dynamic, sophisticated, and complex market-based economic process that generates new and novel goods. Consumer desire rooted in a materialistic conception of the good life features a powerful human drive for the new and the novel. The good life is to be accomplished through the acquisition of goods. Our goods are an extension of ourselves and objects of our deepest desires and passions; goods are a part of our self-identity; they express who we are. Goods connect us to the social groups we identify with, and goods are a vehicle for demonstrating and communicating our status in the world. While Veblen's conspicuous consumption is a part of this larger picture of consumer behavior, it is not the entire story. Self-identification through consumption for some may actually communicate a distaste for symbols of status, such as the disheveled old professor who insists on wearing a well-worn twenty-five-year-old tweed jacket with arm patches. Consumption may be seen by many as simply a tool or means for accomplishing larger ends, such as the writer who needs a computer for word processing. Sensuous, undiminished pleasure may be derived from fairly modest and repeated consumption rituals, such the daily espresso and reading of the local paper at the local coffee house. Still, if a majority or even a significant minority fully accept a materialist conception of the good life, then consumption activity is driven by a constant quest for novelty. Pleasures are fleeting and comforts become boring. More costly novel symbols of status are sought not only to avoid the discomfort of falling behind, but to enjoy the stimulus and pleasure of getting ahead of others in the economic pecking order. Novelties that keep us fashionable, satisfy sensuous pleasures, or fulfill our basic longings for ownership and control of goods are needed to overcome the perpetual problem of insufficient stimulus that comes with affluence.

The predominant metaphor in economics is Adam Smith's invisible hand. Through the pursuit of self-interest, material needs will be met, and through competition, prices will be driven down to the point where they just cover the average costs of production. In such a world, there would be very little interest in investing heavily in new ideas and technology since the resulting profits would be quickly competed away by imitators. The metaphor of creative destruction offered by Schumpeter more or less inverts the invisible hand.[64] The attraction of the marketplace is the opportunity to obtain a very visible monopoly. New products and technologies are invented because they offer the creator a monopoly and the monopoly profits that go with it. In a dynamic world, such monopolies, however, are generally temporary. Others will be motivated to seek still newer and more innovative technologies that replace the old. This vision of how a modern capitalist economy works blends nicely with "the consumption of novelty" that follows from a materialist conception of the good life and Veblen's notion of conspicuous consumption. The novelty-seeking consumer provides the market for the monopoly-seeking entrepreneur. Anyone reasonably familiar with recent economic history, I suspect, will be hard-pressed to reject the creative destruction–conspicuous consumption metaphor as a reasonable description of much of modern economic reality.

If the contents of this chapter offer a reasonable description of contemporary economic life, then a modern affluent economy will exhibit a strong tendency to grow. Growth will be driven by the monopoly-seeking entrepreneur and will satisfy the addictive desires of consumers. If growth were socially benign, then consumer addictions would be like an addiction to caffeine. Nothing much would come of it. If, however, growth leads to larger problems such as environmental decline, then a social addiction to growth could be troublesome. Before assessing the extent to which economic growth can be environmentally debilitating, we need to understand current public policy toward economic growth and stability. Growth, we will see, is essential to the smooth functioning of a modern economy; without it, society will face the pain of unemployment, something governments find politically important to avoid if at all possible.

NOTES

1. Thorstein Veblen, *The Theory of the Leisure Class: An Economic Study of Institutions* (New York: Mentor Books, 1953).
2. Veblen, *The Theory of the Leisure Class*, 70.
3. Veblen, *The Theory of the Leisure Class*, 71.
4. Veblen, *The Theory of the Leisure Class*, 80.
5. Veblen, *The Theory of the Leisure Class*, 81.
6. Veblen, *The Theory of the Leisure Class*, 85.
7. See Juliet B. Schor, *The Overworked American: The Unexpected Decline of Leisure* (New York, Basic Books, 1991).
8. Veblen, *The Theory of the Leisure Class*, 85–86.
9. For a more detailed discussion of this issue, see Robert H. Frank, *Choosing the Right Pond: Human Behavior and the Quest for Status* (New York: Oxford University Press, 1985), 155–67.
10. Tibor Scitovsky, *The Joyless Economy: An Inquiry into Human Satisfaction and Consumer Dissatisfaction* (New York, Oxford University Press, 1976).
11. Scitovsky, *The Joyless Economy*, 15–22.
12. Scitovsky, *The Joyless Economy*, 23.
13. Scitovsky, *The Joyless Economy*, 28–30.
14. Scitovsky, *The Joyless Economy*, 31–58.
15. Scitovsky, *The Joyless Economy*, 61–62.
16. Scitovsky, *The Joyless Economy*, 63–67.
17. Scitovsky, *The Joyless Economy*, 67–68.
18. Scitovsky, *The Joyless Economy*, 68.
19. Scitovsky, *The Joyless Economy*, 70–79.
20. Scitovsky, *The Joyless Economy*, 114–24.
21. Scitovsky, *The Joyless Economy*, 124–45.
22. Ronald J. Faber and Gary A. Christenson, "In the Mood to Buy: Differences in Mood States Experienced by Compulsive Buyers and Other Consumers," *Psychology and Marketing* 13 (1996): 803–19; Aric Rindfleisch, James E. Burroughs, and Frank Denton, "Family Structure, Materialism, and Compulsive Consumption," *Journal of Consumer Research* 23 (1997): 312–25; Ronald J. Faber et al., "Two Forms of Compulsive Consumption: Comorbidity of Compulsive Buying and Binge Eating," *Journal of Consumer Research* 22 (1995): 296–304; Gary A. Christenson et al., "Compulsive

Buying: Descriptive Characteristics and Psychiatric Comorbidity," *Journal of Clinical Psychiatry* 55 (1994): 5–11; Ronald J. Faber, "Money Changes Everything: Compulsive Buying from a Biopsychological Perspective," *American Behavioral Scientist* 35 (1992): 809–19; Elizabeth C. Hirschman, "The Consciousness of Addiction: Toward a General Theory of Compulsive Consumption," *Journal of Consumer Research* 19 (1992): 155–79; Gerhard Scherhorn, "The Addictive Trait in Buying Behavior," *Journal of Consumer Policy* 13 (1990): 33–51; Alain d'Astous, "An Inquiry into the Compulsive Side of 'Normal' Consumers," *Journal of Consumer Policy* 13 (1990): 15–31; Thomas C. O'Guinn and Ronald J. Faber, "Compulsive Buying: A Phenomenological Exploration," *Journal of Consumer Research* 16 (1989): 147–57; Gilles Valence, Alain d'Astous, and Louis Fortier, "Compulsive Buying: Concept and Measurement," *Journal of Consumer Policy* 11 (1988): 419–33.

23. Christenson et al., "Compulsive Buying," 6; d'Astous, "An Inquiry into the Compulsive Side of 'Normal' Consumers."

24. Data for these calculations were obtained from U.S. Executive Office of the President, Council of Economic Advisors, *Economic Report of the President: Transmitted to the Congress, February 2002* (Washington, D.C.: U.S. Government Printing Office, 2002).

25. Russell W. Belk, "Possessions and the Extended Self," *Journal of Consumer Research* 15 (1988): 139–68.

26. Russell W. Belk, "Materialism: Trait Aspects of Living in the Material World," *Journal of Consumer Research* 12 (1985): 265–80; Guliz Ger and Russell W. Belk, "Cross-cultural Differences in Materialism," *Journal of Economic Psychology* 17 (1996): 55–77.

27. In *The Overspent American: Upscaling, Downshifting, and the New Consumer* (New York: Basic Books, 1998), 74, Juliet B. Schor suggests that we are no longer attempting to keep up with our neighbors. Rather, our reference group includes friends, relatives, and coworkers.

28. William O. Bearden and Michael J. Etzel, "Reference Group Influence on Product and Brand Purchase Decisions," *Journal of Consumer Research* 9 (1982): 183–94; William O. Bearden, Richard G. Netemeyer, and Jesse E. Teel, "Measurement of Consumer Susceptibility to Interpersonal Influence," *Journal of Consumer Research* 15 (1989): 473–81; Terry L. Childers and Akshay R. Roa, "The Influence of Familial and Peer-based Reference Groups on Consumer Decisions," *Journal of Consumer Research* 19 (1992): 198–211.

29. Rob Allessie and Arie Kapteyn, "Habit Formation, Interdependent Preferences and Demographic Effects in the Almost Ideal Demand System," *The Economic Journal* 101 (1991): 404–19; Robert L. Bassmann, David J. Molina, and Danile J. Slottje, "A Note on Measuring Veblen's Theory of Conspicuous Consumption," *The Review of Economics and Statistics* 70 (1988): 531–35.

30. Angela Chao and Juliet B. Schor, "Empirical Tests of Status Consumption: Evidence from Women's Cosmetics," *Journal of Economic Psychology* 19 (1998): 107–31.

31. Bruno S. Frey and Alois Stutzer, *Happiness and Economics: How the Economy and Institutions Affect Well-being* (Princeton, N.J.: Princeton University Press, 2002), 25–36.

32. Michael Argyle, "Causes and Correlates of Happiness," in *Well-Being: The Foundations of Hedonic Psychology*, ed. Daniel Kahneman, Ed Diener, and Norbert Schwartz (New York: Russell Sage Foundation, 1999), 353–73.

33. Frey and Stutzer, *Happiness and Economics*, 82; Robert H. Frank, *Luxury Fever: Money and Happiness in an Era of Excess* (Princeton, N.J.: Princeton University Press, 1999), 111; Richard A. Easterlin, "Will Raising the Incomes of All Increase the Happiness of All?" *Journal of Economic Behavior and Organization* 27 (1995): 35–47; Ed Diener et al., "The Relationship Between Income and Subjective Well-Being: Relative or Absolute?" *Social Indicators Research* 28 (1993): 195–223.

34. Frey and Stutzer, *Happiness and Economics*, 75.

35. For a somewhat different view, see Ed Diener and Shigehiro Oishi, "Money and Happiness: Income and Subjective Well-being across Nations," in *Culture and Subjective Well-being*, ed. Ed Diener and Eunkook M. Suh (Cambridge, Mass.: The MIT Press, 2000), 185–218. In this study, the correlation of income and satisfaction was higher for countries with lower incomes, but not at statistically significant levels.

36. Frey and Stutzer, *Happiness and Economics*, 77; Easterlin, "Will Raising the Incomes of All Increase the Happiness of All?" 39–40.

37. Sara J. Solnick and David Hemenway, "Is More Always Better?: A Survey on Positional Concerns," *Journal of Economic Behavior and Organization* 37 (1998): 373–83.

38. David Neumark and Andrew Postlewaite, "Relative Income Concerns and the Rise in Married Women's Employment," *Journal of Public Economics* 70 (1998): 157–83.

39. Frank, *Choosing the Right Pond*, 23.

40. For evidence casting doubt on the significance of relative concerns, see Diener et al., "The Relationship Between Income and Subjective Well-Being."

41. Daniel Kahneman, "Objective Happiness," in *Well-Being: The Foundations of Hedonic Psychology*, ed. Daniel Kahneman, Ed Diener, and Norbert Schwartz (New York: Russell Sage Foundation, 1999), 3–25.

42. Daniel Kahneman, "Objective Happiness," 14.

43. Daniel Kahneman, "Objective Happiness," 14.

44. Joseph Schumpeter, *Capitalism, Socialism, and Democracy*, 3rd ed. (New York: Harper and Brothers Publishers, 1950), 83.

45. Schumpeter, *Capitalism, Socialism, and Democracy*, 83.

46. Schumpeter, *Capitalism, Socialism, and Democracy*, 83.

47. Schumpeter, *Capitalism, Socialism, and Democracy*, 84.

48. For evidence that the Schumpeterian economic dynamic is at work in the U.S. economy, see Patrick Francois and Huw Lloyd-Ellis, "Animal Spirits through Creative Destruction," *American Economic Review* 93 (2003): 530–50.

49. James Wallace and Jim Erickson, *Hard Drive: Bill Gates and the Making of the Microsoft Empire* (New York: John Wiley & Sons, 1992); Daniel Ichbiah and Susan L. Knepper, *The Making of Microsoft: How Bill Gates and His Team Created the World's Most Successful Software Company* (Rocklin, Calif.: Prima Publishing, 1991); Charles H. Ferguson and Charles R. Morris, *Computer Wars: How the West can Win in a Post-IBM World* (New York: Random House, 1993).

50. Michael L. Katz and Carl Shapiro, "Antitrust in Software Markets," in *Competition, Innovation and the Microsoft Monopoly: Antitrust in the Digital Marketplace*, ed. Jeffrey A. Eisenach and Thomas M. Lenard (Boston: Kluwer Academic Publishers, 1999), 29–81.

51. It is true that file conversion from WordPerfect to MS Word is possible, but the conversion process is time-consuming and seldom works with complete accuracy.

52. Katz and Shapiro, "Antitrust in Software Markets," 32–34.

53. Thomas Penfield Jackson, *United States v. Microsoft Corporation: Findings of Fact* (Washington, D.C.: United States District Court for the District of Columbia, 1999, http://usvms.gpo.gov/findings_index.html), 17–19.

54. Katz and Shapiro, "Antitrust in Software Markets," 34–36.

55. Wallace and Erickson, *Hard Drive*; Ichbiah and Knepper, *The Making of Microsoft*.

56. Microsoft could have profited from the Windows 98 upgrade at a price of $49 but chose the revenue-maximizing price of $89 as any good profit-maximizing monopolist would. See Jackson, *United States v. Microsoft Corporation*, 32.

57. Jackson, *United States v. Microsoft Corporation*, 16. This figure includes Apple operating systems installed in the total.

58. Jackson, *United States v. Microsoft Corporation*, 35–38.

59. Thomas C. Rubey, "Profile of Computer Owners in the 1990s," *Monthly Labor Review* 122 (1999): 41–42.

60. Rubey, "Profile of Computer Owners in the 1990s," 41.

61. U.S. Executive Office of the President, Council of Economic Advisors, *Economic Report of the President: 2002*, Table B-18.

62. Bob Davis and David Wessel, *Prosperity: The Coming Twenty-Year Boom and What it Means to You* (New York: Random House, 1998), 90–102.

63. Davis and Wessel, *Prosperity*, 105–38; Erik Brynjolfsson and Lorin Hitt, "Paradox Lost? Firm-Level Evidence of the Returns to Information Systems Spending," *Management Science* 42 (1996): 541–58; Erik Brynjolfsson and Lorin Hitt, "Beyond Computation: Information Technology, Organizational Transformation and Business Performance," *Journal of Economic Perspectives* 14 (2000): 23–48.

64. Leonard I. Nakamura, "Economics and the New Economy: The Invisible Hand Meets Creative Destruction," Federal Reserve Bank of Philadelphia, *Business Review*, July/August 2000: 15–30.

3

The Macroeconomics of Being Hooked on Growth

The novelty- and status-seeking consumer and the monopoly-seeking entrepreneur blend together to form the underpinning of long-run economic growth. Growth in the short run, however, is modulated and shaped by public sector fiscal and monetary policies. The federal government, through its control over spending and taxation, and the Federal Reserve Bank, through its control over interest rates, attempt to influence the path taken by the economy as a whole. The intention of such policies is to limit unemployment by keeping the economy charging ahead at its growth potential while at the same time avoiding the problem of inflation. Pulling this off involves a critical balancing act that is only imperfectly achieved in practice. Growth is essential to prevent excessive unemployment, but too much growth will bring inflation. If the economic growth rate is persistently below the growth rate of the economy's full employment potential output, then unemployment and the pain and social disruption that go with it will build over time. Growth is indispensable as the economy is currently arranged to avoid the debilitation of unemployment. To explain all this in the simplest terms possible is the purpose of this chapter.

GDP AND FULL EMPLOYMENT OUTPUT

To make sense of the growth–unemployment connection, certain concepts from macroeconomic theory need to be introduced. First and foremost, discussion of ideas about the economy as a whole must run in terms of some kind of output measure. For better or worse, the standard measure—inflation adjusted Gross Domestic Product or GDP—will be used. Anyone who watches television news or reads a newspaper has no doubt heard of GDP, since reports about its growth or decline are awaited with much anticipation and discussed extensively in the media. Briefly put, real GDP is the inflation adjusted dollar value of all goods and services newly produced within the borders of a country over the period of a year. If GDP were not adjusted for inflation, then it would be an inaccurate measure of economic output. For instance, if all prices went up by 5 percent from one year to the next, unadjusted GDP would also rise by 5 percent if output happened to remain unchanged. If we looked just at unadjusted GDP, we might think that output increased by 5 percent when in fact it didn't; only the prices charged for output went up. Inflation-adjusted (real) GDP has significant flaws as a measure of output, particularly when environmental quality is brought into account, but such issues needn't be of much concern here. No widely accepted alternatives are available, and real GDP will do as a rough measure of output for the purpose of considering relationships between output, unemployment, and inflation.

A second concept that will be highly useful is the notion of full-employment real GDP. This is the most output our economy could produce if everyone who wants to work is employed at the most hours in a year their employers can get them to work.[1] This is a potential output level that is seldom if ever reached in practice but serves as a benchmark for the amount of output the economy can potentially supply at a given point in time. Full-employment output is in turn dependent on two critical variables: (1) the total number of hours that potentially can be worked with everyone fully employed; and (2) the average output per hour worked. This later measure is usually referred to as "productivity," or sometimes "labor productivity," and is defined as real GDP per hour worked. Full-employment GDP is equal to the product of total potential hours of work and productivity. Forces influencing productivity are a subject of considerable debate, but they include the educational and skill level of the labor force, the volume of capital goods available to workers in the form of machinery, equipment, and various other tools and facilities, and the kind of technology embodied in those capital goods.[2]

Productivity is especially important because it ultimately determines a society's average material affluence. If productivity increases, then in theory workers can on average be paid more in inflation-adjusted terms and can increase their purchases of goods and services. Real (inflation-adjusted) wage growth that is in balance with productivity growth does not necessarily occur, however, as historically demonstrated by a decline in real wages for hourly workers since the mid-1970s despite the occurrence of significant productivity growth.[3]

To reiterate, full-employment real GDP depends on the total labor amount of labor hours that can be worked by the labor force and the amount of output produced by the typical worker. Full-employment real GDP is simply the product of labor hours supplied and output per hour worked. The annual growth rate of full-employment real GDP is thus dependent on the growth of the labor force measured in hours supplied and the growth of labor productivity. Because of the mathematics of growth rates, the growth rate of full-employment real GDP will equal the sum of the growth rates for the labor force and labor productivity. If, for example, the growth rate of the labor force is 1 percent annually and the growth rate of labor productivity is 2 percent annually, then the growth rate for full-employment real GDP will be 3 percent annually. If the economy were fully employed, this is the most it could grow in a year in terms of actual output. In other words, this is the economic-growth speed limit.

The speed limit varies over time, depending on actual labor-force and productivity growth. In the booming 1960s, for example, productivity grew at around 3.2 percent per year while the labor force was expanding at about 1.7 percent per year for a speed limit of a substantial 4.9 percent. In the 1970s, the labor-force growth rate increased to 2.6 percent as the baby boomers entered the labor force, but productivity growth slumped to 1.8 percent, resulting in a lowering of the speed limit to 4.4 percent. Productivity growth got even worse in the 1980s, falling to 1.7 percent. The labor force growth rate also slowed with the end of the baby boomer bulge to 1.6 percent, resulting in a decline in the growth speed limit to 3.3 percent during the 1980s. In the high-technology boom of the 1990s, productivity growth recovered to 2 percent a year while labor-force growth continued declining, reaching 1.1 percent.[4] The current view is that potential full-employment economic growth is running somewhere in the 3 to 4 percent range.[5]

The full-employment growth rate, or growth speed limit, is an important benchmark. If the growth rate for actual real GDP is persistently less than the benchmark, then unemployment will build. If the growth rate of real GDP demanded by the public is persistently greater than the benchmark, inflation will accelerate. Why? This all requires further explanation. As a simplifying convention, the term "GDP" will henceforth refer to the inflation-adjusted variety.

INFLATION, UNEMPLOYMENT,
AND THE GROWTH SPEED LIMIT

For the sake of argument, assume that the economy is fully employed. What if full-employment GDP grows by 3 percent over the next year while actual or measured GDP grows by only 2 percent? With everyone who wants to work fully employed, 3 percent more output can be produced. However, only 2 percent more output needs to be produced to supply the actual purchasers. The economy can get along with 1 percent less output than is feasible and roughly 1 percent fewer labor hours than are available, meaning that unemployment will rise either because businesses shed workers through layoffs or new entrants to the labor force don't find jobs.[6] No doubt some of the reduction in labor hours will be spread over workers who remain employed because of a decline in the average workweek, but much of the reduction is bound to take the form of layoffs and declines in hiring. Why the latter occurs instead of a simple reduction in hours for everyone is an interesting question in its own right and will be taken up in a chapter 6. For now, layoffs and reduced hiring are accepted as the ways employers bring about reductions in labor hours worked. The conclusion is simple. A GDP growth rate below the growth rate of full-employment output will result in rising unemployment. Growth in GDP is indeed required to prevent the pain of unemployment.

In order to talk about the inflation issue, the notions of desired expenditures and actual expenditures for newly produced goods need to be distinguished from one another. The public could attempt to buy more goods than the economy can produce at full employment, but the actual amount purchased can never be more than full-employment GDP. Desired expenditures (in inflation-adjusted terms) can be more than full-employment GDP, but actual expenditures cannot. If desired expenditures exceed full-employment GDP, upward pressure on product prices is likely. Businesses will either take advantage of the situation by raising prices to improve their profit margins, or else they will face rising wages and labor costs as they compete with one another to hire more workers in an attempt to meet consumer demand. Higher wage rates will translate into higher labor costs per unit of output and higher prices as businesses raise prices to cover higher costs and protect their profit margins. So if desired expenditures persistently grow more rapidly than full-employment GDP, inflation will accelerate.[7]

In sum, keeping the economy on a full-employment, inflation-free growth path involves a critical balancing act. To avoid inflation once the labor force is fully employed, GDP can't grow more quickly than the growth rate in full-employment GDP. This growth rate, equal to the sum of the labor force and productivity growth rates, is the ultimate economic speed limit. To avoid rising unemployment, however, GDP growth must at least equal the growth speed limit.

THE GROWTH SPEED LIMIT
AND MONETARY AND FISCAL POLICY

History demonstrates that growth along a path that minimizes unemployment as well as inflation is by no means assured. Advocates of unfettered markets guided only by the "invisible hand" would argue that the best that can be expected will be achieved in the absence of any kind of government intervention. Governmental agencies, however, don't seem to see things this way. Clearly, the Federal Reserve Bank, through its board of governors, manipulates the money supply and interest rates so as to modulate economic expansion and price inflation.[8] The federal government itself also attempts to alter the direction of the economy from time to time through either its spending or taxation practices. In the early 1960s the Kennedy administration cut tax rates for the purpose of stimulating the economy.[9] The Reagan administration in the early 1980s did the same thing, although it hoped to stimulate the supply side as opposed to the demand side of the economy.[10] The effectiveness of such efforts needn't be of concern for the moment. The point is, the goal of public policy is to keep the economy growing in order to limit unemployment while avoiding excessive growth that leads to inflation.

Public policy in the 1990s illustrates clearly the balancing act between too much and too little growth. Until the recession beginning in 2001, the big debate at the Federal Reserve was over the magnitude of the growth speed limit and the amount of growth allowable without causing increased inflation. Alan Greenspan, the chairman of the Federal Reserve, argued that the rate of productivity growth had permanently increased as a consequence of the application of new technology, such as computers, high-speed communications, and robotics, to the task of productivity improvement. In the early 1990s, the Federal Reserve (the Fed) staff was arguing that growth much above 2.5 percent a year would kindle inflation. Contrary to the conventional wisdom, actual growth during the period 1996–1998 ran in the 3.6–4.4 percent range without fostering higher inflation rates. Although some at the Fed remained skeptical that such high rates of growth could be sustained, Greenspan convinced his colleagues to keep interest rates stable for much of the 1996–1999 period despite relatively rapid growth rates for real GDP. Only in 1999 when inflation fears increased did the Fed begin to increase interest rates. By this time even the skeptics began to believe that the economy could grow in the 3–4 percent range without sparking inflation. But the bursting of the high-tech bubble and the resulting sharp decline in high-tech capital equipment orders in 2000 set the stage for the recession of 2001 and also reduced the Fed's optimism on the growth speed limit. At the end of 2001, the Fed's researchers estimated that the maximum potential growth rate for the economy had dropped to around 3 percent. The whole issue became academic in 2001 as the Fed reversed course and madly began to slash interest rates in order to forestall declining growth rates and a slide into recession.[11] With the events of September 11, 2001, accentuating the plunge into recession, Congress and the Bush administration jumped into the policy fray with proposals to stimulate economic recovery through increased spending and reduced levels of taxation.[12] Recession and negative economic growth brought with it rising unemployment.[13] The goal of both the Federal Reserve and the federal government shifted to fighting unemployment.

This recent monetary and fiscal policy experience supports the notion that the central economic concern in this country is with economic growth. If growth falls below the economic speed limit, the Federal Reserve and the federal government pursue policies to turn growth around, suggesting that too much pain from unemployment is politically unacceptable.

DEPENDENCY ON GROWTH

Growth is needed for more reasons than to just keep up with labor-force and productivity expansion. Without growth, economic decline is a distinct possibility. GDP is composed of basically four pieces: consumption, gross domestic investment, government spending, and exports minus imports. Investment mainly includes spending by businesses on those things that ultimately expand their capacity to produce, such as computers, machinery, and new buildings. Common sense suggests that businesses won't enlarge their spending on such items unless they foresee expansion in markets for the goods they produce and sell. Simply put, economic growth requires more and new kinds of productive capacity. A one-time investment in plant capacity is required for each permanent addition to GDP. A constant investment level requires constant annual additions to GDP; a growing investment level requires expanding additions to GDP. If GDP is not expanding, then investment in new plant capacity falls. As long as Chrysler can sell more minivans each year, it will add to production capacity to meet sales expansion. If minivan sales stabilize, then investment in new capacity will go to zero. The point is simple; without growth, investment spending and GDP will be less than otherwise and so will employment. Less growth can cause a downward cascading of economic activity and even push growth into negative territory. Growth is essential just to keep the economy from sliding into a downward spiral.

Because growth is so central to the health of the modern macroeconomy, the forces behind growth are of critical importance. Fiscal and monetary authorities can modulate economic activity at the margin, but deeper phenomena are responsible for the underlying tendency to economic expansion, as suggested in chapter 2. Veblen's conspicuous consumption, Scitovosky's novelty-driven psychological stimuli, and Schumpeter's creative destruction are at the heart of the economic growth process. Without them, growth is likely to fail, and the result under existing social arrangements will be the pain of unemployment.

Linkages between the demand and the supply sides of the economy are critical for continued economic growth. Veblen's conspicuous consumption on the demand side of the economy requires a periodic infusion of new kinds of status goods from the supply side of the economy. Individuals wear certain clothes, drive certain cars, and live in houses with a certain style in a certain neighborhood to demonstrate their economic position in the social pecking order. The status demonstrated with a particular commodity depends on its rarity. But as average incomes increase, particular status goods become more affordable and less rare. At one time simply owning an automobile or a television was a sign of economic status. With reductions in costs from mass production and advances in incomes, ownership of such products widened. New kinds of status goods are now required. A television set alone won't do; a house full of electronic devices is needed now to keep up with the Joneses. Schumpeterian-style entrepreneurs on the supply side of the economy create the new kinds of goods that offer new ways of demonstrating status and keep conspicuous consumption advancing on the demand side. Conspicuous consumption on the demand side requires creative destruction and entrepreneurial action on the supply side.

The connection between conspicuous consumption and creative destruction is just as easily turned around. In the absence of conspicuous consumption, consumers will not demand the full cornucopia of new goods turned out by Schumpeterian creative destruction. Entrepreneurial investment spending to fund new product development will atrophy and GDP will lessen, dragging down employment. If the latest expensive hand-held computer devices are unwanted, businesses won't create them. In this way, creative destruction and growth on the supply side depend on conspicuous consumption on the demand side of the economy.

More than just status is at stake in the world of consumption. Goods offer comfort and the stimulus of pleasure. Once acquired, the stimulus of pleasure from a new good tends to wane and the experience of comfort it offers eventually gives way to boredom. A new stimulus will be needed from a still newer and more novel consumption experience. Novelty is a central element in the day-to-day existence of the modern consumer.

Without a new restaurant, electronic gadget, video game, perfume, or brand of sport utility vehicle, life would just not be as interesting and stimulating. Entrepreneurial energy is essential on the supply side of the economy to feed the desire for novelty on the demand side. In the absence of the desire for novelty on the demand side, contentment with existing consumption may well dampen spending, reducing GDP and employment. With little interest in the new and novel, the monopoly-seeking entrepreneur on the supply side of the economy would face more limited outlets for market-capturing innovations. This in turn would mean less investment spending to transform innovative ideas into new products. Not only would consumption be less in such a world, but so would investment spending. The final result would be less GDP, less employment, and more unemployment. Again, the supply and demand sides of the economy are interdependent. Novelty seeking on the demand side and the entrepreneurialism of creative destruction on the supply side need one another.

The point of all this is simple. The modern economy depends on growth to forestall economic decline and rising unemployment. Without conspicuous consumption and the desire for consumer novelty on the demand side of the economy, GDP and its growth would suffer. The same can be said for the novelty-creating energy of creative destruction on the supply side of the economy.

THE PAIN OF UNEMPLOYMENT

Once again: Economic growth is essential to avoid the pain of unemployment. Growth is also essential in order to enjoy the novelty of new goods and to have new means for demonstrating status. Getting unhooked from the desire for novelty and status goods without undue sacrifice is a distinct possibility, as chapter 6 will argue. Dealing easily with the pain of unemployment is another matter. As the economy is currently constituted, an actual economic growth rate below the growth of full-employment GDP will mean rising unemployment, and rising unemployment is a serious matter because of resulting economic, social, and psychological disruptions.

Unemployment and Bankruptcy

The reduction of income flows brought on by unemployment causes financial stresses and strains in the best of circumstances. Unemployment insurance payments usually replace only a part of lost income and are of limited duration. The unemployed are often faced with the dilemma of having to skip a mortgage payment in order to put groceries on the table or avoid the embarrassment of a motor vehicle repossession. The most extreme form of financial trauma faced by the unemployed is personal bankruptcy.

Any discussion of personal bankruptcy and unemployment must be placed in the larger context of household debt and its relationship to bankruptcy. Between 1980 and 1994 the ratio of household debt to annual income increased from 65 percent to 81 percent. Over a similar period (1979–1997) consumer bankruptcy cases increased fourfold or 400 percent.[14] Despite the dramatic rise in bankruptcy filings, the tipping point for the debt-to-income ratio at which households tend to declare bankruptcy has remained remarkably stable at around 150 percent. Simply put, the proportion of households reaching an unchanging tipping point has increased significantly in the last two decades.[15] The single most important reason for this is the rise of credit card debt. The flood of credit card applications sent through the mail is familiar to us all. Obtaining lines of credit these days is incredibly easy. The logic of lending is now akin to the life insurance business. All who hold credit cards pay a premium in the form of relatively high lending rates, but some will fail to pay their credit card debt. Credit is extended essentially on an actuarial basis. The earnings from those who do pay are enough to cover the losses of those who don't and provide for a significant profit for credit card companies and banks.[16] This new system makes credit immediately available and easy to use.[17]

When this system of easy credit is combined with Veblen's concept of conspicuous consumption and Scitovsky's ideas on the pursuit of comfort and novelty through consumption, the danger becomes clear. Additional status goods and novelties are readily obtainable with an impulsive flick of the wrist. Ready cash is unnecessary. If one's income is lost, pleasure and status can still be defended through the use of credit, at least for a while. For some, the siren song of consumption overpowers financial prudence, and the end result is a trip to the bankruptcy courts.

While the conventional wisdom is that personal bankruptcy is largely confined to those at the lower ranks of socioeconomic status, bankruptcy is in practice a middle-class phenomenon. The ranks of the bankrupt have noneconomic demographic characteristics that mirror the larger population. The educational attainment of those who have gone through personal bankruptcy, for example, is about the same as for the society as a whole. The central difference between those who suffer bankruptcy and everyone else is not socioeconomic status but rather the former's poor financial condition relative to the latter. The phenomenon of bankruptcy is important because it affects a relatively large portion of the population. With bankruptcy filings running about a million a year in the 1990s, over a decade roughly ten percent of all households are affected.

The connection between bankruptcy and unemployment is obvious and substantial. Of all survey respondents in a major study of bankruptcy, 67.5 percent indicated that job problems were a reason for filing bankruptcy.[18] Among the reasons listed for bankruptcy, including creditor, medical, family, and housing problems, job problems were mentioned most frequently. Job problems include unemployment, a recent interruption of employment, reduced earnings, and reduced hours. Of the primary petitioners for bankruptcy among survey respondents, 48 percent report a recent employment interruption.[19] Clearly, unemployment is a significant initiator of bankruptcy. A rise in unemployment increases financial stress and results in increased bankruptcy.

For some who are otherwise in good financial shape, a long period of unemployment is undoubtedly the primary cause of bankruptcy. For many, unemployment is simply a precipitating event that puts them beyond the financial tipping point into bankruptcy. The real problem is excessive debt caused by excessive credit card use or too large a mortgage. One-half to two-thirds of bankruptcy filers are homeowners. While only 6 percent of filers indicate that their home is a reason for their financial problems, homeowners appear to be more vulnerable to job loss. Among homeowners, job loss is listed more often as a reason for a bankruptcy filing. Homeowners will go to great lengths to keep their homes when unemployment hits. They will try to avoid selling in a local market that is depressed by unemployment, and they will reduce their reemployment prospects by refusing to move to other locations where prospects for finding a job are better. Moving costs are also a barrier to relocating because they tend to be substantially higher for those saddled with home ownership than they are for renters. Simply put, unemployment can be an especially traumatic event for homeowners.

Whether caused by excessive housing costs or excessive use of credit for purchases of consumer goods, a high debt level makes adjusting to the shock of unemployment difficult.[20] Unemployed workers are also frequently reluctant to adjust their standard of living downward and attempt to maintain consumption standards as long as they can through the use of credit cards. Ultimately, such financially dangerous behavior can lead to bankruptcy. Even unemployed workers who find new jobs fairly quickly are vulnerable to bankruptcy because of the debt they may run up while out of work.

Unemployment and Health

The most immediate effects of unemployment on individuals are clearly going to be financial in nature. First and foremost, the unemployed are going to have trouble paying their bills. In a society where financial prudence is an important virtue, the inability to meet financial obligations is likely to result in mental anguish and physical stress. Economic stress and deprivation have the potential to damage physical and mental health. Those who can't pay their bills may sleep badly at night, fight with their spouses, drink more alcohol or eat more than they should, or suffer from depression or anxiety. Accumulated stress and resulting behaviors can lead to deterioration of mental and physical health.

Although the primary role of employment for most people is to provide a source of income, a job can also serve a variety of noneconomic or psychological functions. Participation in meaningful work can be a source of personal identity, self-worth, and social recognition. Employment offers opportunities for shared experiences and contacts with others and exposure to larger goals and purposes beyond the strictly personal. Finally, employment imposes a time structure on the day and requires activity, functions that may well be especially important to younger workers.[21] Not all types of employment fulfill every one of these psychological functions. Boring, repetitive jobs are less likely to do so than those featuring a variety of tasks, teamwork, and the opportunity for creativity and independent decision making. Apart from its economic remuneration, the quality of employment is largely dependent on how well the psychological functions are fulfilled.

To the extent that psychological needs are fulfilled by employment, the loss of a job can be an emotionally traumatic event. Unemployment can mean a loss of a sense of self-worth or personal identity, a reduced sense of control over one's fate, and a decline in social connections to others.[22] If such psychological needs are not met by a job or are fulfilled elsewhere, then the loss of a job may be stressful for economic reasons but less so for psychological reasons. In short, employment will be important in meeting psychological needs for some, but not for all.[23]

Studies of the relationship between unemployment and physical and mental health generally find significant correlations. Correlation, however, does not imply causation. Poor health could be a cause of unemployment just as readily as unemployment could cause a deterioration in health. Researchers have addressed this problem by looking at the experience of workers over time and statistically evaluating whether a shift from being employed to being unemployed causes a deterioration in health independently of initial health status.

For younger workers, unemployment appears to increase the incidence of physical illness, but its predominant effect for them seems to be increased psychological disorders, including declines in life satisfaction, self-esteem, and happiness, and increases in distress, anxiety, and depression.[24] Whether young workers are satisfied with their jobs significantly affects the status of their reported mental health and the extent of its deterioration as a consequence of unemployment. Satisfied workers report a significant rise in mental disorders once they are unemployed and a significant decline upon returning to work. Those dissatisfied with work report relatively high levels of mental disorder that changes little with employment status. In other words, an unsatisfying job is no better than unemployment for mental health.[25]

For the working population in general, health and employment interact; good health increases the prospects for employment, and employment increases health.[26] According to researchers, unemployment increases the number of physician visits and the incidence of heart attacks.[27] In one key study, unemployment was found to increase the reported level of both physical illness and depression. This same study found that elevated depression from unemployment was confined entirely to the college educated, although education didn't affect reported physical illness related to unemployment. For the poorly educated, high local unemployment rates and low prospects for reemployment substantially increased reported physical illness and depression. The college educated experienced the greatest residual effects of depression for those who were currently employed in the study but had been previously unemployed. This is consistent with the view that stress from unemployment is primarily financial for the poorly educated and primarily psychological for the well educated. Employment need matters in the connection between health and unemployment. For those with little economic or psychological need for employment, losing a job is of little significance for mental health; for those with high needs, mental health is significantly impaired by unemployment.[28]

Alcohol abuse related to unemployment is not only a potentially serious health problem but can cause dangerous social problems, such as increased domestic violence, as well. While reverse causation is a potential issue in studying the link between unemployment and alcohol abuse, researchers have largely discredited reverse causation by comparing job losers over time with those who remain employed. Most studies show that job loss increases alcohol consumption, although the relationship is weaker in countries that pay unusually high unemployment benefits. One study did find a reverse relationship between unemployment and alcohol consumption and argues that this was a consequence of a reduction in discretionary income. While most studies focus on simple alcohol consumption, one explicitly addresses the question of alcohol abuse, using data from face-to-face interviews for a relatively large sample of individuals from several large cities in the United States. Alcohol abuse was found to increase among those who were laid off between a first and second interview, taking into account the survey participants' alcohol-abuse histories. Surprisingly, the study also found that unemployment in the local area had a disciplining effect on alcohol consumption among those who remained employed. This finding suggests that employees faced with a declining local economy are likely to "clean up their act" and reduce alcohol consumption because employers are most likely to lay off known alcohol abusers first. Whether overall alcohol abuse actually increases with unemployment cannot be established with certainty. Because unemployment affects a small proportion of the total population, it is conceivable that aggregate alcohol abuse actually declines as unemployment rises. Purposely increasing unemployment to reduce alcohol abuse, however, would be a perverse and painful way of solving the problem.[29] Clearly, more research needs to be done to gain a clearer understanding of the effects of unemployment on alcohol abuse.

While the question of whether unemployment increases aggregate alcohol abuse remains to be settled, deterioration of health from higher unemployment is well documented. The decline in physical or mental health caused by unemployment can be traced to both financial stress and the trauma of losing the psychological benefits of employment.

Unemployment and Social Support

In the modern world individuals are largely defined by the work they do. When people meet for the first time, the first question that often comes up is "What do you do?" The loss of a job results in the loss of a big piece of one's identity. Also, in the modern world, primary social networks outside of the immediate family are likely to be rooted in the workplace. Friendships and social ties are frequently developed on the job. Although businesses sometimes discourage it, lovers and spouses are also frequently found on the job. The point is a simple one. Work is a critical connection for many to the larger social world.

The problem with unemployment is that it weakens basic social ties. Not surprisingly, those who become unemployed experience a reduction in contacts with those they consider to be a part of their social network.[30] An important function of our social connections and friendships is to provide assistance in dealing with life's stressful events. Adjusting to a divorce, for example, is made much easier with support from friends. Unemployment is an especially traumatic life event because it disconnects people from the very networks they need to adjust to their new circumstances. For this reason an especially heavy burden is placed on the family as a buffer against the stresses of unemployment, and evidence suggests that families have trouble bearing the strain. In a study of husbands' responses to job loss, the level of hostility, anxiety, and depression increased with unemployment and caused a reduction in the quality of family relationships. This in turn reduced social support received by husbands. In short, unemployment

damages the social network, within as well as outside the workplace, that
people need to get through life's harder moments.

CONCLUSION

The Federal Reserve and federal government administrations are right to
pursue policies that minimize the amount of unemployment a society
must bear. Unemployment is damaging to personal finances, individual
health, and social well-being. If economic growth is a requirement for the
prevention of unemployment, then policies that facilitate growth are to be
applauded. A problem arises, however, if growth itself brings its own
problems with it. Then society is caught in the dilemma of the addict.
Growth brings the euphoria of consumption and avoids the pain of unemployment but leads to long-term debilitation. Whether there really is
long-term debilitation associated with economic growth is the topic of the
next chapter.

NOTES

1. We have to be a little careful with the term "full employment." Some who
want to work may simply lack the minimum skills that employers require. These
individuals will remain unemployed even when the economy is operating at its
maximum potential output. Such individuals are referred to in macroeconomic
textbooks as "structurally unemployed." Structural unemployment is often the result of technological changes in the economy rendering certain kinds of work
skills unneeded. Similarly, "frictional unemployment" may exist if there are temporary problems matching workers with certain skills and jobs. Skilled construction workers may be unemployed in one part of the country, for example, while
construction jobs go begging in another part. Remaining unemployment is referred to as "cyclical" and can in theory be eliminated by operating the economy
at its maximum potential output. The term full employment really means zero
cyclical unemployment. Measured unemployment is the sum of structural, frictional, and cyclical unemployment. Consequently, full employment defined as
zero cyclical unemployment is consistent with positive (structural and frictional)
measured unemployment. For a more extensive discussion of this issue, see Karl
E. Case and Ray C. Fair, *Principles of Macroeconomics, Sixth Editions* (Upper Saddle
River, N.J.: Prentice-Hall, 2001), 136–37.

In practice, full employment, or zero cyclical unemployment, may be unattain-
able for either economic or political reasons. Businesses may pay workers above
the going market rate to induce workers to be more productive. The idea is simple: If you pay people above the going rate, they will work harder and want to
avoid being fired for shirking their work. If you are being paid above the going
market wage rate and get fired, you won't be able get a job that pays as well. This

idea is known as efficiency wage theory. Because of the payment of a wage above the going market equilibrium rate under efficiency wage theory, not all workers desiring employment will be hired. The amount of labor supplied by workers will exceed the amount demanded by employers and the wage rate paid will not decline in order to close the gap. The end result is unemployment. See Case and Fair, *Principles of Macroeconomics*, 286, for a discussion of efficiency wage theory. Efficiency wage theory is one case of a more general collection of problems involving limitations on the ability to fully define contracts between individuals and businesses and is discussed in Samuel Bowles and Herbert Gintis, "Walrasian Economics in Retrospect," *Quarterly Journal of Economics* 115 (2000): 1411–39. Simply put, higher unemployment and higher wage rates have a disciplining effect on workers. Business managers and owners will favor a certain amount of unemployment in order to sustain labor efficiency. This may politically prevent policymakers from attempting to drive cyclical unemployment to zero. For purposes of argument here, we will assume that the full employment output is in fact attainable. The discussion in this chapter would not be much changed if something less than full employment output were the feasible maximum level in practice.

2. Case and Fair, *Principles of Macroeconomics*, 127–30.

3. U.S. Executive Office of the President, Council of Economic Advisors, *Economic Report of the President: Transmitted to the Congress, February 2002* (Washington, D.C.: U.S. Government Printing Office, 2002), Tables B-47 and B-49.

4. U.S. Executive Office of the President, Council of Economic Advisors, *Economic Report of the President*, Tables B-35 and B-49.

5. Jon E. Hilsenrath, "Economy Is Falling Short of Potential, Economists Believe," *Wall Street Journal*, August 31, 2001, A2.

6. We are assuming a proportionality between output at the margin and labor hours required that may occur only approximately in practice. Even if proportionality is not perfect, labor requirements will no doubt decline as output is reduced.

7. There are other sources of inflation than desired expenditures growing more rapidly than full-employment GDP. Some argue that inflation will in fact hit before full employment is reached. Below some unemployment rate, wages, and prices will start to rise because of labor market bottlenecks. In short, unemployment will be eliminated in some occupations before others, and growing demand will cause rising wages in the fully employed occupations. Also, inflation can occur independently of unemployment if energy or raw materials prices are driven up as the consequence, for instance, of the formation of a cartel or, perhaps, because of shortages.

8. The Federal Reserve has an official mandate to pursue both price stability and maximum employment. For an interesting discussion of this mandate by a Fed insider, see Laurence H. Meyer, "Comparative Central Banking and the Politics of Monetary Policy," *Business Economics* 36 (2001): 43–49. To pursue both simultaneously is not always possible. For many years economists argued that unemployment could not be driven below 6 percent without causing inflation to accelerate. The Federal Reserve appeared to buy into this analysis and seemed reluctant to reduce interest rates for the purpose of driving measured unemployment below the 6 percent (see Case and Fair, *Principles of Macroeconomics*, 294–95,

304–306). This hints at a political bias in actual Fed behavior in the direction of fighting inflation. A little extra cyclical unemployment can be a good thing to keep the threat of inflation at bay. A little unemployment is also a good thing for the owners of capital and financial markets because it encourages workers not only to keep their wage demands in check to the benefit of profits, but also to sustain their work effort and productivity for fear of losing their jobs and being unable to find new ones. A little unemployment is a good thing as well for wealthy creditors who would see the real value of the money owed them shrink if inflation accelerates. Conversely, less wealthy working-class debtors would do better in a world of inflation that raises their wages and shrinks the real value of their debts. In the latter half of the 1990s, measured unemployment fell to 4.1 percent and the inflation rate continued to decline. The Fed changed its tune and seemed more willing to accept lower unemployment rates. This was a rare period when the wants of both capital and labor could be satisfied with an expansionary monetary policy. Rapid productivity growth in this period of time served to offset any rises in labor costs.

There may be a political bias to fiscal policy as well. Unemployment rates under Democratic administrations tend to be lower than under Republican ones. Democrats appeal more to a working-class debtor constituency dependent on wages, while Republicans appeal to a wealthier business-oriented creditor constituency focused on profits. Whoever is in charge of the government, Democrat or Republican, there will likely be an upper political limit to the unemployment rate beyond which the regime in power will be kicked out of office. A rise in unemployment above this threshold can only be prevented by keeping the economy growing at its economic speed limit. No matter who holds the reins of power, economic growth is ultimately necessary.

9. Martin F. J. Prachowny, *The Kennedy–Johnson Tax Cut: A Revisionist History* (Cheltenham, U.K.: Edward Elgar, 2000).

10. Anandi Prasad Sahu and Ronald L. Tracy, *The Economic Legacy of the Reagan Years* (New York: Praeger, 1991).

11. Greg Ip and Jacob M. Schlesinger, "Great Expectations: Did Greenspan Push High-Tech Optimism on Growth Too Far?" *Wall Street Journal*, December 28, 2001, A1.

12. Shailagn Murray and John D. Mckinnon, "Consensus Builds to Help the Economy," *Wall Street Journal*, September 27, 2001, A2; Greg Ip, "It's Official: Economy Is in a Recession," *Wall Street Journal*, November 27, 2001: A2.

13. Greg Ip, "Jobless Rate Rose to 5.8% in December," *Wall Street Journal*, January 7, 2002, A2.

14. Teresa A. Sullivan, Elizabeth Warren, and Jay Lawrence Westbrook, *The Fragile Middle Class: Americans in Debt* (New Haven, Conn.: Yale University Press, 2000), 3, 18.

15. Sullivan et al., *The Fragile Middle Class*, 128.

16. Sullivan et al., *The Fragile Middle Class*, 244–52.

17. Alain d'Astous, "An Inquiry into the Compulsive Side of 'Normal' Consumers," *Journal of Consumer Policy* 13 (1990): 15–31

18. Sullivan et al., *The Fragile Middle Class*, 16.

19. Sullivan et al., *The Fragile Middle Class*, 75–83.

20. Sullivan et al., *The Fragile Middle Class*, 205–31.

21. Anne Hammarstrom, "Health Consequences of Youth Unemployment— Review from a Gender Perspective," *Social Science and Medicine* 38 (1994): 699–709; Catherine E. Ross and John Mirowsky, "Does Employment Affect Health?" *Journal of Health and Social Behavior* 36 (1995): 230–43; J. Blake Turner, "Economic Context and Health Effects of Unemployment," *Journal of Health and Social Behavior* 36 (1995): 213–29; Mikael Nordenmark and Mattias Strandh, "Towards a Sociological Understanding of Mental Well-Being among the Unemployed: The Role of Economic and Psychosocial Factors," *Sociology* 33 (1999): 577–97.

22. For evidence that unemployment reduces subjective well-being, see Andrew E. Clark and Andrew J. Oswald, "Unhappiness and Unemployment," *Economic Journal* 104 (1994): 648–59.

23. Nordenmark and Strandh, "Towards a Sociological Understanding of Mental Well-Being among the Unemployed."

24. Hammarstrom, "Health Consequences of Youth Unemployment."

25. Brian Graetz, "Health Consequences of Employment and Unemployment: Longitudinal Evidence for Young Men and Women," *Social Science and Medicine* 36 (1993): 715–24.

26. Ross and Mirowsky, "Does Employment Affect Health?"

27. Ralph Catalano, "The Health Effects of Economic Insecurity," *American Journal of Public Health* 81 (1991): 1148–152.

28. Nordenmark and Strandh, "Towards a Sociological Understanding of Mental Well-Being among the Unemployed."

29. Ralph Catalano et al., "Job Loss and Alcohol Abuse: A Test Using Data from the Epidemiologic Catchment Area Project," *Journal of Health and Social Behavior* 341 (1993): 215–25.

30. Thomas Atkinson, Ramsay Liem, and Joan H. Liem, "The Social Costs of Unemployment: Implications for Social Support," *Journal of Health and Social Behavior* 27 (1986): 317–31.

4

Economic Growth and Environmental Change

Under conventional economic arrangements, economic growth is essential to minimize unemployment and its associated social traumas. Avoidance of the pain of unemployment requires continuous economic expansion. The conventional wisdom is that economic growth is unequivocally a desirable phenomenon. Once environmental concerns are brought into the picture, the benefits of growth are more debatable. If growth indeed results in environmental deterioration, then the avoidance of unemployment through growth comes at a price. Growth truly takes on the characteristics of an addiction. Growth is necessary to avoid the withdrawal pains of unemployment, yet a price is ultimately paid for the addiction to growth in terms of environmental deterioration.

This line of reasoning is obviously contingent on a direct connection between economic growth and environmental decline. The nature of the connection between the economy and the environment depends on how prevailing economic and political arrangements actually function. The conventional view is that environmental quality declines initially as an economy develops but that, beyond some level of development—measured in terms of per capita income—the environment begins to improve, either because of structural changes in the economy or because of a growing middle class making political demands for a cleaner environment. The urban environment in an early industrial economy of the kind described by Charles Dickens is filled with environmental horrors, but as the modern British economy attests, the worst of the problems eventually get cleaned up. In short, affluence brings environmental improvement. This is the central hypothesis of the environmental "Kuznets" curves literature and is adapted from empirical work by Simon Kuznets, who finds that income inequality first increases and then diminishes as incomes rise in the process of economic development.

Understanding the actual relationship between the economy and the environment requires more than offering a simple hypothesis about the connection between income and the environment. A more fruitful approach is to consider the actual environmental consequences that flow from a modern capitalist economy, taking into account the ability of business institutions to influence the politics of environmental regulation. The starting point taken here for this task is Joseph Schumpeter's conception of modern economic reality summarized in his notion of creative destruction, presented in chapter 2. Before revisiting and expanding the Schumpeterian vision to account for the environment, a more general understanding of the linkage between the economic system and the global ecosystem is needed. For this we will turn to a truly original thinker on the topic, Herman Daly.

ECONOMIC CIRCULAR FLOW AND THE ENVIRONMENT

Anyone who has studied macroeconomics is familiar with circular flow analysis. Households purchase commodities produced by businesses, the expenditures of households become the revenues of businesses, and businesses use those revenues to purchase productive services (labor, capital, and natural resources) from households. The incomes of households in turn sustain expenditures on purchases from businesses. In the opposite direction, commodities and services flow from businesses to households and the factors of production flow from households to businesses. Groceries are purchased from supermarkets with incomes earned from employment by householders, and supermarkets in turn use a portion of their revenues to hire householders needed to do the work of selling groceries. Commodities and money flow in a circle that never runs down, and, with continuous investment in additional productive capacity, the flow can be ever expanding. More supermarkets can always be added and more workers hired.

This perception of the macroeconomy is misleading because it ignores scientific laws that place constraints on the flow of inputs to the economic system from the natural environment.[1] The flow of energy and matter through the economic system is in reality linear and unidirectional, not circular. Energy and matter flow from the environment to the economic system and waste heat and matter flow from the economic system to the environment. Supermarkets need energy flows for lighting, heating, and cooling, and they generate flows of waste material that require disposal. The flow begins with the depletion of energy and material resources and ends with the pollution of the environment by waste matter and heat. There is no return flow of energy back to the economic system once it has been transformed into waste heat. Waste matter is in theory recyclable, but in practice recycling potential is limited, as we will now see.

Herman Daly and Nicholas Georgescu-Roegen have gone to great lengths to demonstrate how economists, in their construction of macro-economic models, have failed to recognize that the laws of thermodynamics dictate an absolute scarcity of energy and matter.[2] It is this absolute scarcity that in turn negates the macroeconomic concept of circular flow.

The essence of the first law of thermodynamics is that energy and matter can neither be created nor destroyed. The stock of matter is fixed in availability as is the maximum flow rate for energy. There is an absolute scarcity of both. If energy and matter could be infinitely rearranged without loss, then this law would matter little for economic activity. The disordering of matter created by consumption could simply be compensated for by the reordering of matter through production. Perpetual circular flow, at a constant or even growing rate, would indeed be possible. The problem is that, whenever energy is used to reorder matter, something is permanently lost. This is explained by the second law of thermodynamics.

The second law of thermodynamics basically says that, when performing work, energy is converted to a more dispersed, less useful form. To put it another way, whenever energy is used, it is given off in the form of waste heat. The entropy of energy increases. Entropy is the amount of energy in a system that is not available to do work. An automobile burning a gallon of gas converts energy in a concentrated form into motion and waste heat. The automobile moves, but energy in the gasoline is converted into waste heat unavailable for work.

The flow of matter in production and consumption is also an entropic process.[3] Highly concentrated forms of matter are converted into useful artifacts in production, and in consumption those artifacts are converted into dispersed waste material. The energy of nature—sun, wind, rain, oxidation—causes materials to break down and become more dispersed. A house, for example, slowly deteriorates over time. The paint chips off, wood rots, and the roof deteriorates. As the house deteriorates its material contents become less ordered. Any homeowner is familiar with the process. An increase in entropy is a decrease in order. To reconcentrate all dispersed matter from a consumption process would require an impossibly large amount of energy, rendering 100 percent recycling an impossibility. Matter, like energy, is subject to entropy.

The extent to which the entropy of energy and matter impinges on the circular flow of commodities in the macroeconomy, or damages the natural environment on which the macroeconomy depends, is a fundamental issue that must be addressed by a more broadly based environmental approach to macroeconomics. The entropic, linear flow of energy and matter results in changes to both biotic and abiotic components of what can be called the global ecosystem. Abiotic components include the earth's atmosphere and climatic patterns, the input of solar energy, and the reserves of energy and materials in the earth's crust. The biotic components include a vast array of species and biological communities created and shaped by the interaction of natural evolutionary forces and ecological processes.

In short, the fundamental problem facing an environmental approach to macroeconomics as an area of intellectual inquiry is this: the global economy is growing while the global ecosystem is stable in terms of its capacity to supply energy and materials, absorb wastes, and provide a host of ecosystem services.[4] As a result, stocks of nonrenewable resources in the earth's crust are being depleted, waste sinks are filling up, and human-created ecosystems (i.e., agriculture) are taking over a larger and larger percentage of global biotic productivity. Further consequences of these events include a plunge in global biotic diversity, the disappearance of natural habitats (such as tropical rain forests), and numerous environmental problems, including global warming, air and water pollution, toxic wastes, and destruction of the protective ozone layer. To fully understand the impact of economic activity on ecosystems, we need to know something of the services they provide. Then we will be able to move forward and consider the economy–environment relationship in detail.

ECOSYSTEM SERVICES TO HUMAN BEINGS

Human beings as members of the biotic community are dependent on the materials and services provided by ecological systems. We as biotic consumers need access to the primary productivity of plants. In the modern world this has been accomplished mainly through the creation of anthropogenic (human-made) agricultural ecosystems that favor monocultures composed of species with high net primary productivity (net fixation of carbohydrates through photosynthesis). Nonetheless, we do still rely on natural ecosystems for some food resources, such as fish and other marine organisms. Successful agriculture also indirectly relies on natural ecosystems. The most productive agricultural regions in the world are located on old grasslands with their legacies of extraordinarily rich soils, and the soils themselves constitute an essentially natural ecosystem, albeit one that is in danger of destruction from agricultural practices that cause erosion. Although much modified through plant breeding, the genetic stocks of favored agricultural species have their ancestral origins in natural ecosystems, many of which today no longer exist or are threatened with extinction.[5]

In addition to foodstuffs, a variety of fibers and chemicals are extracted from natural and anthropogenic ecosystems. For much of the nineteenth century, old-growth virgin forests supplied most of the timber used in construction and served as the country's primary energy resource. Now that old-growth supplies are depleted, timber harvesting has shifted to second-growth plantation forests. Although many modern drugs have their origins in the flora and fauna of the tropical rain forests,[6] other ecosystems are potential sources as well, as demonstrated by the discovery of taxol, a cancer-fighting chemical, in the Pacific yew, an understory species in Pacific Northwest old-growth forests.[7] In sum, ecosystems, both natural and anthropogenic, are essential sources of food, fiber, and chemicals for human use, actual as well as potential.

Ecosystems perform a variety of additional functions beneficial to human beings. Wetlands serve as nurseries and habitats for a variety of species and also purify water and reduce the intensity of floods. Wetlands are both sponges and filters. Forests, like wetlands, are beneficial because they limit the rapidity of storm water runoff and the erosion that goes with it by storing moisture in their canopies and soils. Old-growth forests often contain streams that are ideal habitats for fishes having both recreational and commercial value, such as salmon and trout. Forests also store up carbon and reduce the potential for global warming caused by the buildup of carbon dioxide and other greenhouse gases in the earth's atmosphere. Together anthropogenic and natural ecosystems are responsible for the maintenance of the balance of gases in the earth's atmosphere necessary to sustain life.[8]

These are tangible, material services that ecosystems provide us. Human beings also enjoy a variety of intangible benefits, especially from natural ecosystems. Natural habitats are frequently the setting for outdoor recreation, including camping, hiking, mountain climbing, photography, bird-watching, nature study, fishing, and hunting.[9] Such intangible uses of the natural world are increasingly important in affluent urban societies where individuals hunger for contact with nature and can afford to devote time and money to its pursuit. Natural ecosystems are also important as the setting for the scientific study of organisms and biotic processes. Finally, natural areas and certain species have cultural significance. In the last century, some of the early national parks were preserved in the United States because of their monumental qualities.

Wilderness remnants with their dramatic natural and geologic features remind U.S. citizens of their pioneer heritage, as do certain species that are national symbols, such as the bison and the Bald Eagle.[10] The point is a simple one. Ecosystems provide us with numerous tangible and intangible services, some of which are indispensable.

Because of its propensity for expansion, the economic process can easily disrupt ecosystem services. Global warming induced by excessive CO_2 emissions can cause damage and destruction to both natural and anthropogenic ecosystems.[11] Excessive liquid waste emissions can overload the nutrient recycling capacity of aquatic ecosystems, inhibiting their ability to function and support a diversity of life.[12] Acid rain and other forms of air pollution can harm the health of both terrestrial and aquatic ecosystems.[13] Deforestation and poor agricultural practices can cause soil erosion in amounts that exceed the capacity of ecosystems to produce new soils.[14] The conversion of natural to anthropogenic ecosystems can reduce biodiversity and, as a consequence, the potential range of chemicals and drugs that can be extracted from nature.[15] Destruction of wetlands can reduce the supply of clean water, diminish biodiversity, and increase flooding.[16] The reduction of natural habitat as a consequence of logging or land development can reduce wildlife populations and cause species extinctions.[17] All such events together reduce tangible and intangible human benefits supplied by ecosystems.

The central argument of this book is that forces leading to economic growth cause the kinds of environmental disturbances just described. The global economy is prone to growth while the global ecosystem is stable in terms of gross productivity and its capacity to provide ecosystem services. While ecosystems individually are subject to disturbance and change, at a global level there is no known natural growth trend in global ecosystem productivity or capacity for service provision. As the global economy expands, it places increasing demands and stresses on the global ecosystem, reducing its capacity to serve the human species.

ECONOMIC GROWTH AND THE ENVIRONMENT

To invoke the laws of thermodynamics as the basis for environmental scarcity and to describe stresses to life-sustaining ecosystems from economic activity says nothing about why modern economic arrangements cause such scarcities and stresses in the first place. This can only be discerned from the logic of the modern economic growth process. As argued in chapter 2, Joseph Schumpeter's metaphor of creative destruction offers a compelling description of modern economic reality.

Let's begin our quest for the link between economic growth and the environment by reiterating some of Schumpeter's key conclusions. Capitalism is by its nature a form or method of economic change—a capitalist economy never is, and never can be, stationary. The fundamental impulse that sets off the economic growth process comes from new consumer goods, new methods of production or transportation, new markets, and new forms of industrial organization. The process of change is qualitative as well as quantitative. Old industries are constantly being reduced in scope or even destroyed and new ones created. The result is not only a quantitative expansion of the economy but a qualitative change in its structure as well. New forms of economic activity are created, and the old decline and sometimes even disappear.

While new industries indeed experience more rapid expansion than old, Schumpeter probably overemphasized the destructive side of the growth process. Old industries, such as printing, paper manufacture, food processing, lumber, and steel, seldom disappear entirely because they serve key economic functions in society. They get transformed from time to time by new technologies, but they remain an essential part of the economy. Creative destruction no doubt operates with full force at the level of the firm, but to a lesser extent at the level of the industry. As Nell has emphasized in his work, economic growth is based on pulling social and economic functions into the market arena that were previously served through nonmarket arrangements (i.e., in household production).[18] Clothing was once produced largely in the home; now it is largely factory produced.

Schumpeter's theory of creative destruction suggests that industries have life-cycle patterns of development characterized by initial rapid growth, a subsequent slowing of growth, and in some instances decline. An industry grows rapidly until it reaches market saturation, that point at which all those who desire a product at a given income are consuming it. This part of the growth process involves diffusion of information about the new industry's product or technology, including advertising to convince the public of the product's importance. Once this period has ended, growth in demand for the product is related to income and population growth and the rate at which competing new products and technologies enter the market and attract consumer attention away from the old. As already suggested, older industries don't necessarily disappear, because they often continue to serve essential economic functions. They may disappear, however, from a particular country as their production facilities are located offshore to take advantage of lower production costs.[19]

The Schumpeterian growth process has found empirical support in the work of Arthur Burns, who established in his pathbreaking work sixty years ago that retardation of growth in specific industries is a universal phenomenon.[20] Burns also established that the economy as a whole does not experience growth retardation, even though individual industries inevitably do. The inference of this conclusion is that new industries step into the breach and take on the job of growth engines and, in the process, prevent a retardation of growth in the aggregate economy. Without the addition of new sectors to the economy, the economic growth rate would decline. A central feature of the long-run economic growth process is the creation of new industries. Economic growth proceeds by adding new forms of activity to the economy.

All forms of economic activity will have some kind of environmental impact, according to the laws of thermodynamics. Whether that impact is substantial or trivial is a matter for history to decide, and history suggests a rather steady pace of new industry creation resulting in a stream of new environmental stresses.[21] The economy is constantly adding new forms of economic activity, according to the Schumpeterian view, and new forms of economic activity are constantly creating new kinds of environmental stress. Some such stresses are reversible and disappear when their source disappears. Urban smoke pollution largely disappeared with the diminished use of coal for home heating and to fuel industrial boilers. Cleaner forms of energy, such as fuel oil and natural gas, displaced a dirty form in this instance. At the other extreme, certain environmental stresses are irreversible. Some kinds of toxic synthetic chemicals, such as DDT or PCB, cannot be broken down through the usual biotic processes and become a permanent fixture in the environment. Even if the source of such chemicals disappears, their presence in the environment, along with their toxicity, does not disappear. Regulatory measures can reduce the damage caused by reversible sources of environmental stress, but they can do nothing for irreversible stresses except to prevent further damage beyond that already done. The scope of regulation occurring after new forms of economic activity have been created and new kinds of environmental stress have been introduced is limited by the presence of irreversibility. Although some forms of economic activity causing significant environmental harms have disappeared, the list of new kinds of economic activities causing environmental stresses is ever lengthening.[22]

That businesses and consumers will voluntarily attempt to modify their economic practices in order to diminish environmental harms is at least a theoretical possibility. The concept of cost externalization, unfortunately, suggests that they won't.

ECONOMIC GROWTH AND THE PROBLEM
OF COST EXTERNALIZATION

Individual businesses and consumers are the agents whose activities not only foster economic growth but bring forth environmental change as well, much of which is detrimental to human beings, ecological systems, species, and populations of plants and animals. If such activities are indeed damaging, why don't economic agents exercise restraint in order to minimize the resulting costs of such damage?

The reason they don't is fairly simple. In the framework of a capitalist economy, where the seeking of material gain by economic agents is the central principle, individual businesses and consumers will attempt to avoid the costs of their actions by externalizing them. Profits for individual businesses and utility for individual consumers can be maximized by emitting pollutants into the air or water rather than bearing the cost of emissions control equipment that would limit the discharge of pollutants. In this fashion the costs of the emissions are externalized and borne by the society as a whole. Gain seeking promotes cost externalization.[23]

This is even the case when the cost of environmental damage to society (assuming that it is measurable) greatly exceeds the internal costs of pollution controls. We all contribute to the problem of air pollution when we drive our automobiles, but the decline in air quality as a result of our own individual actions is imperceptible, while emissions control devices are quite expensive. Few are willing to voluntarily install control devices on their own even though the collective costs of damage from air pollution much exceed the total cost of control devices. This line of reasoning applies as well to businesses that emit pollutants or cause other forms of environmental damage. The tendency is to push the burdens of limiting environmental damage off on others in a society, and the net result is that everyone suffers.

Some argue that if property rights to pollution are assigned to someone, then the problem will be self-correcting.[24] Those who experience damage from pollution need only bargain with those emitting the pollutants to reach an agreement by which the former compensates the latter for the cost of reducing emissions to the net benefit of both. Suppose the reduction in pollution damage costs from a 50 percent decline in electrical power plant sulfur dioxide emissions amounts to $100 billion annually, while the cost of emission controls equals $40 billion per year. Those damaged by pollution could improve their well-being to the tune of $60 billion by paying polluters to cut their emissions by 50 percent. The problem with this approach is that the parties involved in a given negotiation could easily number in the millions, resulting in astronomical transactions costs.[25] A voluntary agreement to fund pollution control costs among a large group is highly improbable. Anyone refusing to participate in the agreement can still benefit from pollution controls without paying the cost. This creates a powerful incentive for opting out of the agreement. If the polluter has the right to pollute, emissions will not be limited because transactions costs will likely exceed any benefits to be achieved from negotiations.

This analysis assumes the polluter has the right to pollute. If the property right is reversed and everyone has a right to clean air, then in order to undertake any emissions at all, the polluter would have to compensate damaged parties for costs incurred from pollution in order to avoid emissions control costs. Starting from a position of zero pollution, suppose the emission control costs for the last 50 percent of emissions reduction by electrical power plants equal $90 billion a year, while the reduction in damage costs for the last 50 percent amount to $50 billion. In these circumstances, allowing some emissions benefits society as a whole. The polluter could gain by paying the damage costs instead of incurring emission control costs. If individuals have a right to a pollution-free environment, in all probability no emissions at all will be undertaken even though some emissions would be to society's benefit. Since all must agree to forgo their rights to clean air, individuals will be tempted to hold out for a bigger piece of the compensation pie, causing transactions costs to be excessive. Again, transactions costs will likely exceed benefits from a negotiated solution because of the large number of parties involved. Discussions of voluntary solutions to pollution are largely academic, because in practice the costs of voluntary negotiation are simply too high. The reality is that environmental problems are not voluntarily resolved.

To put the problem of cost externalization into the framework of creative destruction: As new industries emerge and experience growth, they externalize the costs of environmental damage rather than bear them internally. By default, industries have the right to pollute. Damaging uses of the environment crowd out benign uses. Externalized environmental costs take form as social costs borne by members of the larger society. As economic growth proceeds in the absence of significant environmental regulation, such social costs grow.

VESTED INTERESTS AND ENVIRONMENTAL REGULATION

The roots of environmental problems are deeply embedded in the processes that generate economic growth, according to the discussion so far. The logic of the basic argument presented to this point is simple: Long-run economic growth relies on the creation of new kinds of economic activity and these new kinds of economic activity create new kinds of environmental problems. To complete the story, a final piece of the argument needs to be added: New kinds of economic activity foster vested political interests that oppose environmental regulation. If regulatory measures in practice either substantially prevented or repaired environmental problems, then the economic growth–environment connection would be of little importance, but environmental history suggests otherwise.[26] Because of interest-group opposition, environmental regulation so far has not been up to the task of preventing ecological decline.

The problem of organizing interest groups for the purpose of pursuing political ends plays a key role in explaining the limited effectiveness of environmental regulation. In general, small groups with large per capita interests have much less difficulty organizing politically to pursue their interests than large groups with small per capita interests.[27] Consider a group of ten businesses that stand to lose $10 million from environmental regulation and a group of one million individuals who stand to gain $40 million in reduced external costs from regulation. The loss per business from regulation is one million dollars, while the gain per person is forty dollars.

The business group is going to be relatively easy to organize. If a single business fails to voluntarily participate in an interest group, the total amount of interest group activity would be reduced by 10 percent, a significant amount that could influence the group's effectiveness. Each business will have a strong incentive to participate and avoid being the cause of the group's failure to achieve its goals. Transactions costs in forming a voluntary political lobby against regulation will be relatively low.

The group of individual citizens, on the contrary, will have great difficulty organizing. The nonparticipation of any one individual in the group will reduce the total effort by only .0001 percent, a trivial amount. Hence, individuals will be tempted to act as "free riders," hoping to benefit from group efforts while avoiding membership costs. Transactions costs for a joint agreement on voluntary participation will be very high. Environmental problems tend to affect very large numbers of individuals, while industries that externalize costs tend to be composed of relatively small numbers of businesses. The opposition to regulation is likely to have an easier time organizing than the proponents of environmental regulation. Proponents suffer from the problem of "large numbers."

As already outlined, industries are born, grow rapidly, and experience a retardation of growth as they age. These same industries create new environmental problems that are usually dependent in some way on production levels. As such industries emerge and grow, they create vested industry interests—managers, workers, stockholders, customers, and local communities where production facilities are located. Each industry, with its relatively small number of firms, forms a natural political interest group that can organize relatively easily to fight regulation. The economic growth process, and the new industries it depends on, create vested political interests opposed to regulation.

Despite the large-number problem, well-organized environmental groups have emerged and have become effective advocates of environmental regulation in the United States. These groups include the Audubon Society, Environmental Defense Fund, National Wildlife Federation, Sierra Club, and Wilderness Society, and they have been very active in lobbying for environmental legislation since the 1960s. All major environmental lobbying organizations together had over three million members in 1990.[28]

Why have environmental groups been able to successfully organize in the face of the free-rider and large-number problems? The value orientation of the environmental movement is part of the explanation for its organizational success. Most people in the movement are concerned about the harms that humans inflict on nature and see humanity as morally responsible for the world's ecological integrity.[29] In effect, the value foundations of the movement are ethical. Both human beings, who are ultimately dependent on nature, and nature itself are seen as valuable in their own right and deserving of ethical concern.[30] Members of environmental groups who accept this viewpoint likely see their contributions as a part of their moral obligation to conserve the natural world. If they do, then the free-rider problem diminishes in importance. Support for environmental groups is an end in itself, as opposed to being strictly a means to environmental improvement.

To put it differently, individuals who come together to form voluntary organizations such as environmental groups engage not in the calculus of a private intentionality but in what the philosopher John Searle refers to as "collective intentionality."[31] In the case of collective intentionality, individuals do not see themselves as individuals separate from the group. Group members internalize the goals and purposes of the group, foregoing their own private interests. Just as individual intentionality is a primitive form of behavior in some circumstances, collective intentionality is in others. Where different individuals have a common vision to which they feel duty-bound to contribute, collective intentionality is a likely outcome. Of course, not everyone will feel so strongly and not everyone who benefits from the goods created or preserved by the efforts of an environmental group will voluntarily contribute. But the potential for overcoming the free-rider problem through voluntary collective efforts is a distinct possibility, given the presence of collective intentionality.

Substantial support for environmental groups emerged only after environmental problems had gained a significant amount of public attention.

The process by which aroused public concern occurred for environmental issues is rather elegantly explained by Anthony Downs's widely quoted model of the "issue-attention cycle." According to Downs, social problems proceed through a five-stage cycle: (1) the "pre-problem stage" where a social issue has aroused the interests of experts or interest groups but has yet to attract much public attention; (2) the "alarmed discovery and euphoric enthusiasm" stage, where dramatic events or crises bring the problem to the public's attention and create widespread enthusiasm for solving the problem; (3) a "realization of the cost of significant progress" stage, where public enthusiasm diminishes; (4) a gradual "decline in intense public interest" stage, where costs are recognized, the public becomes bored with the problem, and media attention to the problem declines; (5) the "post problem stage" where the problem is forced off center stage by new problems and moves into "a twilight realm of lesser attention or spasmodic recurrences of interest."[32] Downs did note the possibility that interest in environmental issues might persist at relatively high levels because they affect a relatively large proportion of the population, unlike many other issues.

Perhaps the single most important event in mobilizing the environmental movement and bringing environmental issues into Downs's stage (2) of "alarmed discovery" was the publication in the 1960s of Rachel Carson's *Silent Spring*, where the dangers of emitting toxins such as DDT into the natural environment were established in a manner that was at once eloquent and convincing, yet frightening.[33] With the publication of this book, greater interest in environmental regulation by key political leaders, and increasing media attention to environmental problems, public support in the United States for environmental preservation grew rapidly, peaking in the early 1970s.[34]

Beginning in the mid-1970s, environmental issues were forced out of the limelight by the energy crisis and resulting economic problems and were moved to the latter stages of Downs's issue-attention cycle. Public support for environmental issues in the United States revived in the 1980s, however, with Reagan administration threats to turn back the regulatory clock and publicity from a lengthy list of newsworthy environmental disasters, such as Bhopal, Chernobyl, and Times Beach. By 1990, U.S. public support for environmental regulation had reached unprecedented levels, exceeding those achieved in the wake of Earth Day in 1970.[35] Downs was right in suggesting that the environmental issue may prove to be the exception to the issue-attention cycle.[36]

Nonetheless, the intensity of public support for solving environmental problems has never been very deep, except among a significant minority of the population. To date, 22 percent is the highest percentage of respondents listing environmental issues in polls asking an open-ended question about the most important problems facing the country.[37] For most people, other problems, such as crime or threats to economic security, take precedence over the environment. When push comes to shove, for many people the economy comes first. This in all probability has permitted vested interests in the United States to limit and inhibit environmental regulations.

The combined economic and political cycle can now be summarized. Specific industries emerge and grow, creating new environmental problems. Inside interests, or, as Christopher Bosso calls them, subgovernments, rule the regulatory process in the early stages of industry development before environmental issues enter the glare of wide public awareness.[38] Problems are quietly solved by concerned parties and a few affected politicians. When publicity brings environmental problems to broad public attention, environmental interests favoring regulation organize and win legislative and legal victories against industry interests. When the issues recede from public attention and concern, the newly organized environmental interest groups remain, but vested industry interests are able to recover, and regulatory stalemate results. The regulatory war continues, battles are won and lost, but the rate of real regulatory change slows dramatically.

CREATIVE DESTRUCTION AND
ENVIRONMENTAL KUZNETS CURVES

The Kuznets curve theory of environmental change takes an inherently benign view of the link between growth and the environment. While economic growth is initially harmful to the environment, beyond some per capita income level environmental improvement commences as further economic expansion occurs. While the theory is essentially ad hoc as commonly used, a plausible theoretical underpinning can be provided for environmental Kuznets curves using Schumpeter's notion of creative destruction. In Schumpeter's view, new forms of economic activity emerge periodically as a consequence of the forces of capitalist economic development. In many instances pollution increases in the wake of an expanding new form of economic activity. In short, new forms of economic activity create new kinds of environmental problems. New forms of economic activity are also a stimulus for economic growth and increases in per capita income. As pollution levels rise, the public ultimately reacts. Eventually environmental interest groups overcome the free-rider problem and begin to lobby for regulatory legislation. Initially, environmentalists may be no match for the concentrated power of industry lobbying organizations, but as public awareness of the pollution problem widens, environmental groups ultimately gain a foothold in the political process and are able to influence public policy. They may well be helped by politicians who now see support of environmental legislation as a means for garnering votes at election time. In the Downsian alarmed discovery stage, legislation is passed and pollution emissions are brought under regulation.

This process is perhaps best illustrated by the implementation of regulation for air pollutants in the United States associated with the expanded use of fossil fuels for energy production and especially the increased use of the motor vehicle. The two technologies most responsible for transforming the way we live and use energy are electricity and the internal combustion engine. These two together caused an explosion in the growth of fossil fuel consumption and the pollution that goes with it.[39] The first serious attempt at air pollution control in the United States was manifested in passage of the Clean Air Act Amendments of 1970. This act passed under the highly effective tutelage of Senator Edmund Muskie of Maine and pro-environment congressional staffers. The Natural Resources Defense Council and other environmental groups lobbied for passage of the Clean Air Act. Public opinion was strongly in favor of doing something about air pollution. Industry interest groups that had prevented the passage of clean air legislation in the past, such as the National Coal Association, leading auto makers, and the American Petroleum Institute, were shut out of the decision-making process by Muskie, and suffered a major defeat.[40] In the early 1970s, clean air and other environmental issues were at the peak of the alarmed discovery and euphoric enthusiasm stage of the Downsian issue-attention cycle.

As a consequence of intense public interest and support, environmentalists were successful in obtaining relatively stringent provisions in the Clean Air Act and were able to toughen regulations through legal action in the courts. Unlike past regulatory measures, specific standards and regulatory requirements were written directly into the legislation with the hope of avoiding domination or "capture" of the regulatory agency by industries being regulated.[41] In the Clean Air Act, ambient standards for the purpose of protecting public health were set for sulfur oxides, particulates, carbon monoxide, ozone, nitrogen dioxide, and lead, and states were required to implement these standards. The EPA was charged with defining and enforcing emission standards for all new sources, and new motor vehicles were required to achieve a 90 percent reduction in emissions. Emissions limits were enforceable by both state and federal governments, and citizens were given the right to sue the EPA if provisions of the act were not enforced. The Sierra Club successfully sued the EPA on the grounds that the agency was required by law to prevent any significant deterioration of air quality in addition to enforcing ambient standards.[42]

Shortly after the passage of the Clean Air Act, regulated emissions reached their historic peak and began slowly declining. The one exception is nitrogen oxide emissions, which instead reached a plateau after regulation and remained there. More recently in the late 1990s, sulfur dioxide emissions rose again after bottoming out in 1995. Environmentalists succeeded in obtaining relatively strict regulations for air quality from both Congress and the courts at a point of high public concern in the Downsian issue-attention cycle. However, once public attention turned to other issues, such as the energy crisis in the 1970s and economic problems in the 1980s, industry interests were able to turn some of these regulations to their advantage, to extract delays from Congress, and to take advantage of the EPA's limited enforcement budget and the friendliness of local courts to weaken and forestall air pollution regulations.[43]

The historical economic dynamic described by Schumpeterian creative destruction offers an explanation for the rise and decline of pollution emissions as economic growth proceeds. New industries create environmental problems and foster the formation of vested political interests opposed to regulation, but eventually public concern with environmental decline and political action result in regulation and an improvement in environmental quality. Schumpeterian creative destruction actuates the Downsian issue-attention cycle. Simple decline in polluting older industries as a part of the creative destruction process can also partly explain the cycle of environmental improvement.[44] Rising political concern with environmental deterioration and the decline of older polluting industries are part and parcel of the same economic development process that leads to rising per capita incomes. Combining Schumpeterian creative destruction and the Downs's issue-attention cycle yields an explanation for environmental Kuznets curves.

New industries bring growth and with it, usually, rising affluence. Prosperity reinforces the issue-attention cycle and increases pressure on politicians from their citizenry for a cleaner environment.[45] The hypothesis that politics matters is supported by findings that lower levels of economic inequality, higher rates of literacy, and greater political rights and civil liberties are associated statistically with lower levels of air and water pollution.[46] Not only prosperity is associated with environmental improvement; so is less economic and political inequality.

In support of the Kuznets curve hypothesis, for several different pollutants researchers have found statistical evidence that ambient contamination increases as per capita income rises up to a threshold level (unique to each pollutant) and then declines thereafter as per capita income rises further. The air pollutants for which this behavior occurs include sulfur dioxide, smoke, suspended particulate matter, and carbon monoxide.[47] Similar behavior has also been found for water pollutants such as fecal coliform and heavy metals, including lead, cadmium, and arsenic.[48] The lack of a clean water supply and urban sanitation services appears to diminish as income increases for all levels of per capita income.[49] These results are based on cross-country comparisons of per capita income and various measures of pollution or pollution emissions, and they are consistent either with increases in the ability of environmentalists to organize politically and bring pressure to bear for environmental improvement or with structural shifts in the economy toward more environmentally benign kinds of economic activity. The presence of environmental Kuznets curves is confirmed for a number of pollutants characterized by reversibility. Simply put, as people get richer, they want a cleaner environment, and in a political democracy they will get at least some of what they want.

Kuznets curve researchers themselves recognize that the statistical evidence they find is not perfect. Because most studies compare different countries at a given point in time, they cannot be directly applied to a single country like the United States. It is true that conventional air pollution emissions have mostly trended downward since the 1970s in the United States, suggesting consistency with the Kuznets curve results based on cross-country comparisons. Conversely, indicators of water quality in the United States for the most part suggest an absence of any trend over time, positive or negative.[50] While point sources of water pollutants have been reduced, nonpoint sources remain largely unregulated and appear to be expanding. Kuznets curve results and the actual experience with water quality in the United States appear to be at odds. Kuznets curves accurately describe the U.S. experience with some air pollutants, but not for water pollutants. The United States has done much better in controlling air pollution than water pollution.

Even if the Kuznets curve theory holds in practice for individual countries, it does not mean that declines in pollutants at the global level are guaranteed to occur. If the negative slope of the pollution-emission Kuznets curve for countries with relatively high per capita incomes like the United States is the consequence of a structural shift in the economy, on a global scale pollution emissions won't necessarily decline. As technologies age and stabilize, access to sophisticated engineering talent and skilled factory floor workers declines in importance in the selection of a production facility location. Minimizing labor costs for such aging industries as steel or textiles becomes critical in such choices. These industries increasingly locate in less developed countries where labor and other costs are lower. As affluent countries like the United States lose aging industries through this process, they gain industries based on newly emerging technologies that require highly educated workers to develop.[51] For pollutants related to energy use, statistical evidence suggests that less affluent industrializing countries have increased their use of energy and related pollution emissions as a consequence of increasing their exports of manufactured goods, while affluent industrialized countries have reduced their use of energy and related pollution emissions by importing more manufactured goods.[52] Through trade, affluent countries are shifting pollution emissions to less affluent developing countries. In this way consumers in affluent countries may be able to "distance themselves" from the environmental consequences of their consumption.[53]

In sum, the Kuznets curve hypothesis is perfectly consistent with a Schumpeterian economic dynamic combined with a Downsian issue-attention cycle. New industries drive economic development and per capita income growth as well as environmental deterioration. Environmental problems become visible and gain public attention. Political organization around environmental issues commences, and eventually such issues become a part of the public agenda. At the same time, rising prosperity and associated improvements in education and political access expand the public capacity for political action. Environmental improvement associated with growing prosperity is attributable either to the shedding of dirty industries to less developed countries or to the improved environmental regulation brought on by a political reaction to environmental deterioration, or to a mixture of the two.

We must be clear that this connection between Schumpeterian economic growth and the environmental Kuznets curve is by no means a necessary one. The creation and growth of new industries can just as easily lead to irreversible environmental changes or to staunch regulatory resistance that prevents environmental improvement, as we will now see.

THE LIMITS OF PROSPERITY-INDUCED
ENVIRONMENTAL IMPROVEMENT

The Kuznets curve view of the link between economic growth and the environment suggests that "alarmist" cries of environmental decline are overblown.[54] Simple growth in per capita income will bring forth solutions to environmental problems and improvement in environmental quality. What could be easier? Growth is not only good for its own sake, but it is good for the environment.

A deeper look at environmental and ecological trends paints a different picture. Environmental problems characterized by invisibility, strong regulatory resistance, and irreversibility refute the Kuznets curve pattern. The attractiveness of the Kuznets curve idea turns out to be insidious. The danger is that because the Kuznets curve pattern is valid for some visible environmental problems, it will be generalized to all, both visible and invisible. If the public believes and accepts the idea that economic growth will solve all environmental problems, then the willingness to politically impose significant environmental regulations will doubtlessly weaken. Significant but less visible environmental problems will go unresolved. This is the reason why it is important to put time and effort into refuting the Kuznets curve idea.

Kuznets Curves Are Limited to Visible Problems with Local Impacts

Kuznets curves have been found for only the most visible environmental problems that tend to have local impacts. As prosperity rises, the first environmental tasks that developing economies undertake are the improvement of sanitation and water supply and the reduction of visible smoke. These environmental problems have immediate and visible public health impacts and tend to decline continuously as per capita income increases across countries, according to Kuznets curve statistical results.[55] Other environmental problems, such as sulfur dioxide and suspended particulate pollution, that diminish in intensity only after certain thresholds of per capita income are reached, also have visible and local impacts.[56] Visibility and the presence of local effects seem to matter in the reduction of environmental problems.

Contrary to the standard inverted-U pattern followed by conventional pollutants, greenhouse gas emissions, the volume of municipal wastes, and the number of threatened species all appear to increase continuously as per capita incomes rise across countries, according to statistical studies.[57] The impacts of greenhouse warming and threats to species are largely invisible and global in extent, and they mostly affect the future. Similarly, the disposal of urban waste tends to be out of public view in remote landfills or ocean dumps. These problems are much less likely to attract public attention, and for this reason political organizing efforts around such issues are more likely to be afflicted by the free-rider problem. Political support for regulation of a pollution problem that is local and has immediate effects is more easily generated than it is for one with widely dispersed impacts that will manifest in the future. "Out of site, out of mind" is a pun that clearly applies to global warming, solid waste, and endangered species.

The Limits of Environmental Regulation in Practice

Even where environmental problems have come under regulation, resistance by industry groups to implementation of specific regulatory measures has sometimes been strong and, as a consequence, significant pollution problems persist.[58] The success of regulatory efforts is mixed, as the U.S. experience with air pollution control suggests.

Since 1970, emissions of all the key conventional air pollutants covered by the 1970 Clean Air Act in the United States have fallen significantly, with the notable exception of nitrogen dioxide.[59] Lead emissions have been completely eliminated, the measured ambient concentrations of carbon monoxide have dropped substantially and are no longer a significant environmental threat, and concentrations of large-diameter particulate matter in urban areas are below EPA ambient limits. These are the primary successes of air pollution regulation.

For other pollutants, regulation has been less successful. Ozone—an air pollutant that is created by the interaction of sunlight, volatile organic compounds, and nitrogen oxides—has decreased somewhat over the past twenty years,[60] but more than half the EPA monitoring sites continue to violate ozone standards annually, and little improvement in ambient ozone concentrations occurred in the 1990s.[61] Ozone is potentially damaging to the human respiratory system as well as to cultivated and natural vegetation. For many localities ozone concentrations have yet to be reduced to healthy levels. While emissions of one of the precursors to ozone, volatile organics, has been successfully reduced, the other, nitrogen oxides, continues to increase.

Success in dealing with the problem of acid rain has also been mixed. Because of emissions caps instituted under the EPA's Acid Rain Program beginning in 1995, sulfur dioxide emissions declined by 36 percent between 1990 and 1999. Eventually, this program will cap emissions at about 50 percent of their 1980 levels for power plants, the primary source of such emissions.[62] Acid rain is created when sulfur dioxide and nitrogen oxides in the atmosphere react with water and oxygen to form acidic compounds that eventually fall to earth in either a dry or wet form. Such precipitation raises levels of acidity in some water bodies, rendering them inhabitable by certain kinds of fish and other organisms, and in soils, causing damage to vegetation. While control of sulfur emissions to reduce acid rain has been fairly successful, nitrogen oxide emissions continue to increase, worsening the problem.

So the most notable failure of air pollution regulation is the EPA's inability to reduce emissions of nitrogen oxide, a pollutant that is not only a precursor to the formation of ozone, but a significant cause of acid rain. Without reducing nitrogen oxide emissions, the acid rain and ozone problems will remain. Since regulation began, nitrogen oxide emissions have increased by about 17 percent.[63] Industry interests have successfully resisted the measures required to reduce nitrogen oxide emissions. The lesson of air pollution regulation in the United States suggests that it is indeed possible to significantly reduce reversible environmental problems, but interest-group resistance can prevent the final solution to those more intractable problems requiring a somewhat higher level of economic sacrifice. While certain environmental problems diminish as per capita income increases, there may well be an upper limit for environmental improvement imposed by the power of key economic interest groups.[64]

The Problem of Environmental Irreversibility

The most critical limitation of the Kuznets curve approach linking environmental improvement to prosperity is its failure to recognize the significance of environmental irreversibility. In such cases a rise in per capita income cannot lead to increased environmental quality. Economic growth can foster increases in per capita income, but per capita income growth cannot alter the fact of irreversible environmental decline. Once irreversible environmental damage is done, it is either impossible or prohibitively costly to make amends. To illustrate, four historical cases of environmental irreversibility in the United States will be briefly summarized: the loss of the tallgrass prairie; the decline of Pacific Northwest old-growth forests; dam construction on rivers; and the loss of wetlands. Those who accept the idea of environmental irreversibility are welcome to skip ahead to the conclusion and the next chapter.

Irreversibility and the Loss of the Tallgrass Prairie

While most think of various forms of pollution in reference to environmental problems, the destruction and fragmentation of natural habitats in the United States and elsewhere is a long-standing environmental issue, one that is closely associated with agricultural settlement and production, the extraction of wood fiber and other natural resources, and urbanization. The loss of tallgrass prairie habitat can be traced directly to the settlement of the Midwest on the foundation of commercial agriculture.[65]

Agriculture was the dominant sector in the U.S. economy in the last half of the nineteenth century, and a significant portion of its growth in this period can be attributed to settlement of the Midwest. The fourfold rise in U.S. agricultural production from 1850 to 1900 resulted primarily from a threefold expansion in the amount of land in farms, much of which occurred in the prairie states.[66] From 1850 to 1880, the Midwestern prairie states' share of total U.S. farmland increased from 21 percent to 39 percent.[67] Prairie settlement was driven in turn by the single most influential change in transportation in the nineteenth century, construction of the steam railroad.

Transportation improvements, especially the expansion of the railroad, were necessary for the commercialization and growth of prairie-state agriculture. Since overland transportation costs quickly absorbed the market value of such commodities as wheat and corn as distance to urban markets increased, the transporting of agricultural commodities by wagon was too costly for long-distance shipment. Midwestern commercial agriculture was therefore water-oriented before the coming of the railroad. Population density tended to be heaviest along navigable waterways, and the flow of commodities was predominantly to the south, following the flow of Mississippi watershed rivers.[68]

After 1840 commodity flows began to be redirected to the East through the Erie Canal as a consequence of waterborne transportation improvements in the Great Lakes region.[69] This process was accelerated in the 1850s with the development of an extensive rail network emanating from Chicago.[70] Chicago became the linchpin of the Midwestern economy, funneling commodity flows from west to east, manufactured goods from east to west, and lumber, essential for farm building, from the north woods to the prairie. In the 1850s, the populations of interior counties in Illinois lacking access to navigable waterways grew faster than peripheral, water-oriented counties as a consequence of gaining railroad service.[71] Moreover, these same interior counties increased wheat production at a much more rapid rate than the state as a whole.[72] With the coming of the railroad, settlers who had previously been attracted to the river valleys were now moving into the rich upland prairies.[73]

The coming of the railroad solved the problem of transporting commercial crops to market at bearable costs and the problem of obtaining reasonably priced lumber for farm building. The development of the railroad significantly accelerated the settlement of the prairie.[74] Railroad construction did not mean immediate cultivation of all of the prairie, however. Prairie lands within the boundaries of the Wisconsin glaciation were very fertile but often too wet for cultivation because of poorly developed natural drainage systems. Except for relatively dry uplands, the cultivation of these areas had to await the development of artificial drainage technologies in the 1880s.[75]

How much of the original prairie remains today and how much is protected from exploitation? The tallgrass prairie, comprising some 351,000 square miles, covered much of Illinois, all of Iowa, the northwestern half of Missouri, the western edge of Minnesota, and the eastern edges of the tier of states beginning with North Dakota and extending south to Oklahoma.[76] A recent survey suggests that only 4 percent of the original tallgrass prairie remains. Large tracts of tallgrass prairie can be found only in the Flint Hills of eastern Kansas and northeast Oklahoma and on the glacial moraines of northeastern South Dakota, and much of these areas lack any form of protection from exploitation. Otherwise, most prairie remnants are quite small.[77] In his survey of protected prairie preserves, Madson lists 149 in the tallgrass prairie states containing approximately 88,000 acres with an average size of 590 acres.[78] This is an infinitesimal proportion of the original tallgrass prairie, covering some 228 million acres.[79] While the size of these protected prairie patches range from one acre to 8,600 acres, most are at the small end of the scale. Certainly all prairie patches are not included in current surveys. Unrecorded prairie relicts can no doubt be found in old cemeteries and alongside railroad rights-of-way and country roads, but even if these were taken into account, the proportion of the original prairie remaining would still probably be miniscule.[80]

Much was to be gained by settlement of the prairie. Settlement and expansion of the agricultural sector was a driving force in nineteenth-century U.S. economic growth. The tall- and mixed-grass prairies continue today to be the nation's breadbasket, supplying U.S. consumers with most of the grains and much of the meats that they consume. But what was lost?

While much reduced in scale, the prairie was not totally destroyed by settlement because of the inadvertent preservation of remnants. Is the essence of the prairie ecosystem retained in these remnant patches? If it is, then the extent of the loss is diminished. To answer this question requires an understanding of certain ideas from the discipline of conservation biology.

The breaking up of a single continuous habitat into relatively isolated fragments is akin to creating small habitat islands. The theory of island biogeography suggests that habitat islands will have fewer species than continents and that the number of species present will bear a positive relationship to the area of a habitat island.[81] Because smaller islands have smaller and less diverse habitats than larger islands, they support fewer species. To put it somewhat differently, smaller islands will have a greater species extinction rate for a given number of species than larger islands will have. A herd of bison, for example, would be more likely to eventually die out on a small prairie remnant of a few hundred acres than they would in a large area, such as the Flint Hills of Kansas. In a fragmented landscape, species requiring large habitat areas to survive will more likely face extinction. Also, a small prairie remnant will have less variation in habitat features and will support fewer species; whereas a large area may contain both uplands and wet areas supporting both upland bird species and waterfowl, a small area may contain only one of the two habitat types. A small, isolated habitat island will have a smaller species immigration rate for a given number of species than a larger, less isolated island. Small islands are harder to find than large and are less likely to receive wind-transported migrants from other areas. Small isolated prairie remnants, for example, will receive a less diverse influx of prairie flower seeds than larger areas. As a consequence of the interplay of two forces, species immigrations and extinctions, the equilibrium number of species on a small habitat island will tend to be smaller than on a larger habitat island.

The theory of island biogeography suggests that bringing the prairie under cultivation and leaving behind a few isolated prairie fragments would result in a reduction of the number of species within any given preserved area once fragmentation is complete. Before fragmentation, a given area would contain more species because of a higher species immigration rate from the surrounding area and a lower species extinction rate. Afterwards, the number of species would eventually decline because of a drop in the immigration rate and a rise in the extinction rate on remaining habitat islands.[82]

An endemic species occurs only in a given local type of habitat. Because the tallgrass prairie is rather young in evolutionary terms, it is made up of many species that can be found elsewhere. Given the absence of a large number of prairie endemics, the decline of the prairie would be unlikely to result in the endangerment or extinction of a large number of species, unless similar habitats elsewhere were also in decline. John T. Curtis, a prairie plant expert, suggested in the 1950s that the full complement of prairie grasses and forbs are preserved in remnants, although it is at least a possibility that some species were lost prior to detailed botanical surveys of prairie plants.[83] Since Curtis's survey work in the 1940s and 1950s, resurveys of fifty-four sites found that around 14 percent of the original species documented by Curtis have disappeared, and the rate of disappearance has been greater on the smaller habitat patches.[84] Habitat fragmentation and decline are placing serious stresses on native prairie species. Unsurprisingly, many prairie species are threatened with extinction locally, and at least a few are threatened globally. In Minnesota, for example, 105 vascular native plant and animal species associated with the prairie biome are either locally threatened or endangered.[85] Two species that find their greatest abundance in Minnesota prairie fragments, the prairie fringed orchid and the prairie bush clover, are threatened at the federal level. Other tallgrass species that are imperiled globally, according to the Nature Conservancy, include Mead's milkweed, western prairie white-fringed orchid, and prairie moonwort.[86] The problem is that there may not be enough remnant habitat to ensure the future of these species.

Even though avian prairie endemics are few in number, two prairie species, the Prairie Chicken and the Sandhill Crane, are apparently endangered. The Sandhill Crane ranged over the prairie for food and nested in marshy areas, and the Prairie Chicken also found its optimum habitat in the prairie.[87] According to the Nature Conservancy, two other prairie species, Baird's Sparrow and Henslow's Sparrow, are, respectively, vulnerable and uncommon. Of the nine endemic prairie bird species, six are faced with serious population declines.[88] While invertebrates don't get much public attention, a number of them are endemic to the tallgrass prairie region, and some of these are threatened, including a butterfly, the regal fritillary.[89] For the ultimate survival of these species, prairie remnants may be too small or too few and far between.

For someone who believes that the bounty of nature exists for strictly human exploitation, the loss of the tallgrass prairie habitat and the threats to species requiring tallgrass landscapes may not seem like much. For someone who is fascinated by the idea of a sea of tall grasses rippling in the wind, a pageant of colorful wildflowers beginning in early spring and continuing to late fall, or a unique collection of species living in an increasingly rare and unusual landscape, the loss of the tallgrass prairie is more deeply felt. While one can perhaps get a sense of what the prairie might have been like from a few of the remaining remnants, a small piece of the prairie can be only an imperfect substitute for the vast stretches of tallgrass landscape that once existed.

A really serious challenge for prairie species protection is that remaining prairie fragments may not last in the long run. Without periodic fire, prairie patches are invaded by fire-sensitive shrubs and woodland species, and the native species adapted to fire suffer losses. The tallgrass prairie ecosystem and its grasses and wildflowers are adapted to the phenomena of drought, wind, and fire and ultimately require a recurrent cleansing through burning.[90] With settlement and the development of commercial agriculture came fire suppression, eliminating a force of nature central to the existence of the tallgrass prairie. Without fire, remaining prairie remnants will eventually disappear. In a world of climate change and a fragmented landscape, as climatic zones shift to the north, prairie species intolerant of warmer temperatures will be unable to migrate northward for lack of a continuous suitable habitat. If the lack of fire doesn't eliminate many of the remaining prairie remnants, then perhaps global warming will. While prairie restoration on a small scale is feasible, it seems unlikely that significantly continuous, large areas of tallgrass habitat could ever be brought back. The tallgrass prairie as a fully functioning ecosystem appears to be forever lost as a consequence of the human history of economic development in America's breadbasket. The loss of tallgrass prairie habitat is fundamentally an irreversible phenomenon.

Irreversibility and the Decline of Pacific Northwest Old-Growth Forests

Prior to the 1940s, timber harvesting in the Pacific Northwest had been confined largely to privately owned forestlands. By 1940 about half the ultimate harvest of virgin timber by volume was complete and most remaining unharvested old-growth timber was to be found on public lands.[91] At this point in history, the option of preserving large blocks of undisturbed old-growth forests was still available, but it was not to be exercised. The decline of old-growth forests in the decades since World War II has been predominantly driven by the growth of suburbs around major cities and the resulting growth in demand for lumber.

The spreading out of population through suburbanization increased the supply of urban land and reduced its average price. Population spreading was facilitated by the adoption of the motor vehicle as the principal means of transportation, allowing for reductions in time spent commuting per unit distance. The motor vehicle allowed homeowners to live farther from their places of work. With increases in commuting distances, greater volumes of land were brought within the sphere of suburban development. As a result of increased land supplies and reduced land prices, the amount of land consumed per dwelling increased, and a shift from multifamily to single-family dwellings occurred. For an equal amount of floor space, single-family units consume more lumber than multifamily units, and with lower land and transportation costs more funds could be devoted to increasing floor space, further stimulating the consumption of lumber.[92] The point is simple. Lower transportation and land costs resulted in population spreading out in more spacious detached dwellings that required more lumber.

At the same time as the beginning of the suburban housing boom in the 1950s, the lumber industry was turning increasingly to relatively untouched forests on public lands for its timber supply. In 1929, approximately 1.6 billion board feet of timber was cut from the national forest system, or about 4 percent of the U.S. timber supply. By 1952, national forest timber production was up to 4.5 billion board feet and 13 percent of the U.S. timber supply, and by 1962 it was up to 9.2 billion board feet and 22 percent of the total.[93] The suburban housing boom coincided with increased cutting of virgin timber from the national forests.

One region in particular, the Pacific Northwest, was significantly affected by expanded demand for lumber. Log production in western Oregon and Washington increased from an annual average of 9.6 billion board feet in the 1920s, the historical peak production period prior to World War II, to an annual average of 14.4 billion board feet in the 1960s.[94] From 1949 to 1970, log production from the national forests in this region increased from 10 percent of the total harvest to 24.6 percent, and log production from all public lands increased from 22 percent to 40 percent of the harvest.[95] By the 1950s, low-elevation, privately owned old-growth forests (two hundred years and older) had been largely cut, leaving higher-elevation old growth as the primary source of large, old trees.

The U.S. Forest Service, charged with the management of the national forests, had operated primarily in a custodial capacity prior to World War II. Because ample timber supplies were available before the war on private lands at low elevations in the Pacific Northwest, little interest was shown by the lumber industry in the higher-elevation public lands, where timber harvesting was relatively more costly. With surging timber demand after the war, the Forest Service expanded its scope of activity, and the size of its bureaucracy and its budget, through dramatic increases in timber sales. This meant that previously untouched old-growth fell to the ax, even in localities that had been previously set aside as primitive or wilderness areas. This brought the Forest Service into sharp conflict with a burgeoning wilderness and forest preservation movement. A lengthy series of struggles followed over preservation of upland forests, involving wilderness advocates, the Forest Service, and the forest products industry. These struggles culminated in lawsuits in the 1990s over the preservation of an old-growth-dependent endangered species, the Spotted Owl, that virtually halted logging on the national forests in western Oregon and Washington. By then, however, less than 13 percent of the original old growth probably remained and only about 5 percent of the original was explicitly protected from harvesting.[96]

As of the early 1990s, 87 percent or more of the original stands of old growth in the Pacific Northwest were gone and along with them elements of an ecosystem with unique structural and functional characteristics that served as a habitat for certain rare species such as the spotted owl, the marbled murrelet, and the western yew. For many years, old-growth was viewed with disdain by foresters as a biotic wasteland containing decaying timber. The conventional thinking was that such forests should be harvested as quickly as possible and converted to young rapid-growth stands of timber.[97]

The research of Jerry Franklin and many others, however, has substantially altered this view.[98] The most apparent feature of an old-growth forest is its large coniferous trees. In the Pacific Northwest, conifers are able to dominate over deciduous trees because of their ready ability to adapt to the moderate wet winters and warm, dry summers characteristic of the area. Deciduous trees are at a relative disadvantage because of their high rates of water loss in the droughty summer months and their inability to undertake photosynthesis in the wet, mild winter months. Large trees in old-growth forests are the dominant primary producers, transforming atmospheric carbon into organic material through photosynthesis. The large trees in old-growth stands, with their massive accumulations of organic material, ultimately become the source of energy that drives the entire forest ecosystem, particularly when they are transformed through tree death into standing snags or fallen logs on the forest floor.[99]

As structures, large living trees have an important role to play in the functioning of the old-growth ecological system. The upper branches of large trees are prime habitat for nitrogen-fixing lichens, which draw their nutrients from rainwater and convert atmospheric nitrogen into a form useful to plants. Because of its large capacity to store water from rainfall and to buffer temperatures, the canopy of old-growth forests provides an ideal microclimate for lichens. Old-growth forests also make a large contribution to local terrestrial water flows through the interception of fog and mist by the branch and needle system of large trees, particularly in coastal areas where fog and mist are common. The irregularity of the crown of large trees and their relatively distant spacing from one another contribute to the availability of light on the forest floor and the patchiness of the understory. In densely packed young stands, the understory may be entirely absent or composed of a relatively few species adapted to low light conditions.[100]

Large old-growth trees, with their tall, large-diameter trunks, their heterogeneous crowns and branch systems, and their diverse microclimatics, beginning with the cool damp forest floor and ending at the exposed weather conditions at the top of the crown, provide a wide variety of habitat niches for a range of vertebrate and invertebrate animal species. The cavities and irregularities of the crown are attractive nesting habitats for the rare Spotted Owl, and large protruding branches near the treetop serve as perches for the Bald Eagle along waterways. An abundance of insects are found around, on, and within the bark of large, old-growth trees and serve as a food source for a variety of birds and mammals, including bats that feed on flying insects above the crown. Birds and mammals also feed on the abundant foliage. As many as 1,500 species of invertebrates can be found in, on, and around a large oldgrowth Douglas fir.[101]

The unique role of large trees in old-growth ecological functioning by no means ends with tree death. Dead trees become standing snags, downed logs on land, or downed logs in streams, and in these capacities continue to play a major ecological role for many years. Snags are common in forests of all ages, but only old-growth forests and recent burns contain large snags. Large snags with their substantial accumulations of biomass become the feeding ground for a variety of bacteria, fungi, and insects. The unique function of snags, however, is as nesting sites for cavity-excavating birds, such as the Pileated Woodpecker. Cavities are often created by primary excavators in snags and are then used by other hole-nesting birds and mammals.[102]

In addition to the creation of snags, tree death can lead to an abundance of downed large logs on land in old-growth forests. Downed logs perform important nutrient and hydrologic cycling functions. They are principal energy sources for a variety of decomposer organisms that recycle phosphorus and nitrogen for use by primary producers. Downed logs are also an important habitat for nitrogen-fixing bacteria, which convert atmospheric nitrogen into a form usable by primary producing plants. Both nitrogen and phosphorus concentrations in downed logs increase as decay progresses. The volume of water in downed logs also increases with decay, making them more attractive as habitat for both plants and animals.[103]

Downed logs perform a variety of habitat functions for a wide range of organisms, including mycorrhizal fungi, moisture-loving amphibians and reptiles, mammals, and birds. The logs are used as food sources, rearing and food storage sites, perches and lookouts, and paths for travel. They play an important role in the recolonization of fire-disturbed sites by providing a store of nutrients protected from fire by a high moisture content and by providing a pathway for small mammals from the surrounding forest into the burned-over area. Mycorrhizal fungi form a symbiotic relationship with tree roots, absorbing sugars produced by the tree and supplying nutrients to the tree roots from the surrounding soil. In a burned-over area, mycorrhizal fungi disappear completely and must be reintroduced for successful tree growth. Downed logs play a role in reintroduction by providing a pathway into bare areas for small animals that eat mycorrhizal fungi and spread the spores to new areas through defecation.[104] Fallen logs are also an important habitat for tree seedlings for such species as western hemlock, Sitka spruce, and Pacific silver fir. Seedlings are generally more numerous on nurse logs than the adjacent forest floor, particularly in the damper coastal forests. Tree seedlings seem to encounter difficulty competing for space with the mosses and herbs of the forest floor and are more successful rooting in recently fallen logs where competition is less intense.[105]

Downed logs also play a major ecological role in forest streams. Large logs in streams affect the carbon and nutrients available to aquatic organisms, and they also significantly influence the physical profile of small- and medium-sized streams. In small streams, logs act like dams, creating a stepped profile of pools and riffles. In the process, the energy of the flowing water is dissipated and the potential for stream bank erosion is reduced. The pools and riffles are ideal habitats for a variety of invertebrate and vertebrate organisms, including trout and juvenile salmon. While large logs may persist in streams through the development of second growth forests after major disturbances, in managed stands converted to a short rotation, logs will eventually disappear as major structural elements.[106]

Recent research on old-growth forests suggests that they are not biological deserts of over-mature timber as once thought. Rather, old-growth forests are unique biological structures with unusual physical characteristics that carry out key biotic functions in ways that are much different from forests in earlier successional stages. They also support a variety of species that appear to be dependent on old-growth, including the western yew, Marbled Murrelet, and Spotted Owl. Old-growth forest ecosystems have unique structural and functional characteristics and contain a unique collection of species. As a result of the cutting of these forests, something of significance has indeed disappeared. Although it is not immediately apparent to the casual observer, U.S. suburbanization with its expanded use of lumber in housing has played a significant role in the decline of old-growth forests that constitute an increasingly rare and threatened ecosystem type.

Irreversibility and Dam Construction and Riparian Habitat Loss

Along with timber harvesting, dam construction ranks very high as a phenomenon bringing forth significant environmental changes. Almost 70 percent of freshwater mussel and crayfish and close to 40 percent of freshwater fish species are at risk of extinction according to a recent Nature Conservancy report.[107] Some of these species are at risk because of water pollution problems, but many are threatened by riparian habitat modification, of which dam construction is among the most damaging.[108]

Dams have been constructed for centuries for flood control and, more importantly, for irrigation. Civilization marks its birthplace in irrigation agriculture, and the control of irrigation, some argue, has been the foundation stone of highly centralized, despotic societies whose centrality of control was directly related to the scale of their irrigation systems.[109] Irrigation and aridity go together, and irrigation was integral to the development of the arid regions of the western United States. Even in a laissez-faire capitalist economy, irrigation requires centrality of power, and the dominant institution in the irrigating of the West was a government agency, the U.S. Bureau of Reclamation. The beneficiaries of irrigation, subsidized by interest-free government loans for project capital costs, were more often than not land speculators and relatively large-scale farmers, rather than the small-holders originally intended as such by the legislation that established the Bureau.[110] The bureau was not the only government dam builder on the scene, however. In the name of flood control and navigation, the Army Corps of Engineers competed with the bureau to control and reshape the rivers of the West.

Dam construction accelerated around the turn of the century because of improvements in cement technology and, more notably, because of the growing demand for electricity, one that could be supplied in part by hydroelectric projects.[111] Since they were relatively lucrative, hydroelectric projects were incorporated into most large-scale Bureau of Reclamation projects. Many reclamation projects were economically feasible only because of the revenues generated from electricity sales.[112] The number of hydroelectric projects operated by the bureau has grown continuously, and the rate of growth has diminished only recently.[113]

Dams alter river hydrology, water quality, sediment flows, erosion patterns, floodplains, and the diversity and composition of plant and animal life. The most significant physical change induced by dams is the alteration of water flow patterns. First and foremost, a dam converts a part of a river into a lake. The reservoir behind a dam is used to store water for electricity generation, irrigation, urban water supply, or flood control. In the process, the flow patterns of a river are significantly disrupted. On entering the reservoir, water velocity slows and suspended sediments drop out, causing the reservoir to become a sediment trap. This in turn reduces the sediment load of the river below the dam and increases the clarity of the water. The flow pattern of the river below the dam is also altered, depending on the purpose of the dam. If the dam is used for flood control, flooding below the dam is eliminated or at least mitigated; if the dam is used for electricity generation or irrigation, pulses of water flow from the dam according to peak load demands for electricity or irrigation requirements. The absence of flood waters below the dam shrinks the physical extent of the floodplain, the area previously inundated in flood episodes. The rate of erosion immediately below the dam often increases because of the absence of suspended sediment in the flowing waters and the river's attempt to restore its equilibrium sediment load.[114]

The replacement of part of a river by what is essentially a lake reduces the flow rate of water in the river and increases the potential for biological production. In fast-flowing turbulent waters that characterize the upper reaches of watersheds, free-floating planktonic forms of algae have difficulty surviving. In the quiet waters of a dam reservoir fed by nutrient imports from upstream, biological productivity can flourish. Given that a reservoir thermally stratifies, the cold lower layer often becomes depleted of oxygen by the decomposition of dead organic matter descending from the sunlit (photic) zones where plant growth takes place. In these waters various chemicals, such as iron, manganese, and hydrogen sulfide, become suspended along with other toxins and plant nutrients. Water quality below dams that release from the bottom of the reservoir is frequently impaired, while water quality below dams that release from reservoir surface waters will be relatively high, although such reservoirs may discharge significant volumes of algae into downstream waters.[115]

The physical changes to rivers caused by dams bring forth substantial biological changes. Dams eliminate important floodplain habitat, alter thermal regimes and thermal cues on which many species depend, change water flow patterns to which many species are adapted, and create barriers to migration for anadromous fish species, which spawn in rivers and streams and spend their adult lives in ocean waters.

Naturally flowing rivers can be categorized as either floodplain or reservoir rivers. Reservoir rivers have a relatively stable year-round water flow and only infrequently overspill their banks. Floodplain rivers are characterized by a cycle of flood and drought, overspilling their banks during flood episodes and creating backwaters of residual pools and wetland areas. Dams tend to stabilize water flows and diminish flood episodes and in the process reduce the size of the floodplain. Dams essentially convert floodplain rivers into reservoir rivers. The loss of the floodplain results in the loss of backwater pools and the succession of wetlands to meadows. This in turn reduces habitat for waterfowl, muskrat, beaver, and moose.[116]

Diverse habitats create diverse niches for a variety of species. Dams simplify riparian habitats by reducing the extent of floodplains and in other ways as well. Dams simplify daily and seasonal thermal regimes, evening out temperatures and eliminating thermal cues to which a variety of aquatic insects and other invertebrates are adapted. Hatching, growth, and emergence for a variety of organisms depend on water temperature. Dams also often eliminate the pool and riffle habitat to which many invertebrates are adapted and change the substrate from rock and gravel characteristic of fast-flowing waters to sand and silt, associated with slower water flows. Studies have found that while the biomass of invertebrates tends to increase on rivers with dams relative to their natural counterparts, the number of species present tends to diminish.[117] Reduced biodiversity is a central result of habitat simplification caused by the construction and operation of dams.

Riverine fishes have probably suffered the most of all biotic organisms from dam construction. River impoundment in all probability has markedly increased the rate of extinction of freshwater fishes. The central problem for fishes created by dams is the inundation of spawning grounds and the construction of barriers to migration. Trout and salmon, for example, spawn in relatively fast-flowing stretches of rivers with gravel-covered bottoms. Dam reservoirs often flood such habitats and inhibit migration upstream to remaining spawning beds. Not all fishes are harmed by dams, such as those that are adapted to slow-flowing waters and certain introduced exotics able to take advantage of increased food supplies in the tailwaters of dams. The elimination of floodplains, however, removes important spawning and rearing areas for a variety of fish species, and the variation in water levels below dams caused by dam operations can eliminate stable habitats for endemic species. Shifts in temperature regimes after dam construction have often harmed native fish populations whose spawning and growth patterns are temperature determined.

The impact on migratory fish from dam construction is perhaps best illustrated by the historical experience with dams on the Columbia River in the Pacific Northwest region of the United States. Chinook salmon runs into the mouth of the Columbia River—runs that historically were among the largest in the world—have declined significantly since the mid-1920s.

Mature chinook salmon migrate upriver to the spawning grounds of their birth, lay and fertilize their eggs in gravel river and stream bottoms, and then die. Juvenile salmon, or smolts, emerge, spend up to a year in local waters, and then migrate downriver to the waters of the Pacific Ocean, where they remain until they mature and repeat the spawning cycle. The decline in chinook salmon runs are the result of both overfishing and a decline in habitat conditions in the Columbia River and its tributaries.

The most dramatic alteration to Columbia watershed habitat has been the construction of numerous dams. While the construction of dams for irrigation and electric power generation on the smaller tributaries of the Columbia date back to the early 1900s, main stem dam construction on the Columbia and a major tributary, the Snake River, did not commence until the 1930s. Between 1933 and 1969, twenty-two main stem dams were constructed on the two rivers. On the Columbia, the Grand Coulee Dam was constructed without fish ladders and blocked upstream migration of salmon to northern Washington state and Canada. The upper and middle reaches of the Snake River were also blocked from salmon migration by dam construction. Even though fish ladders were installed at many dams, these structures are still formidable barriers to upstream and downstream migration of salmon. Both upstream and downstream migrants face the danger of nitrogen poisoning in the super-saturated waters just below spillways, and downstream juvenile migrants confront the additional danger of injury and death from passage through electrical turbines. The large reservoirs behind dams reduce spawning opportunities by inundating the original spawning beds, where relatively cool, well-oxygenated waters flowed across gravel bottoms. Normally downstream migrants face upstream and simply float with the current. In the stagnant reservoirs behind dams, juvenile salmon are forced to expend more energy than otherwise in swimming downstream, face increased exposure to predators, and sometimes have trouble discerning the appropriate direction in which to swim. Although mortality varies from one dam to another and with flow conditions, fisheries researchers have estimated that upstream mortality for each dam is roughly 5 percent, while downstream mortality is approximately 20 percent. A conservative estimate of the chinook salmon run lost because of dams is approximately 3 million fish out of a run of 3.5 million.[118] The impact of dams on fisheries is clearly a serious matter.

Irreversibility and the Loss of Wetlands

One of the most profound of all changes to the American landscape is the loss of wetlands. Wetlands originally covered about 221 million acres in the lower forty-eight states. By 1996, over half of these wetlands were lost, with only about 102 million acres remaining. While the rate of loss has slowed, wetlands are still being destroyed at a pace of about eighty thousand acres per year.[119] The amount of loss is anything but uniformly distributed. States such as California, Illinois, Iowa, Missouri, and Ohio have lost more than 80 percent of their wetlands.[120]

While early European settlers in the eastern United States benefited from the abundance of waterfowl and other wildlife available virtually for the taking, what are known as wetlands today were referred to as swamps and were seen as an impediment to economic progress.[121] Swamps were difficult to traverse, possessed of a dark and foreboding interior, and featured rich soils that, once drained, made for highly fertile agricultural land. Swamps were a wasteland that hindered the creation of a vibrant rural economy. Some went so far as to suggest that the draining of swamps was a moral imperative.[122]

With improved understanding of the way wetlands work in the natural scheme of things, the early view of swamps as wastelands has been largely overturned. Wetlands today are viewed as essential for the protection of environmental quality, the conservation of fish and wildlife, and the enjoyment of key economic benefits. Most important of all, wetlands serve as nature's sponge and filter. Wetlands along rivers absorb and store pulses of stormwater, preventing downstream flooding and erosion. Water is stored by wetlands and slowly released downstream or finds its way into local groundwater aquifers. Wetlands also remove nutrients, process chemical and organic wastes, and filter out excess sediments, improving the quality of downstream water flows. The abundant plant life in wetlands extracts nutrients such as nitrogen and phosphorus from waters that could otherwise feed algae blooms and weedy plant growth in downstream waterways. The slowing of water flows in wetlands allows suspended sediments in stormwater to settle out, further improving downstream water quality.[123]

In terms of the conversion of sunlight into plant matter through photosynthesis, wetlands are among the most productive ecosystems in the world.[124] This abundance of plant matter serves as the base for a complex food web that serves a diverse array of animal species, especially waterfowl. The connection between waterfowl and wetlands is today relatively well known, especially among hunters. Waterfowl migrate to and from breeding grounds along the Pacific and Atlantic coasts, up through prairie pothole region of the central United States, and along the Mississippi River. Wetlands serve as key feeding grounds as well as final destinations for breeding on each of these flyways. The prairie pothole region of North and South Dakota is famous for its productivity as a waterfowl breeding area. The bottomland forest wetlands of the southern United States serve as an important overwintering ground for waterfowl.[125] A complex of strategically located wetlands is clearly essential to maintaining healthy waterfowl populations on the North American continent.

In addition to waterfowl, including familiar ducks such as Mallards, pintails, and Blue-winged Teals, a variety of other bird species make use of wetlands, among them wading birds (herons and egrets), shorebirds (oystercatchers and plovers), a variety of nesting birds (Red-winged Blackbirds, Marsh Wrens, Least Bitterns, Indigo Buntings, and Yellow Warblers), and raptors (Peregrine Falcon and Marsh Hawks). Wetlands are also vital habitat for numerous mammals including furbearers such as muskrats, nutria, and beavers. Large mammals using wetlands include black bear, deer, moose, and caribou. Most of the 190 species of North American amphibians, such as frogs and salamanders, are wetland dependent, as are many reptiles, including the American crocodile.[126]

Coastal wetlands are of the critical importance for saltwater fish populations, including around two-thirds of U.S. commercial species. Wetlands are important spawning or nursing grounds for such species as menhaden, bluefish, fluke, sea trout, and striped bass, among others.

Coastal wetlands are often important habitats for shellfish as well, such as shrimp, blue crabs, oysters, and clams. Shrimp populations appear to be dependent on the presence of healthy coastal wetlands. Marshes and backwater wetlands along streams and rivers are also critical spawning and nursery habitats for a variety of freshwater fishes, including bass, bluegill, muskies, and walleyes. Fish populations also benefit significantly from the clean waters produced by the filtering function of wetlands.[127]

The array of species supported by wetlands provides important economic benefits. Both commercial and recreational fishing opportunities are substantially expanded by the presence of wetlands. Waterfowl hunting is a major wetland-dependent leisure pursuit, as is bird-watching. Such activities are of direct value to people and generate significant supporting economic activity.

Perhaps the most important economic benefit of wetlands is the reduction of flooding damage that would otherwise occur in their absence. Of great economic importance, too, is the water-cleansing function of wetlands, as well as the ability of wetlands to recharge groundwater supplies.[128] The global economic value of wetlands for all these purposes is substantial.[129]

Given the economic value of wetlands, at first glance it is a little surprising that so much has been lost. This loss is less surprising once the nature of the economic benefits flowing from wetlands and the specifics of the wetlands property holding system are better understood. The benefits are public rather than private, while landholding is often private as opposed to public. The benefits of wetland flood control accrue to downstream residents as a group but not to the wetland owner. Since the flood control benefits cannot be withheld from downstream residents, there is no way for the upstream wetland owner to realize any kind of economic gain from the wetland flood control function. The wetland owner can perhaps realize an economic benefit from the wetland by filling it in and using it for agricultural land. If this occurred the flood control benefit would be forgone, and, prior to enforcement of the Clean Water Act, downstream landowners would have no recourse. The wetland owner would simply be legitimately exercising rights of property ownership. In theory, downstream residents could agree to pay the owner to refrain from filling in the wetland, but in practice the costs of organizing such an effort and the potential for free riding would be too great. Any residents who didn't contribute to the cost of preserving the wetland could still enjoy the benefit of wetlands flood control. All downstream residents would be tempted to act as free riders, precluding voluntary organizing to save wetlands. Even with the Clean Water Act precluding filling in wetlands associated with navigable waterways, wetland losses are still fairly substantial because of lax enforcement and because not all wetlands are covered.[130] Prior to serious Clean Water Act enforcement in the mid-1970s, few legal impediments to wetlands conversion existed. The institution of private property assumes that parcels of land are functionally disconnected. In legal theory, what one property owner does is presumed by property rights law to have no consequences for anyone else. Apart from using property to directly harm others, landowners are free to use their land as they see fit. In practice, parcels of land are ecologically interconnected. The use to which one parcel of land is put has consequences for other parcels of land and the people who occupy them. The private-property system results in land being used for private benefits even though the benefits of public use may be much greater.

The progressive loss of wetlands historically reflects the creation of new kinds of industries based on new forms of technology. The single most important cause of wetland loss is the drainage for agriculture. The historical pattern of wetlands loss reflects the spread of commercial agriculture along waterway transportation routes and rail lines. Applications of steam technology in river shipping as well as the railroad opened up the Mississippi bottomlands, the Midwest, and the West for settlement and the development of commercial agriculture. While wet areas were initially bypassed for the dry uplands, by the 1880s drain tile and ditch digging technology had been perfected and draining for cropland accelerated. In the Mississippi bottomlands as well as in the Central Valley of California, rivers had to be lined with levees to keep flood waters off the valley bottoms so that they could be permanently drained. No single farmer could do this successfully alone. Ultimately, the task of flood control fell to large government bureaucracies, such as the Army Corps of Engineers. In the name of navigation and flood control, the Corps has reshaped the major rivers in the United States and in the process has removed the source of water for many floodplain wetlands. Flood control reduced fears of annual inundations and stimulated drainage of land for agriculture. All this was facilitated by the presence of gigantic steam-powered dredges capable of building massive levees.[131] In less than twenty years beginning in 1906, Illinois, Indiana, and Iowa saw almost 30 percent of their wetlands disappear to agricultural drainage, and by 1922 California had lost 70 percent of its wetlands, mostly to agricultural drainage in the Central Valley.[132]

Steam technology also played a role in the disappearance of the bottomland cypress forests in the South. These swampland forests were difficult to log by conventional means but were rapidly exploited after the invention of steam-powered "pullboats" capable of pulling large logs to central gathering points, where they could then be floated to sawmills.[133] By the 1920s, virgin stands of cypress had been logged out.[134]

While agricultural drainage and resource extraction continue to play a role in the decline of wetlands, new economic trends are contributing to wetlands loss. Industrialization is essentially an urban phenomenon requiring spatial concentrations of both labor and interconnected businesses. Because moving around within cities in the early days of industrialization was time-consuming and costly, the early industrial city was built at a relatively high population density. With the introduction of the motor vehicle and the construction of highways and freeways, movement across urban landscapes was substantially eased and cities began to spread out, as noted earlier. Wetland areas previously avoided near urban centers became attractive sites for both business and residential development. With the growing popularity of air travel after World War II, cities desired airports, and the only large open spaces left near cities were wetlands. Most new airports in this period were constructed on drained wetlands.[135] Urbanization is playing an increasing role in wetland decline.

CONCLUSION

New forms of economic activity are the engines of both economic expansion and environmental change. The steam railroad stimulated agricultural development in the previous two centuries, leading to both the decline of the tallgrass prairie and the filling in of wetlands; the motor vehicle helped to foster suburbanization, a housing boom, the cutting of old-growth forests, and the filling in of wetlands for residential and business development; the increased use of electricity helped accelerate the damming of America's rivers. Along with new kinds of economic activity come defensive political interest groups opposed to environmental controls, although an associated increase in environmental problems has resulted in the formation of environmental groups on a voluntary basis that advocate more regulation.

Some regulatory efforts have been successful, diminishing or reversing certain types of environmental deterioration. Political resistance to regulation nonetheless remains intense, dampening the extent of environmental improvement. For certain kinds of environmental stresses, the Kuznets curve pattern—rising environmental deterioration followed by decline as per capita incomes increase—holds. This pattern is most evident for environmental stresses that are highly visible and reversible.

Unfortunately, generalizing the pattern is dangerous. Some environmental changes associated with economic development and growth are simply irreversible or reversible only at an unacceptably high cost. This is the case with the loss of the U.S. tallgrass prairie, the decline of Pacific Northwest old-growth forests, dammed-up rivers, and filled-in wetlands. Old-growth forests in some areas may grow back in two hundred years, but it is disputable whether we have the patience to allow that. Prairie and wetland restoration at the margins is a possibility but is undoubtedly too costly to undertake on a sufficient scale to restore fully functioning ecosystems. Removing dams upon which we have come to rely is also likely to be too costly. Still other environmental trends associated with modern economic patterns of development and growth are also effectively irreversible, including global warming, the introduction of exotic species, and the spreading of human population into natural habitats. These trends will be taken up in more detail in the next chapter. The goal will be to explain with some care the linkage between economic growth and irreversible environmental change in the world today.

NOTES

1. Herman E. Daly, *Steady-State Economics: Second Edition with New Essays* (Washington, D.C.: Island Press, 1991), 195–210.

2. Nicholas Georgescu-Roegen, *The Entropy Law and the Economic Process* (Cambridge, Mass.: Harvard University Press, 1971); Daly, *Steady-State Economics*.

3. Strictly speaking, the law of entropy applies only to energy.

4. Daly, *Steady-State Economics*, 180–194.

5. Norman Myers, "Biodiversity's Genetic Library," in *Nature's Services: Societal Dependence on Natural Ecosystems*, ed. Gretchen C. Daily (Washington, D.C.: Island Press, 1997), 255–73.

6. Edward O. Wilson, "The Current State of Biological Diversity," in *Biodiversity*, ed. Edward O. Wilson (Washington, D.C.: National Academy Press, 1988), 3–18.

7. Myers, "Biodiversity's Genetic Library," 263.

8. Susan E. Alexander, Stephen H. Schneider, and Kalen Lagerquist, "The Interaction of Climate and Life," 71–92; Sandra Postel and Stephen Carpenter, "Freshwater Ecosystem Services," 195–214; and Norman Myers, "The World's Forests and Their Ecosystem Services," 215–35, in *Nature's Services: Societal Dependence on Natural Ecosystems*, ed. Gretchen C. Daily (Washington, D.C.: Island Press, 1997).

9. Holmes Rolston III, "Values in Nature," *Environmental Ethics* 3 (1981): 113–28.

10. Douglas E. Booth, *Valuing Nature: The Decline and Preservation of Old-Growth Forests* (Lanham, Md.: Rowman & Littlefield, 1994), 173–95.

11. Dean E. Abrahamson, "Global Warming: The Issue, Impacts, Responses," in *The Challenge of Global Warming*, ed. Dean E. Abrahamson (Washington, D.C.: Island Press, 1989), 3–34.

12. E. B. Welch and T. Lindell, *Ecological Effects of Wastewater: Applied Limnology and Pollutant Effects* (London: Chapman & Hall, 1992).

13. Roy Gould, *Going Sour: Science and Politics of Acid Rain* (Boston: Birkhauser, 1985); Alexander, Schneider, and Lagerquist, "The Interaction of Climate and Life," 75–6.

14. Gretchen C. Daily, Pamela A. Matson, and Peter M. Vitousek, "Ecosystem Services Supplied by Soil," in *Nature's Services: Societal Dependence on Natural Ecosystems*, ed. Gretchen C. Daily (Washington, D.C.: Island Press, 1997), 113–32.

15. Paul R. Ehrlich, "The Loss of Diversity: Causes and Consequences," in *Biodiversity*, ed. Edward O. Wilson (Washington, D.C.: National Academy Press, 1988), 21–27.

16. Postel and Carpenter, "Freshwater Ecosystem Services," 207–10.

17. Norman Myers, "Tropical Forests and Their Species: Going, Going, . . . ?" in *Biodiversity*, ed. Edward O. Wilson (Washington, D.C.: National Academy Press, 1988), 28–35.

18. Edward J. Nell, *Prosperity and Public Spending: Transformational Growth and the Role of Public Spending* (Boston: Unwin Hyman, 1988).

19. J. J. van Duijn *The Long Wave in Economic Life* (London: George Allen & Unwin, 1983), 20–32.

20. Arthur F. Burns, *Production Trends in the United States since 1870* (New York: National Bureau of Economic Research, 1934). Also, see van Duijn, *The Long Wave in Economic Life*, 28–29.

21. Douglas E. Booth, *The Environmental Consequences of Growth: Steady-State Economics as an Alternative to Ecological Decline* (London: Routledge, 1998), 20–54.

22. Booth, *The Environmental Consequences of Growth*, 20–54.

23. Karl W. Kapp, "Environmental Disruption and Social Costs: A Challenge to Economics," *Kyklos* 23 (1970): 833–47.

24. Ronald Coase, "The Problem of Social Cost," *Journal of Law and Economics* 3 (1960): 1–44.

25. Liability law is generally ineffective in limiting pollution for similar reasons. Evidence of damage is often hard to demonstrate, and the damage experienced by any individual is often too small to justify the costs of litigation.

26. For example, see the historical materials in Booth, *The Environmental Consequences of Growth*.

27. Mancur Olson Jr., *The Logic of Collective Action: Public Goods and the Theory of Groups* (New York: Schocken Books, 1971).

28. Robert C. Mitchell, Angela G. Mertig, and Riley E. Dunlap, "Twenty Years of Environmental Mobilization: Trends among National Environmental Organizations," *Society and Natural Resources* 4 (1991): 219–34.

29. Walter A. Rosenbaum, "The Bureaucracy and Environmental Policy," in *Environmental Politics and Policy: Theories and Evidence*, ed. James P. Lester (Durham, N.C.: Duke University Press, 1995), 206–41.

30. See Booth, *Valuing Nature*, 173–95. This issue will be addressed more fully in chapter 7.

31. John R. Searle, *The Construction of Social Reality* (New York: Free Press, 1995), 23–26.

32. Anthony Downs, "Up and Down with Ecology—The 'Issue-Attention Cycle,'" *The Public Interest* 28 (1972): 38–50.

33. Rachel Carson, *Silent Spring* (Boston: Houghton Mifflin, 1962).

34. Christopher J. Bosso, *Pesticides and Politics: The Life Cycle of a Public Issue* (Pittsburgh: University of Pittsburgh Press, 1987), 115–20; Mitchell et al., "Twenty Years of Environmental Mobilization," 1991; Riley E. Dunlap, "Trends in Public Opinion toward Environmental Issues: 1965–1990," *Society and Natural Resources* 4 (1991): 285–312.

35. Dunlap, "Trends in Public Opinion toward Environmental Issues."

36. Downs, "Up and Down with Ecology."

37. Dunlap, "Trends in Public Opinion toward Environmental Issues."

38. Bosso, *Pesticides and Politics*.

39. Booth, *The Environmental Consequences of Growth*, 23–31.

40. R. Shep Melnick, *Regulation and the Courts: The Case of the Clean Air Act* (Washington, D.C.: The Brookings Institution, 1983), 24–52.

41. Bruce A. Ackerman and William T. Hassler, *Clean Coal/Dirty Air: or How the Clean Air Act Became a Multibillion-Dollar Bail-Out for High-Sulfur Coal Producers and What Should Be Done About It* (New Haven, Conn.: Yale University Press, 1981), 1–12; Rosenbaum, "The Bureaucracy and Environmental Policy."

42. Tom Tietenberg, *Environmental Economics and Policy* (New York: Harper-Collins, 1994), 229–95.

43. Booth, *The Environmental Consequences of Growth*, 104–6.

44. An alternative explanation for the Kuznets curve pattern is that conventional air pollution emissions respond to structural changes in the economy. In the world of creative destruction, older industries sometimes fade away and reduce their emissions as a result. Also, older industries with a settled technology sometimes move off shore to low-income countries to take advantage of lower labor costs. Newer industries that emerge to replace the old may well contribute less to conventional air pollutants. The emergence of high technology in the 1990s and the decline of older basic industries such as steel could have resulted in the decline of conventional air pollutants in the United States.

45. Gene M. Grossman and Alan B. Krueger, "Economic Growth and the Environment," *Quarterly Journal of Economics* 110 (1995): 353–77; Joseph N. Lekakis, "Environment and Development in a Southern European Country: Which Environmental Kuznets Curves?" *Journal of Environmental Planning and Management* 43

(2000): 139–53; Joseph Lekakis and Maria Kousis, "Demand for and Supply of Environmental Quality in the Environmental Kuznets Curve Hypothesis," *Applied Economic Letters* 8 (2001): 169–72.

46. Mariano Torras and James K. Boyce, "Income, Inequality, and Pollution: A Reassessment of the Environmental Kuznets Curve," *Ecological Economics* 25 (1998): 147–60.

47. Grossman and Krueger, "Economic Growth and the Environment"; Thomas M. Selden and Daqing Song, "Environmental Quality and Development: Is There a Kuznets Curve for Air Pollution Emissions?" *Journal of Environmental Economics and Management* 27 (1994): 147–62; Torras and Boyce, "Income, Inequality, and Pollution."

48. Grossman and Krueger, "Economic Growth and the Environment"; Torras and Boyce, "Income, Inequality, and Pollution."

49. Nemat Shafik, "Economic Development and Environmental Quality: An Econometric Analysis," *Oxford Economic Papers* 46 (1994): 757–73; Nico Heerink, Abay Mulatu, and Erwin Bulte, "Income Inequality and the Environment: Aggregation Bias in Environmental Kuznets Curves," *Ecological Economics* 38 (2001): 359–67.

50. Booth, *The Environmental Consequences of Growth*, 31–35.

51. This process need not be smooth and balanced. A country could easily lose more to imports in terms of employment than it gains from exports if the new industry creation process is too slow to offset the offshore movement of employment.

52. Vivek Suri and Duane Chapman, "Economic Growth, Trade and Energy: Implications of the Environmental Kuznets Curve," *Ecological Economics* 25 (1998): 195–208.

53. Dale S. Rothman, "Environmental Kuznets Curves—Real Progress or Passing the Buck? A Case for Consumption-Based Approaches," *Ecological Economics* 25 (1998): 177–94.

54. Grossman and Krueger, "Economic Growth and the Environment."

55. Heerink, Mulatu, and Bulte, "Income Inequality and the Environment."

56. Grossman and Krueger, "Economic Growth and the Environment"; Heerink, Mulatu, and Bulte, "Income Inequality and the Environment."

57. Shafik, "Economic Development and Environmental Quality"; Heerink, Mulatu, and Bulte, "Income Inequality and the Environment"; Robin Naidoo and Wiktor L. Adamowicz, "Effects of Economic Prosperity on Numbers of Threatened Species," *Conservation Biology* 15 (2001): 1021–29.

58. Booth, *The Environmental Consequences of Growth*, 104–6.

59. The percentage changes in emissions for the key pollutants are as follows: carbon monoxide, -29 percent; nitrogen oxides, +17 percent; volatile organic compounds, -43 percent; sulfur dioxide, -40 percent; particulate matter, -77 percent; lead, -98 percent. U.S. EPA, *Latest Findings on National Air Quality: 1999 Status and Trends* (Research Triangle Park, N.C.: Office of Air Quality Planning and Standards, August 2000), 2.

60. The decrease is 12 percent based on an eight-hour measurement standard and 20 percent based on a one-hour measurement standard. For a discussion of measurement standards, see U.S. EPA, *Latest Findings on National Air Quality*, 7.

61. U.S. EPA, *Latest Findings on National Air Quality*, 6–8.

62. U.S. EPA, *Latest Findings on National Air Quality*, 15–18.

63. This is for the period 1970–1998. U.S. EPA, *National Emissions (1970–1998)* (Research Triangle Park, N.C.: Office of Air Quality Planning and Standards, March 2000), A-10.

64. There is some evidence that environmental Kuznets curves turn back up after declining as per capita incomes continue to rise. See Torras and Boyce, "Income, Inequality, and Pollution." U.S. EPA, *Latest Findings on National Air Quality*, 7.

65. John Madson, *Where the Sky Began: Land of the Tallgrass Prairie* (Boston: Houghton Mifflin, 1982).

66. Robert E. Gallman, "Commodity Output, 1839–1899," in *Trends in the American Economy in the Nineteenth Century*, National Bureau of Economic Research (Princeton, N.J.: Princeton University Press, 1960), 13–71.

67. U.S. Department of Commerce, Bureau of the Census, *Historical Statistics of the United States: Colonial Times to 1970*, (Washington, D.C.: U.S. Government Printing Office, 1975), 460.

68. William Cronon, *Nature's Metropolis: Chicago and the Great West* (New York: W. W. Norton, 1991), 97–109; Douglass C. North, *Growth and Welfare in the American Past: A New Economic History*, 2nd ed. (Englewood Cliffs, N.J.: Prentice-Hall, 1974), 141–42.

69. North, *Growth and Welfare in the American Past*, 142.

70. Cronon, *Nature's Metropolis*, 55–93.

71. North, *Growth and Welfare in the American Past*, 146–52.

72. Albert Fishlow, *American Railroads and the Transformation of the Ante-Bellum Economy* (Cambridge, Mass.: Harvard University Press, 1965), 205–15.

73. Cronon *Nature's Metropolis*, 109.

74. Cronon, *Nature's Metropolis*, 109–10; James F. Hamburg, *The Influence of Railroads upon the Processes and Patterns of Settlement in South Dakota* (New York: Arno Press, 1981); Clare C. Cooper, "The Role of Railroads in the Settlement of Iowa: A Study in Historical Geography," M.A. thesis, University of Nebraska, 1958.

75. Allan G. Bogue, *From Prairie to Corn Belt: Farming on the Illinois and Iowa Prairies in the Nineteenth Century* (Chicago: University of Chicago Press, 1963), 85; Cooper, "The Role of Railroads in the Settlement of Iowa," 79.

76. Paul G. Risser, *The True Prairie Ecosystem* (Stroudsburg, Pa.: Hutchinson Ross Publishing Company, 1981), 13.

77. Ernest M. Steinauer, and Scott L. Collins, "Prairie Ecology—The Tallgrass Prairie," in *Prairie Conservation: Preserving North America's Most Endangered Ecosystem*, ed. Fred B. Samson and Fritz L. Knopf (Washington, D.C.: Island Press, 1996), 39–52.

78. Madson, *Where the Sky Began*.

79. Risser, *The True Prairie Ecosystem*, 13.

80. Madson, *Where the Sky Began*, 261.

81. Robert H. MacArthur, and Edward O. Wilson, *The Theory of Island Biogeography* (Princeton, N.J.: Princeton University Press, 1967).

82. Mark K. Leach and Thomas J. Givnish, "Ecological Determinants of Species Loss in Remnant Prairies," *Science* 273: 1555–58.

83. John T. Curtis, *The Vegetation of Wisconsin: An Ordination of Plant Communities* (Madison, Wis.: University of Wisconsin Press, 1959), 306.

84. Leach and Givnish, "Ecological Determinants of Species Loss in Remnant Prairies."

85. Barbara Coffin and Lee Pfannmuller, *Minnesota's Endangered Flora and Fauna* (Minneapolis: University of Minnesota Press, 1988), 12.

86. The Nature Conservancy, Northern Tallgrass Prairie Ecoregional Planning Team, *Ecoregional Planning in the Northern Tallgrass Prairie Ecoregion* (Minneapolis, Minn.: The Nature Conservancy, Midwest Regional Office, 1998).

87. Risser, *The True Prairie Ecosystem*, 74–88; A. W. Schorger, "Extinct and Endangered Mammals and Birds of the Upper Great Lakes Region," *Transactions of the Wisconsin Academy of Sciences, Arts and Letters* 34 (1942): 23–44; Madson, *Where the Sky Began*, 137–38.

88. Fritz L. Knopf, "Prairie Legacies—Birds," in *Prairie Conservation: Preserving North America's Most Endangered Ecosystem*, ed. Fred B. Samson and Fritz L. Knopf (Washington, D.C.: Island Press, 1996), 135–48.

89. While there are peripheral populations outside the tallgrass prairie area for the regal fritillary, most of the remaining population is found within the area. Barry L. Williams, "Conservation Genetics, Extinction, and Taxonomic Status: A Case History of the Regal Fritillary," *Conservation Biology* 16 (2002): 148–57.

90. In "Ecological Determinants of Species Loss in Remnant Prairies," Leach and Givnish report that short, small-seeded, or nitrogen-fixing plants are especially vulnerable in prairie remnants because of the lack of fire. Fire opens up the landscape for plants short in stature and increases the dispersal ability for small seeds. Also, where fire volatilizes nitrogen, nitrogen-fixing plants will have an advantage that they don't have otherwise.

91. Booth, *Valuing Nature*, 96.

92. Best estimates of the price elasticity of housing are -.65. When the price of housing declines by 10 percent, the quantity of housing increases by 6.5 percent. See Edwin S. Mills and Bruce W. Hamilton, *Urban Economics*, 5th ed. (New York: HarperCollins, 1994), 209. Thus if land costs on average decline because of an increase in supply caused by reduced transportation costs, then the quantity of housing consumed will increase and hence the amount of construction materials going into housing, such as lumber.

93. U.S. Department of Commerce, Bureau of the Census, *Historical Statistics of the United States*; Robert H. Nelson, "Mythology Instead of Analysis: The Story of Public Forest Management," in *Forest Lands: Public and Private*, ed. Robert T. Deacon and M. Bruce Johnson (San Francisco: Pacific Institute, 1985), 23–76.

94. Booth, *Valuing Nature*, 89.

95. Brian R. Wall, *Log Production in Washington and Oregon: An Historical Perspective* (Portland, Ore.: USDA Forest Service, Resource Bulletin, PNW-42, 1972).

96. Booth, *Valuing Nature*, 111–18.

97. Booth, *Valuing Nature*, 95–110.

98. J. F. Franklin et al., *Ecological Characteristics of Old-Growth Douglas-Fir Forests*, (Portland, Ore.: USDA Forest Service, GTR, PNW-8, 1981).

99. R. H. Waring, and J. F. Franklin, "Evergreen Coniferous Forests of the Pacific Northwest," *Science* 204 (1979): 1380–85; Franklin et al., *Ecological Characteristics of Old-Growth Douglas-Fir Forests*.

100. Thomas A. Spies and Jerry F. Franklin, "Old Growth and Forest Dynamics in the Douglas-Fir Region of Western Oregon and Washington," *Natural Areas Journal* 8 (1988): 190–201; Franklin et al., *Ecological Characteristics of Old-Growth Douglas-Fir Forests.*

101. Spies and Franklin, "Old Growth and Forest Dynamics in the Douglas-Fir Region of Western Oregon and Washington"; Franklin et al., *Ecological Characteristics of Old-Growth Douglas-Fir Forests.*

102. J. F. Franklin, H. H. Shugart, and M. E. Harmon, "Tree Death as an Ecological Process: The Causes, Consequences, and Variability of Tree Mortality," *BioScience* 37 (1987): 550–56; Thomas A. Spies and Jerry F. Franklin, "Coarse Woody Debris in Douglas-Fir Forests of Western Oregon and Washington," *Ecology* 69 (1988): 1689–1702; Franklin et al., *Ecological Characteristics of Old-Growth Douglas-Fir Forests*; R. William Mannan, Charles E. Meslow, and Howard M. Wight, "Use of Snags by Birds in Douglas-Fir Forests, Western Oregon," *Journal of Wildlife Management* 44 (1980): 787–97.

103. Franklin et al., *Ecological Characteristics of Old-Growth Douglas-Fir Forests*; P. Solins et al., "The Internal Element Cycles of an Old-Growth Douglas-Fir Ecosystem in Western Oregon," *Ecological Monographs* 50 (1980): 261–85; Chris Maser and James M. Trappe, *The Seen and Unseen World of the Fallen Tree* (Portland, Ore.: USDA Forest Service, Pacific Northwest Forest and Range and Experiment Station, GTR PNW-164, 1984).

104. Franklin et al., *Ecological Characteristics of Old-Growth Douglas-Fir Forests*; Maser and Trappe, *The Seen and Unseen World of the Fallen Tree*; Chris Maser, James M. Trappe, and Ronald A. Nussbaum, "Fungal–Small Mammal Interrelationships with Emphasis on Oregon Coniferous Forests," *Ecology* 59 (1978): 799–809. Chris Maser et al., "The Northern Flying Squirrel: A Mycophagist in Southwestern Oregon," *Canadian Journal of Zoology* 64 (1986): 2086–89.

105. Mark E. Harmon and Jerry F. Franklin, "Tree Seedlings on Logs in *Picea-Tsuga* Forests of Oregon and Washington," *Ecology* 70 (1989): 45–59.

106. Franklin et al., *Ecological Characteristics of Old-Growth Douglas-Fir Forests.*

107. The Nature Conservancy, *Priorities for Conservation: 1996 Annual Report Card for U.S. Plant and Animal Species* (Arlington, Va.: The Nature Conservancy, 1996).

108. G. E. Petts, *Impounded Rivers: Perspectives for Ecological Management* (New York: John Wiley and Sons, 1984).

109. Karl Wittfogel, *Oriental Despotism: A Comparative Study of Total Power* (New Haven, Conn.: Yale University Press, 1957); Donald Worster, *Rivers of Empire: Water, Aridity, and the Growth of the American West* (New York: Pantheon Books, 1985).

110. Worster, *Rivers of Empire*; Marc Reisner, *Cadillac Desert: The American West and Its Disappearing Water* (New York: Penguin Books, 1987).

111. Petts, *Impounded Rivers.*

112. Worster, *Rivers of Empire*, 241; Reisner, *Cadillac Desert*, 283–84.

113. Booth, *The Environmental Consequences of Growth*, 43.

114. Petts, *Impounded Rivers.*

115. Petts, *Impounded Rivers.*

116. Petts, *Impounded Rivers.*

117. Petts, *Impounded Rivers.*

118. Douglas E. Booth, "Hydroelectric Dams and the Decline of Chinook Salmon in the Columbia River," *Marine Resource Economics* 6 (1989): 195–211. Petts, *Impounded Rivers*.

119. Ann Vileisis, *Discovering the Unknown Landscape: A History of America's Wetlands* (Washington, D.C.: Island Press, 1997), 333–34. The discussion of wetlands to follow relies heavily on Vileisis's excellent work on the topic. Much of what follows is simply a summary, and in some instances a paraphrase, of her conclusions.

120. Vileisis, *Discovering the Unknown Landscape*, 3.

121. Vileisis, *Discovering the Unknown Landscape*, 30–37.

122. Vileisis, *Discovering the Unknown Landscape*, 33–37, 75.

123. Ralph W. Tiner Jr., *Wetlands of the United States: Current Status and Recent Trends* (Washington, D.C.: U.S. Department of the Interior, Fish and Wildlife Service, 1984), 18–23.

124. Tiner, *Wetlands of the United States*, 19–20.

125. Tiner, *Wetlands of the United States*, 14–16; Vileisis, *Discovering the Unknown Landscape*, 163.

126. Tiner, *Wetlands of the United States*, 14–18.

127. Tiner, *Wetlands of the United States*, 13–14.

128. Tiner, *Wetlands of the United States*, 18–25.

129. One estimate puts the number at $4.9 trillion (1994 dollars). See Robert Costanza et al., "The Value of the World's Ecosystem Services and Natural Capital," *Nature* 387: 253–60.

130. Vileisis, *Discovering the Unknown Landscape*, 254–319.

131. Vileisis, *Discovering the Unknown Landscape*, 122–34.

132. Vileisis, *Discovering the Unknown Landscape*, 127, 131.

133. Vileisis, *Discovering the Unknown Landscape*, 118.

134. Vileisis, *Discovering the Unknown Landscape*, 121.

135. Vileisis, *Discovering the Unknown Landscape*, 205–208.

5

Everyday Economic Life
and Environmental Decline

What do we do in our daily life that contributes to environmental decline? The goal of this question is not to make people feel guilty about their behavior. The purpose is enlightenment. Understanding how the way we live affects the natural environment is interesting for its own sake and is necessary for intelligent ameliorative action. Historical experience clearly reveals a link between economic growth and irreversible environmental change (chapter 4). Understanding the role we personally play in irreversible environmental deterioration is essential for assurance that such a link is of continuing importance in the world today. This understanding is also critical for determining what needs to be done to reverse environmental decline and how doing so would change the way we live.

To comprehend how present-day patterns of daily living contribute to the problem of environmental decline, three serious, essentially irreversible, contemporary environmental problems are brought down to the level of daily experience: global warming, the loss of natural habitat from the spreading of human population over the landscape, and the introduction of exotic plants and animals species that pose a threat to native flora and fauna. The key task is to show how ordinary economic activity causes each of these three environmental problems. Understanding that requires the introduction of important ideas from the environmental sciences—something that to the uninitiated could seem a little tedious. The reward, however, of the effort will be a more honest understanding of the connection between patterns of human existence and environmental change.

GLOBAL WARMING

The Evidence

Global warming in the form of an increase in the earth's average surface temperature is a fact of life. Since 1900, the global average surface temperature has increased between 0.4 and 0.8 degrees centigrade. Marine air temperatures and sea surface temperatures have increased by a comparable amount. Temperature increases in the twentieth century were the largest to have occurred in any century in the past one thousand years.[1] Other evidence of global surface warming include increases in clouds, atmospheric water vapor, and precipitation; the retreat of mountain glaciers and the decline in spring and summer Arctic sea ice; a reduction in snow cover and a shortening of seasons for lake and river ice in northerly latitudes; and increased ocean heat content and rising sea levels.[2] The evidence for the occurrence of global warming is difficult to refute. On a cold winter's day, the problem of global warming may seen overblown. A look at the causes and consequences suggests otherwise.

The causes of global warming are increasingly clear. Rising global temperatures appear to be the consequence of increased atmospheric concentrations of so-called greenhouse gases, including carbon dioxide (CO_2), methane (CH_4), nitrous oxide (N_2O), and carbon compounds containing chlorine, fluorine, bromine, or iodine, collectively referred to as halocarbons. Each greenhouse gas occurs naturally at relatively low concentrations in the atmosphere (with the exception of halocarbons), but concentrations have increased significantly in the past two hundred years because of emissions increases caused by economic expansion and industrialization.

The most important of the greenhouse gases is carbon dioxide. Animals and decomposers (such as bacteria) take up oxygen from the atmosphere and return carbon dioxide to it. Plants do exactly the opposite. The result without any kind of human intervention is a rough balance of emissions and absorptions. Human intervention in the form of modern industrial activity has upset that balance. The primary energy sources for modern industrial economies are fossil fuels, and the burning of fossil fuels inevitably results in the emission of CO_2.[3] CO_2 is also being added to the earth's atmosphere as a result of tropical deforestation caused by burning to clear the way for pasture land. The atmospheric concentration of CO_2

increased from approximately 280 ppm (parts per million) in 1750 to 367 ppm in 1999.

Second in importance to CO_2 as a greenhouse gas is methane. Methane is added to the earth's atmosphere naturally from wetlands, but it is also added as a consequence of human activity in the form of rice cultivation, cattle rearing, natural gas emissions from oil fields, and emissions from land fills. About half of all methane emissions are caused by human action, and methane concentrations have increased by about 150 percent since 1750.

Next down the list in terms of importance for greenhouse gases are nitrous oxides and halocarbons. Nitrous oxide emissions result from the use of nitrogen based fertilizers, the burning of biomass, various industrial activities, and cattle feedlot operations, and concentrations are currently 16 percent greater than they were in 1750. Certain halocarbons are implicated in destruction of the ozone layer and are being regulated under the Montreal Protocol. These chemicals are used for a variety of tasks, including refrigeration and motor vehicle air conditioning, and have come into use fairly recently.[4] Since ozone-destroying halocarbon emissions are globally regulated and scheduled for elimination, they are usually excluded from greenhouse gas accounting.

Greenhouse gases are transparent to ultraviolet and short-wave visible radiation received from the sun, but are opaque to infrared radiation reflected back into the atmosphere from the earth's surface. In short, such gases act like a "greenhouse," trapping heat energy. Greenhouse gases absorb and reradiate infrared radiation in all directions, causing a rise in atmospheric and surface temperatures. The measure of the heat-trapping ability of greenhouse gases is radiative forcing. Radiative forcing is roughly analogous to the insulating value of the glass in a greenhouse. Of the total amount of radiative forcing from post-1750 increases in greenhouse gases, CO_2 is responsible for 60 percent, methane 20 percent, nitrous oxide 6 percent, and halocarbons 14 percent.[5] The glass in the global greenhouse has gotten thicker.

The actual amount of global warming occurring as a consequence of increased radiative forcing is uncertain because of the complexities of the global climate system. Forecasts of increasing global temperatures are based on calculations from complex climate simulation models that can be subject to significant error. The critical difficulties in accurately simulating global climate patterns include correctly characterizing feedback effects and properly accounting for all variables that can significantly influence climate. Global warming initiates a number of positive and negative feedback effects that can alter the extent to which warming occurs. A warmer climate, for example, will in turn result in a damper climate as a consequence of increased evaporation. Since water vapor traps heat, the amount of global warming will be greater than otherwise. Climate models estimate that an increase in water vapor will approximately double the amount of warming that would otherwise occur. A warmer climate will also result in less ice and snow cover, causing the planet to be darker and to absorb more solar radiation and reflect less off into space. The most uncertain feedback effect of all has to do with cloud formation. Clouds increase warming by acting as a greenhouse gas, but they also reduce warming by reflecting solar radiation back into space. While there is general agreement that clouds on net cool the climate, there is little agreement about the changes that would result in clouds from additional warming. Warming could increase the altitude of clouds and reduce their ability to reflect solar radiation because of cloud cooling. Warming could also increase the water content of clouds, making them brighter and better able to reflect solar radiation.[6] Despite complexities and uncertainties, with recent improvements in climate modeling, experts now suggest that "most of the observed warming over the last fifty years is likely to have been due to the increase in greenhouse gas concentrations."[7] The actual thickness of the glass in the global greenhouse is not known for certain, but it is clear that the thickness is increasing.

The Intergovernmental Panel on Climate Change, the most widely accepted body of global experts on greenhouse warming, project that the average global surface temperature will increase by 1.4 to to 5.8 degrees centigrade (2.2 to 10.4 degrees fahrenheit) over the period 1990 to 2100 barring any purposeful change in policies that affect the volume of greenhouse gas emissions. This projection is based on a range of alternative scenarios for basic global social and economic trends and their associated emissions of greenhouse gases. None of the scenarios includes explicit measures to mitigate global warming. Anticipated consequences of global warming include rising global precipitation, with increases more heavily concentrated in northerly latitudes; more extreme weather events, including droughts and more intense storms; retreating glaciers; and a rise in the average sea level of 0.11 to 0.43 meters, adding to the sea level increase of .10 to .20 meters over the past century.[8] Simply put, life on earth is going to get warmer, wetter, and stormier.

The Sources of Global Warming in Daily Life

How does each of us contribute to the problem of global warming in our daily life? Again, the purpose of asking this kind of question is enlightenment and understanding, not to attribute blame or to generate feelings of guilt. In order to solve a problem, knowledge of its root cause is essential.

The best way to get a personal sense of our contribution to global warming is to consider greenhouse gas emissions in terms of the average household. The amount of greenhouse gas emissions per American household is about 66.4 metric tons of carbon dioxide equivalents per year, or, to put it in more familiar terms, around 146,385 pounds annually or 401 pounds daily. Given an average household of 2.7 persons, the daily emissions per person is about 150 pounds. In this measure, the amount of methane, nitrous oxides, and halocarbons is included by estimating the global warming potential for each of these emissions and calculating the quantity of CO_2 that would cause an equivalent amount of warming over a hundred-year time horizon.[9] Carbon dioxide emissions themselves amount to 53.3 of the total 66.4 metric tons per household and constitute a very large piece of the total emissions pie. Responsibility for producing greenhouse gas emissions originates in the industrial, transportation, residential, commercial, and agricultural sectors. Within each, CO_2 emissions occur as a consequence of both direct combustion of fossil fuels and the consumption of electricity. Households are directly responsible for greenhouse gas emissions through electricity consumption and space heating in the residential sector and motor vehicle fuel consumption in the transportation sector. By virtue of being the final consumer of goods and services produced in them, households are indirectly responsible for greenhouse gas emissions in other sectors.

The term "responsibility" is used here in a special way. Because of their lack of control over business decision making, households don't necessarily have the ability to alter emissions in the business sector of the economy or the emissions rate for consumer goods whose design is determined by businesses with an eye to maximizing profits. Still, without household consumption of final goods, the business sector of the economy would not exist. To talk in terms of household "responsibility" for emissions makes sense so long as it is clearly understood that households themselves lack full control over what is available for consumption and how it is produced. "Responsibility" refers here to the essential role households play as final consumers. Household action is necessary for emissions to occur, but households don't necessarily have the power to reduce emissions by shifting to alternative emissions-reducing consumer goods or by getting producers to shift to emissions-reducing production technologies. For this reason any attribution of blame to households for greenhouse gas emissions is pointless.

To get a more detailed picture of the consequences of everyday consumption patterns for global warming, let's consider U.S. greenhouse gas emissions patterns sector-by-sector, beginning with transportation. Of the 66.4 metric tons of greenhouse gases emitted by an average household yearly, 17.8, or about 27 percent, come from the transportation sector.[10] Around 9.9 metric tons is attributable to the burning of gasoline for cars and light trucks, around 1.3 metric tons results from airline travel, and the rest comes mostly from the transporting of goods. Every time a gallon of gas is burned, about nineteen pounds of CO_2 is emitted into the atmosphere. For the average household, daily emissions amount to roughly sixty pounds of CO_2 from the consumption of gasoline. Another forty-three pounds is emitted per household for the shipping of goods and transportation not involving household motor vehicles. The grand total daily emissions amounts to 108 pounds for the transportation sector.

Households directly emit another 12.9 metric tons of CO_2 equivalents annually as a consequence of electricity consumption and space heating in their residential dwellings. Of the total residential CO_2 emissions (11.4 metric tons),[11] 7.8 are the result of electricity consumption and 3.6 are due to space heating. This amounts to forty-seven pounds of CO_2 emissions daily for electricity and twenty-two pounds for space heating.[12] Residential electricity consumption and space heating for the average dwelling is responsible for emitting just a bit more CO_2 than the typical household's complement of motor vehicles. The typical residential dwelling is a significant direct source of greenhouse gas emissions at seventy-eight pounds per day of CO_2 equivalents.

Before households can make use of consumer goods, they must be produced. Greenhouse gases not only originate from the daily use of goods in households, but from their manufacture and distribution as well. The industrial sector emits 19.5 metric tons of CO_2 equivalents per household annually of which 14.9 are due to actual CO_2 emissions. The difference of 4.6 metric tons is attributable to the emissions of methane, nitrous oxides, and halocarbons. Methane, for example, is emitted by industry in natural gas production, coal mining, and various other petroleum related processing activities. Of the actual CO_2 emissions, 6.8 metric tons are due to electricity consumption by industry and the remainder is the consequence of direct combustion and various industrial processes. To put the total in familiar terms, 118 pounds of CO_2 equivalent emissions per household are attributable daily to the industrial sector of the economy. This is the amount of emissions associated with the manufacture of all those goods we buy at the mall, the drug store, the big box retailers, and the motor vehicle dealerships.

Such goods need to be manufactured, and they need to be marketed and distributed. This is the job of the commercial sector of our economy. The commercial sector annually emits 10.6 metric tons of greenhouse gases per household with 7.4 of this attributable to CO_2 emissions from electricity consumption and 2.3 attributable to direct combustion for space heating. This amounts to about sixty-four pounds per day, of which forty-five pounds result from the electricity that fuels those brightly lit stores and advertising signs that do so much to illuminate our urban landscapes.

The final sector that needs to be added is agriculture. Much of our grocery bill is attributable to the industrial and commercial sector, but the farm is where it all begins. The fuel used to run tractors is accounted for in the transportation sector, so what's left is mainly emissions in the form of methane and nitrous oxides. The grand total per household from the agricultural sector is 5.3 metric tons per year in CO_2 equivalents, or thirty-two pounds per day. Most of this is in the form of methane from farm animal digestion and manure management and nitrous oxides from nitrogen fertilizer use. Farms account for much of the non-CO_2 greenhouse gases.

To summarize, greenhouse gas emissions per U.S. household on a daily basis in pounds by sector in CO_2 equivalents are as follows: transportation—108, residential—78, industrial—118, commercial—64, and agriculture—32. As already noted, this adds up to about 401 pounds per day, an impressive sum. Again, each household in this country directly and indirectly contributes 400+ pounds of carbon dioxide to the earth's atmosphere daily.

Of course, any single household does not contribute enough in greenhouse gases to really matter, given the overall size of the global atmosphere. When we consider all 105 million American households together, however, the total volume of emissions is huge: 7001.2 million metric tons of CO_2 equivalents annually. Emissions of CO_2 by the United States from fossil fuel sources amount to roughly 23 percent of the global total, while per capita U.S. emissions are about five times the global figure.[13] The United States is the dominant global source of greenhouse emissions, to which each and every household contributes. It is the sum total of economic activity of the average household that results in the United States being a significant part of the global warming problem. Whether the United States can be part of the solution is taken up in the next chapter. Whether the it in fact *will be* part of the solution is another matter that necessarily involves questions of both public values and interest-group politics, issues to be taken up in chapters 7 and 8.

The Environmental Consequences of Global Warming

Global warming is a serious matter that brings with it significant threats to both human beings and natural ecosystems. If you already accept this, then you may want to skip ahead to the problem of population spreading. If you want some details about what global warming will entail, then read on. We begin with agriculture.

Agriculture

The impact of global warming on agriculture is of obvious importance for human welfare. In theory, agriculture can be both harmed and benefited from greenhouse gases. The key benefit to agriculture from global warming will be atmospheric CO_2 enrichment. Since photosynthesis converts CO_2 to sugars essential for plant growth, the efficiency of the process should be enhanced with CO_2 enrichment in the absence of any significant constraints from other limiting resources that would prevent increases in plant growth. The downside of global warming for agriculture is the increased incidence of drought, especially in the lower latitudes. While agricultural production on a global scale most likely can be maintained in the face of greenhouse warming, the distribution of production over the globe will undoubtedly change to the detriment of those who already face challenges growing enough to eat. In a warmer world, more affluent temperate regions in the higher latitudes are projected to experience gains in production while the more impoverished tropical regions are projected to lose production. Studies that serve as the basis for these projections don't explicitly take into account the effect of warming on weeds, pest insects, and plant diseases. The CO_2 "fertilization" effect will benefit weeds just as it does crops, and warming will likely shift the feasible range for insects and disease pathogens farther northward, creating more pest problems for farmers in temperate areas.[14] Projections of gains in temperate-region agricultural productivity could easily be reversed by pests, weeds, and severe weather. The salutary effects of global warming on agriculture are by no means assured.

Forests

Just as for croplands, global warming will bring change to the forests of the world. For forests in the lower latitudes, warming is less of an issue than the process of deforestation. The predominant threat to tropical forests is land clearing and conversion to agriculture, not global warming. Warming is more of a threat to temperate and boreal forests. Particular species in these forests are strongly influenced by temperature and precipitation. As the climate warms, the ideal habitat in terms of temperature range for a given species will shift upward in latitude and altitude. The danger is that the tolerable temperature range for tree survival will move faster than trees can migrate. If this occurs, trees could be lost at lower elevations and latitudes more rapidly than they are added at higher ones. Higher temperatures will also tend to increase pest problems in forests as well as the incidence of fires. Despite these threats from global warming, the total temperate forest area is projected to remain stable, partly because of reforestation occurring in areas of poor agricultural productivity such as the New England states in the United States. The more northerly boreal forests are likely to suffer the most from elevated temperatures, with fire and pests being a special problem. On balance, overall wood fiber production is unlikely to be significantly altered by global warming, but forest composition and the type of wood available for harvest will undoubt-edly change.[15] The forests of the future in the temperate region will look quite different in terms of the type of tree species present, although the to-tal amount of wood volume may not change that much. The impact of warming will be more qualitative than quantitative. If the concern is strictly with wood volume, then warming may not be much of a problem.

Rising Sea Levels

The single most serious threat to human well-being from global warming is a rising sea level. An increase in the sea level will cause inundation of lowlands and low-lying islands, accelerated coastal erosion, increased coastal flooding and storm damage, damage to coastal structures, and salt-water intrusion into freshwater estuaries and aquifers. Because bridges and harbor facilities are designed for certain water levels, some will be ren-dered useless and some will have to be modified as a consequence of a sea-level increase. Since beach profiles tend to be flatter than the land just above sea level, a rise in the sea level will cause erosion of a land area sev-eral times the area initially inundated. Basically, the erosive force of rising ocean waters will eat away at the steeper landscapes above the initial sea level, re-create the flatter beach profile farther inland, and in the process in-undate an expanded area. The same process will result in the inundation of entire barrier islands off coastlines. Needless to say, beach resort areas will suffer significant losses of buildings. With a higher sea level, storm surges will operate from a higher base and do significantly more damage. Higher sea levels will also force the groundwater table upwards, adding to flooding problems, and cause salt water to extend farther up into estuaries and to intrude into groundwater sources. The economic cost of a sea-level increase is difficult to predict but could easily amount to billions of dollars annually for the United States alone.[16] Currently, about 46 million people per year worldwide are at risk for flooding from storm surges on low-lying lands. If the sea level increases by half a meter, those at risk from storm surges rise to around 92 million. Many of these people live in low-lying countries such as Bangladesh that already suffer from very high poverty rates. Protective measures against storm surges are simply too costly for these countries to bear.[17] A warmer, stormier world with higher sea levels will be a special challenge for those trying to eke out an existence in flood-prone landscapes.

Warming and Human Health

The projected overall impact of global warming on the human ability to extract food and fiber from agricultural lands and forests appears to be

fairly modest as noted above. Only coastal dwellers appear to be significantly endangered from the consequences of global warming discussed
so far. Adding the direct effects of climate change on human health gives
a more complete and compelling picture of the dangers of continued
global warming. Human health is endangered by heat waves whose oc-
currences and duration will rise because of global warming. Heat increases the incidence of respiratory and cardiovascular illnesses. Heat
also increases the occurrence of conventional air pollution, such as tro-
pospheric ozone, and the health problems it causes such as asthma and
respiratory disorders. Climate warming can also expand the range of
various tropical diseases. Global temperature increases of three to five
degrees centigrade could expand the proportion of the global population
potentially subject to malaria from 45 to 60 percent. Along with illnesses
induced by global warming, injuries and deaths from extreme storm
events are likely to increase in a warmer world.[18] Global warming is a
clear threat to human health. Heat can be pleasant and comforting, but
too much is dangerous.

Warming, Natural Ecosystems, and Threats to Species

Human beings have the special advantage of being able to explicitly
adapt to threats of the kind posed by global warming. Crop species can be
altered to cope with a warmer world, populations can be moved away
from low-lying coastal areas, health problems and diseases can be treated,
and air conditioning can be installed. Nonhuman species in natural
ecosystems can adjust and adapt to changing climatic conditions, but
most can only do so on a geologic time scale. Plant and animal species can
move to different locations and sort themselves into new biological communities in response to climate change, as they did during the last continental glaciation ten to fifteen thousand years ago. Over this time span,
most plants and animals kept up with geographic shifts in temperature
that occurred as continental glaciers expanded and receded. As glaciers
expanded, plants and animals migrated south, only to turn around and
move back as the glaciers shrunk.

Unfortunately, current climatic change from global warming is occurring much more rapidly than the pace of glaciation in the past.[19] With the
present pace of climate change, some species will be unable to migrate
quickly enough to avoid temperature-related stress or even to survive.
This is especially true for plants that have limited seed dispersal capabilities and the animals that depend on those plants. For this reason, global
warming has the potential to cause significant declines in species populations and ultimately species extinctions. Such losses can in turn damage
and disrupt ecosystems occupied by these species.

The loss and extinction of species and the resulting disruption of ecosystems is a problem for human beings for two reasons. First, we clearly benefit from a wide range of services that ecosystems provide, including climate regulation, the storage and cleansing of water flows, erosion prevention, nutrient cycling, soil formation, pollination, pest control, habitat provision for valued species, food production, raw materials supplies, recreation, and aesthetic appreciation.[20] The decline or loss of key plant and animal species can disrupt the supply of such services. In short, the presence of nonhuman species is good for us, and their loss can harm us.

Second, apart from any material benefits they provide, we may see species as having a right to exist and flourish for their own sake within the larger evolutionary scheme of things.[21] The human species evolved from the same origins as all other plant and animal species. Some of us may see this common origin in evolutionary processes as carrying with it obligations to protect nonhuman species and the natural processes they depend on. A sense of kinship on our part with other forms of life is not an unreasonable proposition. Other species may be good for us materially, but even if they are not, we might want them around anyway.[22]

The potential for global warming to threaten species is sizeable and not easily summarized. A limited discussion of a few of the threats is useful because it will give us an indication of the potential magnitude of the problem. Threats to species posed by global warming arise as a consequence of higher temperatures on land, higher temperatures in saltwater and freshwater, and rising sea levels. Wherever they are found, most species will have to contend with a change in their environment because of the greenhouse effect.

Different species respond differently to climate change. Highly mobile species, like birds and large mammals, can, in the absence of barriers to migration, adapt to global warming simply by moving to more suitable habitats in more northerly latitudes. Less mobile species, such as small mammals and plants, may not be able to respond so readily to shifts in temperature regimes. For plants, temperature changes under global warming may be too rapid for migration. Warming of 1 to 3.5 degrees centigrade over the next century will shift temperate vegetation zones northward by 150 to 550 kilometers and upward in elevation by 150 to 550 meters. Tree species in the past have been able to migrate at only a rate of four to two hundred kilometers per century.[23] Some temperature-sensitive plant species will simply die out in warmer latitudes and be unable to gain a foothold in cooler latitudes because of slow seed dispersal.

As a consequence of such limited migratory abilities, species found in a relatively narrow latitudinal range may be threatened with extinction. Northern hardwood forest species such as sugar maple, yellow birch, northern hemlock, and beech may well disappear from the Great Lakes area. Because of a slow dispersal rate, genotypes of beech needed for survival in a more northerly range may not arrive in time to assure survival of the species.[24] Global warming will, in effect, prune from the forest tree species unable to disperse to the north very rapidly.

Climate change will likely put the nail in the coffin for many prairie species already under threat from habitat loss. Warming does not bode well for Midwest tallgrass prairie species confined to small, fragmented habitats because of massive agricultural land barriers to species migration.[25] In order for species to successfully migrate northward in response to temperature increases, habitat must be continuous. Drought-sensitive species in the highly fragmented tallgrass prairie will be unable to cross vast expanses of corn and soybean fields to reach cooler, more moist habitats. Even if they can in theory head northward fast enough as temperatures rise, a northward march for plants in a fragmented landscape will be impossible. Landscape fragmentation worsens the problem of global warming.

For some species already occupying the coolest latitudes, there is simply nowhere to go. A substantial range shrinkage for the most northerly tundra vegetation type is inevitable in a warmer world. The results of climate modeling research indicate that warming will be greater at higher latitudes and greater still in the Arctic region, where reduced sea ice and snow cover will decrease the amount of energy reflected back into space and increase the amount of local warming.[26] The loss of tundra in turn will reduce populations of tundra-dependent species such as caribou and waterfowl. Boreal forests have been migrating northward in Alaska at the rate of 100 to 150 kilometers for every degree centigrade increase in temperature, causing a shrinkage in tundra vegetation. The structure of boreal forests themselves appears to be changing significantly in response to warmer temperatures. Some boreal forests have been transformed into wetlands because of permafrost melting, and the area of boreal forest burned every year in western North America has doubled over the last twenty years.[27] Higher temperatures mean not only shifting vegetation zones, but an increase in the incidence of wildfire and the consequences for vegetation that go with it. The ecosystems of the higher latitudes where temperature changes will be the greatest are likely to undergo the most substantial changes. Species confined to these areas will be appreciably threatened by global warming.

The movement of vegetation zones in response to warmer temperatures will be in a northerly direction, and in mountainous landscape it will be upwards as well. Just as a northerly movement of vegetation zones squeezes out tundra, a vertical movement of vegetation zones shrinks high elevation subalpine vegetation habitats. In many areas, lower timberline will move upward as well, shrinking the total area occupied by forests.[28] A drier climate in western mountainous forests will also increase fire frequency, shifting forest age in the direction of youth, reducing old-growth forest habitats, and replacing conifers with hardwoods able to sprout quickly after fires. The net result will be a reduction of species diversity in mountainous landscapes.[29] Mountain hikers a century from now will see a type of landscape entirely different from what we see now. Gone will be the beautiful open meadows of subalpine wildflowers, to be replaced by forest species found today only at lower elevations.

Changing climate regimes and landscape patterns will also have significant impacts on animal species. Animals may be able to migrate in response to climate change, but they will still be dependent on what happens to the resources they feed on and the habitats they live in. The probable disappearance of jack pine stands from northern Michigan in the United States under global warming will mean the extinction of Kirtland's warbler, a species dependent on such stands for nesting.[30] Global warming and the upward migration of forest zones will reduce whitebark pine stands in the Yellowstone area, causing a decline in whitebark pinenuts, a critical food resource for the local grizzly bear population.[31] The whitebark pine are a high-elevation species that have nowhere to go. The grizzlies that depend on them are already under threat from human habitat incursions. The loss of sea ice in the Arctic is a threat to seals, walrus, and polar bears dependent on it for habitat.[32] In the spring months, polar bears hunt for seals on sea ice. Animals, no less than plants, will suffer from the consequences of a warmer world.

Another kind of change associated with warmer temperatures that can cause increasing stress for certain species is the altered timing of biological events (phenology). Increased global temperatures means earlier spring warming and later fall cooling. Such a shift in temperature regimes can cause breeding and growing seasons to occur earlier in time. A shift in the climate regime in the direction of earlier spring warming in tundra habitats could result in migratory shorebirds arriving after the peak of insect food availability, reducing their reproductive success.[33] This is equivalent to arriving at a restaurant for dinner only to find that its hours of operation have been changed. Being in the right place at the right time is critical in nature. Global warming has the capacity for resetting the timing of natural events to detriment of those species unable to reset their own internal clocks.

While terrestrial biota will be dramatically affected by global warming, ecosystems most likely to be altered are those found in a marine or coastal environment. Both rising sea levels and increased seawater temperatures pose a threat to numerous marine species. Coastal wetlands are among the most biologically productive ecosystems in the world, serving as nurseries for numerous marine and terrestrial species and as important habitats for migratory and shore birds. As much as one-half of all fish caught by commercial and recreational fishermen spend part of their life cycle in coastal wetlands. Large areas of coastal wetlands have already been lost as a consequence of economic development, and many of the remaining wetlands are threatened by a sea level increase induced by greenhouse warming. Wetlands can keep pace with normal rates of sea level rise through sedimentation and peat formation. However, a greenhouse-induced sea-level rise will exceed the ability of wetlands to keep up. Even if wetlands could keep up, human barriers, such as coastal highways, in some cases will prevent the inland migration of wetlands.[34] A one-meter rise in the sea level could cause a 30 to 70 percent loss of coastal wetlands. Other kinds of threats to coastal species from a sea-level rise will occur as well. In Florida, a number of species, including the Florida panther and key deer, are currently squeezed by human development into coastal habitats that will be inundated as a result of rising sea levels.[35] The loss of important mangrove forests along the U.S. Gulf Coast is also likely as a consequence of sea-level increases from global warming. Mangroves serve as habitat for a variety of marine species and protect coastal areas from erosion.[36] In the simplest possible terms, rising sea levels are bad for coastal species.

Global warming will have other consequences as well for marine biota. Slight increases in temperature disrupt coral reef ecosystems by causing bleaching of the coral and its death. Coral exists in a symbiotic relationship with algae that are highly temperature sensitive. Damage to coral can also occur as the result of water pollution and diseases related to warming. The destruction of coral reefs is especially significant because of the vast array of fish species using coral reefs as prime habitat.[37] In a hundred years the beautiful coral reefs much loved by vacationing scuba divers may well be hard to find.

Not only marine but freshwater ecosystems and their species will suffer stresses as a consequence of higher temperatures. Warming will tend to increase winter moisture, move up the timing of snow melt, and reduce the amount of summer moisture in the northern regions of the United States. The net effect will be to raise temperatures and reduce the volume of summer water flows in streams and rivers. Lake temperatures will be higher than otherwise as well, expanding the upper layers of warm water and reducing deep, coldwater refuges. Warming will also increase biological production in the surface layers of lakes, the downward flow of dead organic materials, and the extent of deepwater oxygen deprivation induced by the decomposition of organic matter. All these trends together will significantly shrink the range of coldwater fishes such as trout.[38] A five-degree centigrade increase in the mean July temperature could cause as much as a 43 percent reduction in trout and salmon populations in the Rocky Mountain region, according to one study.[39] Yet another problem in freshwater ecosystems is the drying of wetlands because of reduced summer stream flows and increased temperatures. Wetland will be replaced by forest and shrubland species and, as a consequence, wetlands and the species they support will shrink in extent.[40] A reduction in wetland habitat for duck populations in the northern Great Plains will likely be aggravated by a drying up of prairie potholes that serve as prime waterfowl breeding grounds.[41] Global warming will reduce the opportunities not only for great fly fishing in mountain trout streams but great duck hunting in prairie potholes and wetlands.

In sum, global warming has the potential not only to do costly damage directly to human beings, but to significantly alter and harm natural ecosystems and the species they contain. This in turn means a loss of species and the services to humankind they provide. The extinction of species, such as the grizzly bear in Yellowstone, or Kirtland's warbler in Michigan, or the key deer in Florida, will make those places less interesting for observers of wildlife to visit. The decline or extinction of marine fish species dependent on coastal wetlands or coral reefs can mean serious economic losses to both commercial fishing and the tourism industry. Similarly, the decline of trout and other coldwater fish species will be much lamented by recreational fishermen in the Rocky Mountain region and the northern woodlands of the United States. The diversity and the beauty of both mountain forests in the western United States and the temperate forests of the Great Lakes region will be reduced by global warming, and naturalists will have increasing difficulty finding remnants of the tallgrass prairie in the Midwest. With a decline in the extent of wetlands, their role as sponges for flood prevention and filters for freshwater supplies will diminish, as will their role as habitat for waterfowl and fish species. These are but a few of services provided by nature to human beings that are likely to suffer as a consequence of global warming.[42]

While human benefits accrue from natural landscapes subject to harm from global warming, such landscapes and the species they contain may also be seen by some as having value in their own right, as suggested above. This means that natural landscapes and the species they contain ought to be defended for their own sake, not just for the human benefits they bring. If this is the case, the problem of global warming is a serious matter not only for economic reasons, but for ethical reasons as well. Human societies may be able to adjust to the losses in services from the natural world, although such adjustments could be costly if studies of the value of such services are at all accurate.[43] If adaptations and adjustments to global warming are indeed possible and affordable, then in the end the only real restraint on human-induced climate change may be a moral commitment not to needlessly cause the extinction of species who, like ourselves, are the product of evolutionary processes.[44]

POPULATION SPREADING

The defining elements of a modern, middle-class style of life in the United States undoubtedly include a large house on a large parcel of land in the suburbs and the automobile as the primary mode of transportation. These elements together require large inputs of energy and are a significant part of the global warming problem. These elements are also "land intensive" and a significant part of the natural habitat loss problem, as we will now see.

The Spreading Process

The history of human society to an important extent is the history of human population expansion and spreading over the global landscape. As noted in the previous chapter, nineteenth-century U.S. population spreading from east to west was motivated by the desire for arable land and was facilitated by the development of transportation, most importantly the railroad. When the industrial revolution took hold in the latter half of the nineteenth century, a profound shift in population from rural areas to urban centers commenced. Industrial activity requires the concentration of population in cities to take advantage of the economies of close proximity. Businesses needed to be close to the workforce to minimize the latter's commuting times and costs and to each other in order to facilitate communications and the movement of goods. At the end of the nineteenth century, 70 percent of the U.S. population was still rural. By the mid-point of the twentieth century, the United States was predominantly urban, with 60 percent of the population living in urban settings, and by the beginning of our current century urban population had risen to 79 percent of the total.[45]

Despite a powerful trend toward population concentration, Americans have never lost their desire to live in landscapes with rural features. This desire fueled extensive outward spreading of population away from urban centers in the latter half of the twentieth century. While cities are the life's blood of industrialization, Americans have always felt ambivalence toward urban living. Cities in nineteenth-century America, essential as they were to economic progress, were tinged not only by the pollution and unhealthy conditions characteristic of a newly industrializing society, but also by the corruption of city government political machines. The good and moral life in the eyes of many was to be found in a rural setting, not an urban one. The rural ideal, as Sam Bass Warner articulates, includes enjoyment of the pleasures of family life, the security of small communities, and a proximity to the world of nature[46] Since in an urban society this ideal was impossible to obtain, it was sought through location on the urban fringe by those who could afford to do so as soon as transportation technology made it possible.

Warner documents the first wave of suburbanization occurring in Boston in the last half of the nineteenth century. The city's original two-mile radius, necessitated by the need for everyone to walk everywhere, expanded to a ten-mile radius by 1900. Outward expansion of the city's boundaries was enabled by the construction of a street railway system and the extension of municipal services to newly developing areas. Achieving the rural ideal through suburbanization in the Boston area turned out to contain an internal contradiction. Any connections to nature were soon lost as the urban edge migrated farther out and construction took place on undeveloped land. The pleasures of family life in suburban havens could be obtained in the newly developing areas of the city, but the early suburbs never really established their own commercial and community centers, and the interactions of community life integral to the rural ideal were seldom achieved. Retailing remained essentially a central city function concentrated at the urban center and along streetcar lines.

The intensity of the desire for suburban living has remained largely unchanged over the past century. Anthony Downs claims that the dominant suburban vision prevailing today includes five key elements: ownership of detached single-family homes on spacious lots; ownership of automotive vehicles; work in low-rise workplaces with convenient parking; residences in small communities with strong local governments; and an environment free from signs of poverty.[47] What has changed since the nineteenth century are the enabling conditions. In the walking city, suburban living was largely precluded by the need to be within walking distance of the urban center, no more than two or three miles. The limitations of the walking city were overturned by the coming of the electric streetcar. In fifty years the electric streetcar expanded Boston's urban radius from three to ten miles. By 1900 a six-mile commute would require about an hour from home to office.[48] The streetcar enabled those who could afford it to move to the urban periphery. This new technology facilitated the outward movement of residential activity, but left the spatial economics of business largely unchanged. Close proximity to customers and other businesses was required because communication was largely limited to office boys carrying notes. Goods could only be moved through the congested streets of the city by handcarts and wagons at a relatively high cost. Manufacturing huddled close to railheads and ports to limit the costs of moving goods within the city, and offices congregated together for ease of communication. The result was that everyone had to commute to the urban center for employment. Under the new pattern of settlement in the streetcar city, the working class lived at high densities in and about the confines of the old walking city, the more prosperous middle class lived in lower densities somewhat farther out, and the richest class lived in the lowest densities on the urban periphery.[49] At first newly developing areas were happy to be annexed to the central city, but soon suburban residents wanted independence from the central cities they no longer controlled politically, and they wanted independent determination of their own level of municipal services while avoiding the burdens of central city problems and taxes.[50]

The movement of the relatively prosperous to the urban periphery was, perhaps, inevitable given the nature of the nineteenth-century American city. Industrialization meant dirty, smoky, gritty cities while immigration, essential for the manning of the industrial system, created overcrowded ghettos repulsive to middle-class sensibilities.[51] In this setting, the suburb provided a peaceful haven from the apparent chaos of the central city. Though the central city and the proximity it afforded were the real source of economic wealth, those who benefited from it most were the first to leave.

Augmentation of the urban land supply by outward extension of streetcar lines took advantage of the mathematical relationship between the radius and the area of a circle—land area increases in proportion to the square of the radius from the center of the city.[52] As the feasible commute expanded from roughly two to six miles for a streetcar system oriented on the urban center like spokes on a bicycle wheel, the possible area for urban development increased roughly ninefold. The streetcar brought relatively cheap land on the urban boundary within the sphere of urban development, making possible suburban housing construction at relatively low densities.

The motor vehicle expanded the supply of land within the sphere of urban influence even more dramatically, not just by reducing commuting times to the central business district but more importantly by disconnecting work from the urban center. Trucks allowed for the movement of goods within an urban area at much reduced costs.[53] This was especially true once the interstate highway system was developed, with spokes running through old urban centers and radial spurs connecting different suburban locations. Any activity depending on truck transportation could now locate advantageously near interstate junctions and have access to the whole metropolitan area as well as interurban shipping routes, while avoiding the congestion of the old central city. The untying of work from the urban center allowed urban areas to be almost boundless. The average commute in the early 1980s was 9.2 miles and took twenty-two minutes, in contrast to the one-hour commute required to cover six miles on the streetcar.[54] Reduced commuting time alone would expand the urban boundary substantially for a core-dominated urban area where commuting is from the urban periphery to the center. With the suburbanization of employment, the nine-mile average commute is more typically between residence and work within the suburban circle. This arrangement allows for the outward movement of work and residence in tandem, bringing potentially vast amounts of rural land into the realm of urban development. Apart from physical barriers, the supply of urban land is limited only by the extent of the urban expressway system. The motor vehicle essentially eliminated constraints on the outward march of urban development.

Numerous other trends aided and stimulated the suburbanization of businesses and residences. The telephone, like the truck, stretched out the lines of interaction between businesses and reduced the need for close proximity. With the growth of auto-accessible suburban shopping malls, suburban residents no longer relied on downtown retailing and could live in more distant locations and continue to have access to urban consumption opportunities. The switch to the motor vehicle wasn't simply a matter of consumer choice but was enabled by an incredible public investment in expressways and highways, brought forth in no small measure through the lobbying efforts of a powerful collection of major industries.[55] After World War II, the suburban dream of a detached, single-family dwelling was no longer confined to the relatively wealthy but could now be afforded by the more prosperous segments of the working class, with the help of relatively low cost VA and FHA insured mortgage loans. Home ownership blossomed as a result to the detriment of the older central cities lacking substantial supplies of single family dwellings qualifying for VA or FHA assistance.[56] Because of annexation-law reforms resulting in the need for local resident approval, suburban residents could avoid annexation by the central city and establish separate municipal jurisdictions instead. Besides avoiding the high tax costs associated with central-city problems, local approval of annexation allowed for the local control of zoning and the use of exclusionary practices, such as minimum-lot-size requirements, that would keep economically burdensome and undesirable low-income residences out. The end result was to confine the poor to the older, filtered-down housing in the central city and create economically and socially homogeneous suburban communities.

Because of the intensity of the desire for suburban living and the growing ability to live and work in the suburbs, central-city population growth stagnated and lost its relative dominance over the past half-century. From 1950 to 2000, suburban population mushroomed, increasing more than threefold from 38.1 to 140.6 million, while central city population grew modestly by comparison, from 51.2 to 85.4 million. The share of suburban population in U.S. metropolitan areas increased from 43 percent to 62 percent as a consequence.

The initial wave of suburbs that developed after World War II consisted largely of bedroom communities. Residents commuted to the central city for work. In this setting, the essentials of the suburban dream—quiet neighborhoods of single-family homes on large lots in a semirural setting—were not hard to maintain. More recently, the suburbs have been transformed.

With the construction of large shopping malls, office complexes, and industrial parks, the majority of jobs in urban areas are now found in the suburbs.[57] Many suburbs now have a sufficient density of office space and employment to be urban centers in their own right. In a book that has received much attention, Joel Garreau documents the development of new centers of employment activity in the suburbs and coined the phrase "edge cities" to describe them. Most suburban residents today commute to other suburbs or edge cities for their employment rather than the central city. As a consequence of this trend, suburbs have taken on increasingly urban characteristics, including traffic congestion, noise, pollution, and crime. Quiet bedroom communities in semirural settings have been transformed into what are essentially cities, but cities that retain quintessentially suburban qualities—the primary one being auto dependence. Moving from one point to another in suburban space mandates the use of the automobile. For this reason, traffic in suburbs is a constant problem, despite the relatively large amount of land devoted to highways and streets. The rise of edge cities further extends the outer boundary of metropolitan commuting and suburban development. The increasingly urban-like qualities of the edge city cause commuters to look farther afield for rural-like residential opportunities. The dynamic in many metropolitan areas now appears to be a continuous outward spreading of population to more distant suburbs, followed by an outward movement of businesses and employment.[58]

The outward spread of population within metropolitan areas is now being augmented by a comparatively new trend—the migration of population to counties outside metropolitan boundaries. If the suburbs have lost their luster, then one option is to move beyond them. The historic pattern of population loss in rural areas as a consequence of out-migration appears to have been reversed. Between 1990 and 2000 nonmetropolitan counties in the U.S. experienced net in-migration, adding 6.9 percent to their total population as a consequence. In the same period, metropolitan counties experienced a slightly lower 6.1 percent net in-migration rate. Only because of a higher rate of natural increase did the total population growth rate of the metropolitan exceed the nonmetropolitan counties (13.8 percent versus 10.3 percent). Despite rural population declines in such areas as the Great Plains and the Mississippi Delta, a large majority (74 percent) of nonmetropolitan counties gained population from 1990 to 2000. Among nonmetropolitan counties, those serving as destinations for retirees and those offering extensive recreation-oriented activity experienced the highest rates of growth (28.4 percent and 19.3 percent). Rural retirement and recreational counties are heavily concentrated in the Northeast, the Upper Great Lakes, and the Mountain West. Recreational counties are attracting not just retirees but rather a broad age range of adults over thirty, including some who have families with children.[59]

Historically, economic necessity dictated population migration from rural areas with declining employment opportunities to urban areas with expanding employment. The emerging reversal of this migration pattern is driven more by the desire for amenities offered by scenic rural areas and to escape the problems of urban life than by economic need.[60] The choice of where to live is increasingly motivated by consumer want in a world where improvements in transportation and communication have made living at low densities in attractive, remote rural locations feasible.[61] Satellite TV, the Internet, the World Wide Web, the interstate highway system, and overnight package delivery all make living in remote areas possible without sacrificing access to the benefits of the global economy.[62] In a recent study of two rapidly growing rural Oregon counties in a scenic mountainous area, 60 percent of households were found to be users of the Internet, a figure that is above the national average of 52 percent.[63] Internet use is apparently a common feature of life in high-amenity rural areas. In a voter survey, the rural residents of the Sierra Nevada Mountains, a region that is experiencing rapid population growth, claim to have chosen where they live predominantly because of the quality of life and the quality of the environment, to be a part of a small community with beauty and charm in a rural area, and to get away from urban and city life.[64] Employers increasingly consider amenities in their location decisions, having discovered that locations with much to offer in natural beauty and recreational opportunities attract high-quality, well-educated employees.[65]

The movement to the suburbs and beyond is inexorably spreading human population out over the landscape. The forces behind the "Schumpeterian" style of economic-growth process discussed in chapters 2 through 4 have created the kinds of "information age" technologies that facilitate population spreading. Computers, the Internet, the fax, the modem, and satellite communications ease the movement of population and economic activity to locations that were at one time too remote for human settlement. The process of innovation behind "creative destruction" and the consumer desire for novelty are again working together to foster economic advance, and the form that advance is taking is to expand the spatial scale of human activity.

Population Spreading and Everyday Low-Density Living

The spreading of human population over the suburban and rural landscape is the expression of a deeply felt American desire to live at low densities. Americans more than almost all other nationalities choose to live at low densities and to consume large amounts of land. For large cities in the United States, the 1990 metropolitan-area population density equaled 14.2 persons per hectare (2.471 acres) while the comparable figure is 49.9 for major European cities and 161.9 for Asian cities.[66] Moreover, the already large amount of developed land per person in the United States, relative to other countries, is on the increase. Between 1982 and 1997, developed land in the United States increased by 34 percent, while population increased by only 16 percent.[67] Americans continue to spread out and are living at lower and lower densities.

So much land is consumed by Americans because of the way they live. Most live in spacious houses in suburbs, commute by automobile to their place of work, and work in suburban office parks, factories, or malls that feature low-rise buildings and acres and acres of parking lots. Between 1980 and 1999 the square footage in the average newly constructed American house rose by 28 percent from 1,740 to 2,225.[68] Between 1980 and 1998 urban highway mileage grew by 35 percent, while the number of motor vehicles on the road grew by 36 percent.[69] Given these numbers, understanding why the amount of developed land has increased so much in recent years is not hard.

Low-density living is enabled by dependence on the motor vehicle as the principal mode of transportation. Americans own more cars, drive more miles, and depend less on public transportation on a per-person basis than any other nationality. Countries that depend more heavily on public transportation systems live at much higher densities.[70] The love affair with the automobile and really big houses on large lots explains why Americans consume so much land. In recent years this love affair has been extended to include living in rural areas on ten-to-a-hundred-acre plots of land in close proximity to landscapes of significant natural beauty. As already noted, such modern innovations as the interstate highway, the personal computer, the modem, the Internet and the World Wide Web, overnight package delivery, the cell phone, and satellite TV have all helped to make living in remote rural landscapes feasible. All these new technologies increase the feasibility of living in remote landscapes while continuing to participate in the global consumer economy.[71] The innovative power of Schumpeterian creative destruction has enabled the continuation of Veblenesque consumption patterns outside of urban settings. A move to the country need not mean forgoing the wonders of the modern consumer economy.

Americans love their wide-open spaces. The problem is, such a love is self-spoiling. The enjoyment of those wide-open spaces through development is causing them to rapidly disappear. The desire for space is also coming into direct conflict with the needs of nonhuman species for habitat.

The Environmental Consequences of Population Spreading

What is the spread of population doing to the world of nature? What are the environmental and ecological consequences of population expansion beyond existing urban boundaries? If these questions interest you, then charge ahead. If you already believe that population spreading has important consequences, then you may want to skip the details and move on to the next environment problem, the invasion of exotic species.

Although the ecology of suburban-style development has only recently come under study, the results offer a clear message—such development substantially alters the environment and imposes stress on populations of native plant and animal species. While the green lawns and shrubs of the suburbs may be pleasant to look at, they are nothing like the landscapes that preceded them.

Whether it occurs within urban areas or in rural settings beyond urban boundaries, low-density residential and commercial development changes the way the landscape works. Such development brings with it acres and acres of impervious surfaces in the form of highways, parking lots, and rooftops. Rather than soaking into soils and adding to groundwater, rainwater collects together into large torrents that can erode hillsides and stream banks and cause downstream flooding. The potential for human harm is significant, although adjustments are possible to diminish damage from unwanted water flows. Drainage systems can be installed and streams channelized with concrete to move water rapidly away and avoid the problems of erosion. Levees can be constructed to mitigate flooding, although they don't always deal effectively with really huge flood events.

Unfortunately, nonhuman native species don't adjust so easily to changes in the landscape caused by the outward spread of human population. Stresses to populations of native species caused by suburban-style development include habitat loss, habitat disturbance, the fragmentation of habitat, and the introduction of nonnative, "exotic" species. The creation of a concrete jungle through the construction of business districts, edge cities, or shopping malls eliminates landscape features and vegetation that serve as habitat for native species. Business areas dominated by streets, parking lots, and buildings are among the most extreme forms of habitat alteration.

While most plant and animal species are absent in such settings, a few actually flourish. As Robert B. Blair notes in a fascinating study of bird species along a gradient involving different types of urban development, so-called urban exploiters, such as the White-throated Swift, Rock Dove, and House Sparrow achieve their maximum densities in the business district. The last two species are well-known introduced exotics found in many urban settings, while the first is a cliff-dwelling native species that can readily adapt to the cliff-like buildings common in business districts.[72] Over 80 percent of the business district in Blair's study is covered by buildings and pavement, while the cover for the residential area in the study is around 20 percent each for buildings and pavement, 10 percent for lawn, and over 40 percent for trees and shrubs. As might be expected, a golf course in the study is about 60 percent lawn and just less than 40 percent trees and shrubs.

The reduced density of development and the more diverse type of vegetative cover in the residential area and on the golf course causes a shift in the mix of bird species present as well as the total number of birds. The abundance and diversity of bird species reaches a peak in the residential area and golf course, but many of the birds found in these two locations are widely distributed species as opposed to local natives. Native species, or "urban avoiders," such as the Wrentit and Steller's Jay, are at their peak in a wooded nature preserve, Blair finds. Residential development and the golf course apparently eliminate the habitat features required by native bird species, although the presence of lawns, shrubs, and trees increase food, perches, and nest sites for "suburban adapters," birds that are attracted to suburban landscape features. Suburban adapters include such familiar species as American Robin, the House Finch, the Mourning Dove, and the European Starling. Development in any form, simply put, is hard on local native species.[73]

Near the outer suburban boundary of metropolitan areas, development usually becomes somewhat discontinuous and patchy. Some landowners choose to keep their land out of development, hoping for higher land prices in the future, while others cash in right away. The resulting patchiness of development divides up and fragments remaining areas of habitat used by native species. An important consequence of this pattern is the creation of more extensive edges around remaining pieces of habitat. Some species avoid edges, while others are attracted to them. Edge-loving species may, for instance, forage in human-created suburban habitats while breeding in undeveloped habitats. Interior species will typically fulfill all their life functions within the boundaries of a habitat patch and face some sort of threat on the edge. Brown-headed Cowbirds, for example, forage in developed landscapes but lay their eggs in the nests of songbirds near forest edges. By this act songbirds are deceived into raising cowbird offspring.[74] Because of this kind of parasitic behavior by cowbirds, songbird reproduction is diminished in fragmented habitats with extensive edges. Habitat fragmentation caused by suburban development suppresses the population of habitat interior-loving native bird species, a conclusion supported by a study of an urbanizing landscape of shrubby habitat near San Diego.[75]

In the same geographic area, a second study finds that house cats create serious problems for local bird populations, especially in small habitat fragments with interiors easily accessible from neighboring residences. Cats put a dent in the population of other species as well. Using results from a survey of cat owners, study authors estimated that cats from roughly a hundred residences surrounding a modest-size habitat fragment returned to their homes 840 rodents, 525 birds, and 595 lizards. Around two-thirds of the rodents, 95 percent of the birds, and virtually all of the lizards were probably native species, according to a subsample analysis of prey species actually returned by cats.

A decline in small animals at the bottom of the predator food chain in suburban areas is partly explained by the local disappearance of large predators such as coyotes. Coyotes normally prey on smaller predators such as gray fox, opossum, raccoon, and the domestic cat, and all of these in turn prey on still smaller animals, including birds. Where coyotes have been reduced in abundance, the presence of small predators increases and populations of native birds decline as a consequence. In short, urban intrusion into natural habitats upsets the usual predator-prey balances.[76]

Another problem being created by suburban intrusion into wildland areas in California is a reduction of mountain lion habitat and increasing conflicts between mountain lions and local suburban residents. Mountain lions are among the few large mammals remaining in the wild capable of instilling real fear in human beings. Juvenile mountain lions avoid crossing areas where housing is fairly dense, but they will bed down during the day near trails heavily used by recreationists. Mountain lions traveling in and near suburban areas are at risk of being killed from motor vehicle collisions and encounters with human beings.[77] California law allows the killing of mountain lions causing damage to property, including farm animals and pets. Permits to kill mountain lions because of pet depredations increased between 1972 and 1975, and the growth of such incidents was concentrated in areas where significant new house construction occurred, primarily in the Los Angeles and San Diego areas. Between 1910 and 1985 there were no verified mountain lion attacks on humans, but between 1986 and 1995 nine attacks were reported, two of them fatal and eight occurring near areas of rapid growth in housing.[78] Increased encounters between human beings and mountain lions in rapidly developing localities in California appear to be the product of human intrusion into mountain lion habitat rather than expanding mountain lion populations. While mountain lion populations are far from being threatened with extinction currently, increased human encounters are bound to increase pressures to remove mountain lions from landscapes near urbanizing areas. Human migration into mountain lion habitat and human fear together could ultimately spell the doom of mountain lion populations in much of the western United States.

The outward spreading of human population beyond urban boundaries to rural areas is causing stresses and strains on native species in much the same way as outward expanding suburbanization does in metropolitan areas. In the valley bottoms of Montana near Yellowstone National Park, ranchlands are being subdivided into smaller, so-called ranchettes. Rural development of this kind is occurring near bird hotspots such as stands of cottonwood and aspen. Unfortunately, the densities of cowbirds and avian nest predators, such as ravens and magpies, associated with the presence of rural housing are reducing the rate of nest success for Yellow Warblers in the Yellowstone area. Warbler hotspots in the urbanizing valley bottoms are needed to provide dispersers to maintain the presence of warblers on higher elevation public lands, where the habitat is not as rich in resources and warbler reproduction is less successful.[79] Ranchettes are indirectly threatening warblers, a species much admired by bird lovers.

Montana rural development is also contributing to problems faced by the state's most well-known animal, the grizzly bear. The single greatest threat to the grizzly is mortality from encounters with homeowners, hunters, anglers, hikers, and others. Habitat space limitations, along with the availability of human-related food sources (such as garbage), are apparently causing some grizzlies to utilize private lands and suffer greater mortality levels as a result.[80] In these areas, mortalities occur both from malicious killing and from the managed removal of habituated or food-conditioned bears. In one case, a new subdivision development is apparently funneling grizzlies into a relatively high-density residential area with abundant food sources in Whitefish, Montana, increasing the potential for human–bear encounters. Residential development and high road densities in nearby Swan Valley may be preventing grizzlies from using an area with high spring habitat potential for females. Development in Swan Valley may also be closing off a migration corridor for bears between the Bob Marshall and Mission Mountain wilderness areas, limiting use of the Mission Mountains by grizzlies.[81]

Of all the Rocky Mountain states, Colorado is undergoing the most rapid pace of rural development and loss of ranchland to subdivisions and ranchettes.[82] The Colorado Natural Heritage Program determined that 14 amphibians and reptiles, 45 birds, 24 mammals, and 255 plant species are locally rare or imperiled as of 1998. Of these species, experts suggest in a survey that 12 amphibians and reptiles, 38 birds, 14 mammals, and 49 plants are stressed by development in rural mountain counties. A number of these development-stressed species are known to be within areas projected to be encompassed in rural ranchette or suburban development (forty acres or less per dwelling) by the year 2020 including 11 of the 12 amphibians and reptiles, 22 of the 38 bird species, 9 of the 14 mammal species, and 30 of the 49 plant species. Rural development in Colorado clearly has the potential for placing added stress on species that are already rare or imperiled.[83]

Mounting evidence indicates that the transformation of rangeland into low-density residences alters the attractiveness of the local landscape for native species. Recent research finds that the species composition of bird and mammal populations is quite different near rural residences than it is in undeveloped habitat. In a study by Eric Odell and Richard Knight, red foxes and coyotes in a rural Colorado county were detected more frequently farther away from residential dwellings, while dogs and house cats were detected closer to residences. As in other studies, Odell and Knight found that bird species composition differs with distance from residential development. Close to residences, "human-adapted" species, such as the ubiquitous American Robin and Brown-headed Cowbird, increased in abundance, while "human-sensitive" species, such as the Dusky Flycatcher and Orange-crowned Warbler, decreased in abundance. Conversely, farther away from residential dwellings, human-adapted species declined in abundance while human-sensitive species increased. Simply put, development reduces the presence of human-sensitive species in the landscape while magnifying the presence of species widely available elsewhere. Nest parasitism by the Brown-headed Cowbird is an obvious suspect in causing reductions in local populations of songbirds.[84]

The spreading of population and housing development over the landscape in rural areas is clearly taking a toll on native species. In addition to the impacts just described, researchers have also noted other effects of rural sprawl and low-density housing development. In Montana's Gallatin Valley near Yellowstone, rural housing development has reduced the use of land by deer and has shifted species composition toward white-tailed deer and away from mule deer.[85] In both Montana and Colorado, valley bottom development appears to be impinging on both wintering and calving grounds for elk.[86] The shores of the comparatively pristine Yellowstone River in Park County, Montana, have become a popular place to put up a new housing. Periodic flooding, however, reshapes the river and threatens new residences with erosion and inundation. Landowners have reacted by armoring stream banks with a layer of large boulders. A consequence of such stream-bank modification is a loss of trout habitat and a decline in trout populations.[87] In rural New Mexico, gray foxes avoid high-density subdivisions even though food and den sites are available. A possible explanation is the presence of unrestrained dogs in these areas.[88] While serious research on the topic is in its infancy, results so far suggest that both suburban and rural residential development are reshaping the landscape to the detriment of native plants and animals. The critical lesson of this research is that some plants and animals need substantial blocks of habitat free of human impacts.

The most immediate result of rural suburbanization and sprawl is visual. Much-loved rural open spaces, punctuated by farmsteads or ranch buildings and framed by a backdrop of snowy mountain peaks or forested hills, are lost to a patchwork of housing developments and ranchettes. The rural farming and ranching culture so much a part of American folklore is a victim of such changes as well. Not so readily noticed is something that may be no less important—a reduction in the diversity of the local flora and fauna. Valley-bottom ranches are by no means great stewards of the land in the mountain West, but their presence may be better than a valley full of fancy houses.

THE INVASION OF EXOTIC SPECIES

The power of innovation in the Schumpeterian mold has not only increased the human ability to spread out over the landscape in the continental United States, but has created a global economy as well, tying all the nations of the world together in one huge transportation and communications network. Communication today between any two points on the globe is virtually immediate, and goods can be transported almost anywhere overnight. An unfortunate byproduct of tying nations together in a global trading network is the tying together of different ecosystems and their plants and animals in a single ecological network. Before addressing the consequences of a globalization of flora and fauna, let's first consider the roots of economic globalization.

Globalization

In a modern global economy, trade is essential to have access to the full array of consumer goods globally available and to generate continuous income growth. Historically, as industries age and see their production technologies stabilizing, they become candidates for relocation offshore to poorer countries where wages are cheaper. Clothing, textiles, and motor vehicle parts are examples of industries participating in the movement offshore. Even for some labor-intensive new technologies, offshore production is favored. This is the case for the production of some kinds of computer chips requiring unskilled labor and for some kinds software code writing that can be done more cheaply using educated skilled labor in countries like India. As a consequence of this process, the United States loses industries to offshore locations. This gets reflected at the macro level in an increase in the propensity to import. Trade is essential to get the goods we want in a world where industrial location options are global in scope. The only way we can get goods and services produced elsewhere is by importing them.

The export side of the trade equation is crucial to generate the income and foreign currency needed to purchase an ever-expanding array of imports. Exports for a country like the United States are driven by the creation of new industries and new kinds of economic activity based on sophisticated products and services, such as personal computers, software, the World Wide Web, the Internet, cellular phones, satellite communication, and biotechnology. Given comparatively high levels of educational achievement in the United States, workers have the background to create relatively sophisticated technologies and products, whereas such skills are usually lacking in less developed countries. This gives countries like the United States a foreign trade advantage in relatively new, technologically complex products. High-technology industries, such as computer software, tend to have large fixed costs and low marginal costs of production. To create a new software program is costly, but to produce and sell another copy costs next to nothing. In a larger market, fixed costs can be spread over more units of sales and profits can be significantly increased as well. Fixed costs per unit sold decline continuously as production and sales are increased. The larger the market the better. Microsoft, for instance, strives to obtain a world market since the marginal cost of producing another copy of Windows is trivial and for this reason the sale price of another copy mostly goes to profit. High-growth, high-technology industries with big fixed costs are strongly driven to obtain a global market.

The ultimate impact of trade on income and GDP depends on a race between rising imports and exports, with exports adding to GDP and imports taking away from it. For long-term economic survival, the pace of new technology creation in this country must keep up with the movement of older and labor-intensive industries offshore. Otherwise, imports rise faster than exports, dampening the growth in U.S. income and GDP. Exports add to GDP since Americans produce them, while imports subtract from GDP since, although they are a part of final sales in this country, they are produced elsewhere. Unfortunately for the United States, imports have been winning the race over exports. Both have risen, indicating the growing importance of trade, but between 1959 and 2000 imports increased from 4.4 percent of GDP to 14.9 percent, while exports increased only from 4.1 percent to 11.2 percent.[89] Since we in the United States don't generate enough in foreign sales to pay for our imports, we have to borrow from our trading partners to fill the gap. This continuing need for borrowing is a significant financial dilemma for us created by the global trading system.

The enabling condition for the expansion of foreign trade has been the growth in the extent and rapidity of the global transportation network. The efficiency of the global transportation system has been further enhanced by the development of modern communications and computer technology. Not only do goods need to be physically moved, but they need to be kept track of as well, something that is most effectively accomplished by the modern mix of computers, rapid global communication, and widely available global positioning systems technology. The advance of technology is a critical element in the tying together of distant locations for the purpose of economic interactions. Sophisticated transportation systems enable the movement of goods between continents and also the quick distribution of goods to their final destinations within continental landscapes. Unfortunately, the same is the case for invading exotic species, which are able to hitch a ride on the various means of transportation used in the shipment of goods around the globe.[90]

Globalization and the Spread of Exotics

Given the separation of continents by oceans, the evolution of species on different continents has proceeded in isolation. Because of this separation, different continents tend to have their own unique collections of species. By providing pathways for movement between continents, the global trading economy has removed barriers between flora and fauna that are the product of differing evolutionary pathways. Geographic barriers are generators of biological diversity.[91] The creation of barriers in a geologic time frame, when the globally extensive supercontinent Pangaea broke up into distinct land masses separated by oceans, resulted in plant and animal species evolving independently on the emergent continents. When separated by barriers preventing gene flows between them, isolated plant and animal populations evolve differently, even if the habitat conditions they face are similar.[92] Without barriers separating populations of different species, fewer species would exist. Where the earth with its separate continents supports around 4,200 mammal species, scientists estimate that a single supercontinent would support only about two thousand.[93]

In the past, species needed to contend only with their continental brethren as predators and competitors for resources; now they also face invading species that may come with special advantages. In their native habitats, exotic species are kept in check by coevolved competitors, predators, and pathogens. Freed of these in new habitats, exotic species populations can expand rapidly. Also, not having evolved in the presence of exotics, native species may lack the defense mechanisms needed to successfully fend off the challenge of exotic invaders as either competitors or predators. The end result is a serious threat to many native species from exotic invaders and a potential reduction in biodiversity caused by exotics-induced native species extinctions.

While some exotic species are intentionally introduced to the United States (Scotch broom as an ornamental plant, for example), most introductions are a byproduct of global commerce. Plants, animals, and pathogens often arrive on imported agricultural products, nursery stock, cut flowers, and timber.[94] The Dutch elm disease, which caused the demise of the tall stately elms that once shaded residential streets in much of urban America, arrived on a load of unpeeled raw logs from Europe.[95] Containerized freight offers a relatively new pathway for plants and animals to make their way to North America. The Asian tiger mosquito, a carrier of several serious viral diseases, entered the United States in containers filled with used tires. Containers have also been the source of a number of exotic snails and slugs. Some invasive species have entered the United States in packing materials, including a threatening bark beetle. Ballast water taken on in foreign ports and pumped out in United States ports has been a major source of exotics, including the infamous zebra mussel now infesting much of the Great Lakes region.[96] Some 4,500 species have been introduced into the United States, with most arriving within the last one hundred years. Between 1980 and 1992, 205 harmful nonindigenous species arrived or were first detected in the United States, according to the Office of Technology Assessment, and most of them were unintentional imports. Although regulatory efforts have reduced the inflow of some exotics, such as weed seeds entering as seed contaminants, the importation of other exotics may be growing as a consequence of expanded global trade and improved transportation efficiency. Whether the total influx of exotics is accelerating in response to growing international trade remains to be seen, but it is clear that the cumulative total of introduced species continues to rise.[97]

Daily Living and the Problem of Exotic Species

To most of us, the problem of invasive exotic species may seem somewhat distant from what we do on a daily basis. How do the normal daily activities of the typical American affect the problem of invading exotic species? The direct support of invading exotics in daily life, such as planting an invasive species in the gardens of suburban or rural homes or putting up a bird feeder that mainly benefits house sparrows and starlings, is a fairly common occurrence but not something that everyone does. Everyone, however, participates to some degree in the global economy. A trip to the mall to buy a new shirt or coat or a DVD player more likely than not involves goods that have spent time in a container or on a cargo plane. The international shipment of goods is a primary source for the transit of exotic species around the world. Participation by the typical American in the global economy increases the likelihood that species adapted to one habitat will find their way to other habitats where they may have some special advantage over native species. The end result will be a decline in the richness of the global biota. Unlike the problem of global warming, with its consequences mostly postponed, the costs of exotics are more immediate. One estimate of such costs totals approximately $137 billion per year for the United States.[98] Exotics are an especially costly problem in agriculture and impact everyone at the grocery store checkout counter.

A Case Study of Spreading Exotics: The Great Lakes

If you want to know more about how exotics get around and reap havoc, take a look at this final section. If you don't, then you're done. Move on to the next chapter on possible remedies for the three key environmental problems of the day.

One of the most dramatic transformations of an ecosystem caused by exotics has occurred right under our eyes in the center of the United States. The Great Lakes have been forever changed by the invasion of an amazing array of exotic species. In the last 180 years, 139 species of exotic algae, aquatic vascular plants, molluscs, and fishes have successfully invaded the Great Lakes.[99] The construction of the Welland Canal, bypassing Niagara Falls between Lakes Ontario and Erie, set off the invasion process. Among the first of the exotics to find its way through the canal was the sea lamprey, a parasitic fish that attaches itself to the body of lake trout and whitefish in order to suck out their body fluids. The end result of the sea lamprey invasion was a significant decline in lake trout populations and the decline and extinction of two endemic whitefish species. Luckily, sea lamprey populations are now effectively controlled through the application of a pesticide in breeding areas, but control came too late to prevent substantial damage to native fish populations.

At about the same time, alewives, small herring-size fish, entered the Great Lakes through the Welland Canal. Alewives preyed on large zooplankton and competed successfully with native species such as whitefish. Alewife populations increased dramatically and, because they are subject to large die-offs in the spring, became a nuisance of major proportions. Beaches became clogged with dead, smelly alewives in such volumes that they had to be removed with front-end-loading tractors. To control the problem, several species of Pacific salmon were introduced to prey on alewives. The final result was a significant modification in the original ecological structure of the Great Lakes.[100] Introduced salmon now play the role of top predator in the Great Lakes food chain instead of the native lake trout. In the absence of natural reproduction, the whole system is maintained through the artificial infusion of juvenile salmon smolt every year.

A direct pathway to the migration of exotics, the Welland Canal opened up the Great Lakes to international trade and exposed the lakes to the ballast water of ships from Europe and elsewhere. Arriving by way of ballast water, the zebra mussel has dramatically altered the ecology of the Great Lakes. The mussel apparently became established in the Great Lakes in the mid-1980s and spread to the entire basin by 1990. The mussel is about thumbnail size, attaches to any solid surface, including water intake pipes, lacks a significant predator, and is prolific. It is able to filter huge volumes of water, decreasing food available for other organisms and increasing water clarity. In some areas, increased water clarity and light penetration have caused abundant growth of weedy algae that are torn from their holdfasts by storms and waves, creating piles of rotting, smelly plant matter on local beaches. The cost of clearing blocked intake pipes of zebra mussels will reach over $3 billion in a ten-year period.[101]

The ecology of the Great Lakes has been irreversibly altered as a consequence of exposure to the global trading economy and serves as just one example of how economic expansion through global trade comes at a significant cost to the natural environment. Exotics are found everywhere and are a problem in every region of the country.[102] This is easily verified by talking to any local naturalist who will no doubt have horror stories to tell about exotics.

CONCLUSION

The two leading causes of species endangerment in the United States, according to a recent study, are urbanization and the invasion of nonnative (exotic) species.[103] While urbanization, in the form of suburban and rural sprawl, and the introduction of exotic species are currently the predominant threats to our native flora and fauna, global climate change is projected to be a critical new threat in the future and will interact with the first two problems, making them worse.[104] The ultimate source of these three problems can be traced to the ordinary economic life of the average American.

Most of us arise on a winter morning to a house of roughly eighteen hundred square feet already warmed by a furnace under the control of an automatic thermostat that accounts for our need for heat at various times of the day. At breakfast, we look out on a large back yard in a suburb where houses occupy about a third of an acre of land. The automatic coffeepot has already done its work, we perhaps use the microwave oven to prepare our frozen waffles, and we turn on the radio or TV to catch the morning news and traffic reports. All these products were probably imported and spent time in a shipping container, perhaps along with a hitchhiking animal seeking a new home. By the time we have completed breakfast, we have enjoyed the benefits of fossil-fuel energy for space heating and running our various appliances. We hop in the car for our daily commute of around twelve miles to work on a local freeway (making use of more fossil-fuel energy) to an office park, a suburban mall, or a single-story suburban factory. The activity of work requires still more fossil-fuel energy for lighting, space heating, running computers and other office equipment, and for operating production lines. Work requires still more land space for the office, the retail outlet, or the production line. Space is the essential ingredient for suburban or rural housing development, highways and freeways, and office parks, factories, and shopping malls with their surrounding expanses of parking lots. The point of this tale is the reliance of our daily routine on fossil-fuel energy, acres and acres of land, and global trade in goods and services. Such reliance in turn results in global warming, a reduction in land available for the nonhuman species of the world, and the invasion of exotic nonnative species into our local environment.

Just because the pattern of daily life explains the presence of significant environmental problems does not mean that it is easily changed through individual action. Most people have little real choice in how they live. They have to accept the economic hand they are dealt in order to survive. If public transportation is unavailable, there is little choice but to commute to work by automobile. If high-density central cities are not pedestrian friendly and are threatening to personal safety, then the low-density suburbs are the only real alternative. These things cannot be changed by any one individual, but they are subject to public decisions by society as a whole. The daily pattern of life is as much a matter of public choice as it is a private one. Whether that pattern of life should be altered and whether it can be is the subject of the remaining chapters in this book.

NOTES

1. Intergovernmental Panel on Climate Change, *Climate Change 2001: The Scientific Basis* (Cambridge: Cambridge University Press, 2001), 2.

2. Intergovernmental Panel on Climate Change, *Climate Change 2001: The Scientific Basis*, 34.

3. Douglas E. Booth, *The Environmental Consequences of Growth: Steady-State Economics as an Alternative to Ecological Decline* (London: Routledge, 1998), 30–31.

4. Intergovernmental Panel on Climate Change, *Climate Change 2001: The Scientific Basis*, 36–43, 248–54, 357.

5. Intergovernmental Panel on Climate Change, *Climate Change 2001: The Scientific Basis*, 37–43. Other chemicals in the atmosphere can affect radiative forcing, but their net impact appears to be small, although their role in global warming is not fully understood.

6. Intergovernmental Panel on Climate Change, *Climate Change 2001: The Scientific Basis*, 46–50.

7. Intergovernmental Panel on Climate Change, *Climate Change 2001: The Scientific Basis*, 61.

8. Intergovernmental Panel on Climate Change, *Climate Change 2001: The Scientific Basis*, 67–75.

9. U.S. EPA, *Inventory of U.S. Greenhouse Gas Emissions and Sinks: 1990–2000* (Washington, D.C.: U.S. Environmental Protection Agency, 2002), ES-3, ES-10-ES-11. The number of households for the year 2000 used in per household calculations in this section was taken from U.S. Bureau of the Census, "American FactFinder," Washington, D.C.: U.S. Bureau of the Census, 2000, http//:factfinder.census.gov/, DP-1. Halocarbons covered under the Montreal Accord to eliminate ozone-depleting substances are not included in data used in this chapter for greenhouse gas emissions calculations.

10. Of the 17.8 metric tons emitted by the transportation sector per household, 17.0 are CO_2 and the remainder is other greenhouse gases (methane, nitrous oxides, and halocarbons).

11. The remainder is due to other greenhouse gases.

12. This leaves about nine pounds per day of non-CO_2 greenhouse gas emissions by households.

13. G. Marland, T. A. Boden, and R. J. Andres, *Trends Online: A Compendium of Data on Global Change* (Oak Ridge, Tenn.: Oak Ridge National Laboratory, Carbon Dioxide Information Analysis Center, 2003, http://cdiac.esd.ornl.gov/trends/trends.htm).

14. Intergovernmental Panel on Climate Change, *Climate Change 1995—Impacts, Adaptations and Mitigation of Climate Change: Scientific-Technical Analyses* (Cambridge: Cambridge University Press, 1996), 429–55.

15. Intergovernmental Panel on Climate Change, *Climate Change 1995—Impacts, Adaptations and Mitigation of Climate Change*, 33–35, 99–122.

16. James G. Titus, "The Causes and Effects of Sea Level Rise, " in *The Challenge of Global Warming*, ed. Dean Edwin Abrahamson (Washington, D.C.: Island Press, 1989), 161–95.

17. Intergovernmental Panel on Climate Change, *Climate Change 1995—Impacts, Adaptations and Mitigation of Climate Change*, 35–37.

18. Intergovernmental Panel on Climate Change, *Climate Change 1995—Impacts, Adaptations and Mitigation of Climate Change*, 11–12.

19. The average warming rate was about 2 degrees centigrade per thousand years. See Intergovernmental Panel on Climate Change, *Climate Change 2001: The Scientific Basis*, 140.

20. Robert Costanza et al., "The Value of the World's Ecosystem Services and Natural Capital," *Nature* 387: 253–60.

21. This issue will be addressed more fully in chapter 7.

22. The ethical case for protecting species is given a full treatment in chapter 7.

23. Intergovernmental Panel on Climate Change, *Climate Change 1995—Impacts, Adaptations and Mitigation of Climate Change*, 6.

24. Robert L. Peters, "Effects of Global Warming on Biodiversity," in *The Challenge of Global Warming*, ed. Dean Edwin Abrahamson (Washington, D.C.: Island Press, 1989), 82–95; Robert L. Peters, "Conservation of Biological Diversity in the Face of Climate Change," in *Global Warming and Biological Diversity*, ed. Robert L. Peters and T. E. Lovejoy (New Haven, Conn.: Yale University Press, 1992), 15–30; Margaret B. Davis and Catherine Zabinski, "Changes in Geographical Range Resulting from Greenhouse Warming: Effects on Biodiversity in Forests," in *Global Warming and Biological Diversity*, ed. Robert L. Peters and T. E. Lovejoy

(New Haven, Conn.: Yale University Press, 1992), 297–308; Daniel B. Botkin and Robert A. Nisbet, "Projecting the Effects of Climate Change on Biological Diversity in Forests," in *Global Warming and Biological Diversity*, ed. Robert L. Peters and T. E. Lovejoy (New Haven, Conn.: Yale University Press, 1992), 277–93.

25. Peters, "Effects of Global Warming on Biodiversity."

26. Intergovernmental Panel on Climate Change, *Climate Change 2001—Impacts, Adaptations and Vulnerability* (Cambridge: Cambridge University Press, 2001), 803–5.

27. Intergovernmental Panel on Climate Change, "Climate Change and Biodiversity," *IPCC Technical Paper* V, 2002: 13; Intergovernmental Panel on Climate Change, *Climate Change 2001—Impacts, Adaptations and Vulnerability*, 290, 313.

28. W. H. Romme and M. G. Turner, "Implications of Global Climate Change for Biogeographic Patterns in the Greater Yellowstone Ecosystem," *Conservation Biology* 5 (1991): 373–86.

29. Peters, "Conservation of Biological Diversity in the Face of Climate Change"; Jerry F. Franklin et al., "Effects of Global Climatic Change on Forests in Northwestern North America," in *Global Warming and Biological Diversity*, ed. Robert L. Peters and T. E. Lovejoy (New Haven, Conn.: Yale University Press, 1992), 244–57.

30. Botkin and Nisbet, "Projecting the Effects of Climate Change on Biological Diversity in Forests."

31. Romme and Turner, "Implications of Global Climate Change for Biogeographic Patterns in the Greater Yellowstone Ecosystem."

32. Intergovernmental Panel on Climate Change, *Climate Change 2001—Impacts, Adaptations and Vulnerability*, 804.

33. J. P. Myers and Robert T. Lester, "Double Jeopardy for Migrating Animals: Multiple Hist and Resource Asynchrony," in *Global Warming and Biological Diversity*, ed. Robert L. Peters and T. E. Lovejoy (New Haven, Conn.: Yale University Press, 1992), 193–200.

34. James G. Titus, "The Causes and Effects of Sea Level Rise," in *Policy Implications of Greenhouse Warming: Mitigation, Adaption, and the Science Base*, National Academy of Sciences, National Academy of Engineering, Institute of Medicine (Washington, D.C.: National Academy Press, 1992), 584–91; Intergovernmental Panel on Climate Change, "Climate Change and Biodiversity," 20–21.

35. Larry D. Harris and Wendell P. Cropper Jr., "Between the Devil and the Deep Blue Sea: Implications of Climate Change for Florida's Fauna," in *Global Warming and Biological Diversity*, ed. Robert L. Peters and T. E. Lovejoy (New Haven, Conn.: Yale University Press, 1992), 309–24.

36. Intergovernmental Panel on Climate Change, "Climate Change and Biodiversity," 21.

37. Intergovernmental Panel on Climate Change, "Climate Change and Biodiversity," 14, 20.

38. Intergovernmental Panel on Climate Change, "Climate Change and Biodiversity," 17–18.

39. Intergovernmental Panel on Climate Change, *Climate Change 2001—Impacts, Adaptations and Vulnerability*, 298–304.

40. Intergovernmental Panel on Climate Change, *Climate Change 2001—Impacts, Adaptations and Vulnerability*, 306–12.

41. U.S. EPA, "EPA Global Warming Site: Impacts—Birds," http://yosemite .epa.gov/OAR/globalwarming.nsf/content/ImpactsBirds.html (accessed October 14, 2002).

42. For an in-depth treatment of the consequences of global warming and the possibilities for adaptation to it, see Intergovernmental Panel on Climate Change, *Climate Change 2001—Impacts, Adaptations and Vulnerability.*

43. Costanza et al., "The Value of the World's Ecosystem Services and Natural Capital."

44. This line of reasoning will be given more attention in chapter 7.

45. Edwin S. Mills and Bruce W. Hamilton, *Urban Economics*, 5th ed. (New York: HarperCollins College Publishers, 1994), 57; U.S. Bureau of the Census, "American FactFinder," Urban and Rural, Census 2000 Summary File 3 (SF 3), P5. http://factfinder.census.gov (accessed October 18, 2002).

46. Sam B. Warner Jr., *Street Car Suburbs: The Process of Growth in Boston, 1870–1900* (New York: Atheneum, 1974).

47. Anthony Downs, *New Visions for Metropolitan America* (Washington, D.C.: The Brookings Institution, 1994), 6.

48. Warner, *Street Car Suburbs*, 2, 52.

49. Warner, *Street Car Suburbs*, 34, 52–56.

50. Warner, *Street Car Suburbs*, 163–66; Kenneth T. Jackson, *Crabgrass Frontier: The Suburbanization of the United States* (New York: Oxford University Press, 1985), 147–55.

51. Jackson, *Crabgrass Frontier*, 69–70; Warner, *Street Car Suburbs*, 162.

52. Jackson, *Crabgrass Frontier*, 129.

53. Jackson, *Crabgrass Frontier*, 183.

54. Jackson, *Crabgrass Frontier*, 10. In 1995 the length of the average trip to work was up to almost twelve miles. U.S. Bureau of the Census, *Statistical Abstract of the United States: 2000* (Washington, D.C.: U.S. Government Printing Office, 2000), 631.

55. Jackson, *Crabgrass Frontier*, 163–70, 248.

56. Jackson, *Crabgrass Frontier*, 204–33.

57. Mills and Hamilton, *Urban Economics*, 82.

58. Joel Garreau, *Edge City: Life on the New Frontier* (New York: Doubleday, 1991).

59. Kenneth M. Johnson, "The Rural Rebound of the 1990s and Beyond," in *Conservation in the Internet Age: Threats and Opportunities*, ed. James N. Levitt (Washington, D.C.: Island Press, 2002), 63–82.

60. Christiane von Reichert and Gundar Rudzitis, "Multinomial Logistic Models Explaining Income Changes of Migrants to High-Amenity Counties," *The Review of Regional Studies* 22 (1992): 25–42; Ray Rasker and Andrew Hansen, "Natural Amenities and Population Growth in the Greater Yellowstone Region," *Human Ecology Review* 7 (2000): 30–40.

61. Glenn V. Fuguitt and Calvin L. Beale, "Recent Trends in Nonmetropolitan Migration: Toward a New Turnaround?" *Growth and Change* 27 (1996): 156–74. For an analysis of population spreading to rural counties of the mountain West, see my own article on the subject, "Spatial Patterns in the Economic Development of the Mountain West," *Growth and Change* 30 (1999): 384–405. Some who are moving

to the rural mountain West appear to be bringing their means of employment with them or are able to get work with employers who are themselves attracted by the amenities of the mountain West or to the growing supply of labor available as a consequence of local population expansion.

62. James N. Levitt, "Networks and Nature in the American Experience," 11–49, and William J. Mitchell, "The Internet, New Urban Patterns, and Conservation," 50–62, in *Conservation in the Internet Age: Threats and Opportunities*, ed. James N. Levitt (Washington, D.C.: Island Press, 2002).

63. James N. Levitt and John R. Pitkin, "Internet Use in a High-Growth Amenity-Rich Region," in *Conservation in the Internet Age: Threats and Opportunities*, James N. Levitt (Washington, D.C.: Island Press, 2002), 99–122.

64. Douglas E. Booth, *Searching for Paradise: Economic Development and Environmental Change in the Mountain West* (Lanham, Md.: Rowman & Littlefield, 2002), 10–11.

65. Joel S. Hirschhorn, "Natural Amenities and Locational Choice in the New Economy," in *Conservation in the Internet Age: Threats and Opportunities*, ed. James N. Levitt (Washington, D.C.: Island Press, 2002), 269–85.

66. Peter Newman and Jeffrey Kenworthy, *Sustainability and Cities: Overcoming Automobile Dependence* (Washington, D.C.: Island Press, 1999), 94–95.

67. Of the new land brought into development in this period, more than half was previously forest land or rangeland, both of which likely supported native plant and animal species. USDA Natural Resource Conservation Service, "Summary Report, 1997 National Resources Inventory," http://www.nhq.nrcs.usda .gov/NRI/1997/summary_report/original/table5.html, revised, December 2000; population data came from U.S. Department of Commerce, Economics and Statistics Administration, Bureau of Economic Analysis, *Regional Economic Information System 1969–1997* (Washington, D.C.: U.S. Department of Commerce, CD-ROM, 1999).

68. U.S. Bureau of the Census, *Statistical Abstract of the United States: 2000* (Washington, D.C.: United States Government Printing Office, 2001), 714.

69. U.S. Bureau of the Census, *Statistical Abstract of the United States: 2000*, 622, 628.

70. Newman and Kenworthy, *Sustainability and Cities*, 80, 94–111.

71. See my *Searching for Paradise*, chapters 1–3.

72. Robert B. Blair, "Land Use and Avian Species Diversity Along an Urban Gradient," *Ecological Applications* 6 (1996): 506–19.

73. Robert B. Blair, "Land Use and Avian Species Diversity Along an Urban Gradient"; see also Jon C. Boren et al "Land Use Change Effects on Breeding Bird Community Composition," *Journal of Range Management* 52 (1999): 420–30.

74. M. C. Brittingham and S. A. Temple, "Have Cowbirds Caused Forest Songbirds to Decline?" *Bioscience* 33 (1983): 31–35.

75. Douglas T. Bolger, Thomas A. Scott, and John T. Rotenberry, "Breeding Bird Abundance in an Urbanizing Landscape in Coastal Southern California," *Conservation Biology* 11 (1997): 406–21.

76. Kevin R. Crooks and Michael E. Soulè, "Mesopredator Release and Avifaunal Extinctions in a Fragmented System," *Nature* 400 (1999): 563–66.

77. Paul Beier, "Dispersal of Juvenile Cougars in Fragmented Habitat," *Journal of Wildlife Management* 59 (1995): 228–37.

78. Steven G. Torres et al., "Mountain Lion and Human Activity in California: Testing Speculations," *Wildlife Society Bulletin* 24 (1996): 451–60.

79. Andrew J. Hansen et al., "Ecological Causes and Consequences of Demographic Change in the New West," *BioScience* 52 (2002): 151–62; Andrew J. Hansen and Jay J. Rotella, "Biophysical Factors, Land Use, and Species Viability in and around Nature Reserves," *Conservation Biology* 16 (2002): 1112–22.

80. Hansen et al., "Ecological Causes and Consequences of Demographic Change in the New West," 159–60; Vanessa Johnson, *Rural Residential Development Trends in the Greater Yellowstone Ecosystem since the Listing of the Grizzly Bear* (Bozeman, Mont.: Sierra Club Grizzly Bear Ecosystem Project, 2000); Richard D. Mace and John S. Waller, "Demography and Population Trend of Grizzly Bears in the Swan Mountains, Montana," *Conservation Biology* 12 (1998): 1005–16.

81. Michael Jamison, "Whitefish-Area Growth May be Funneling Grizzlies into Town," *Missoulian*, November 23, 1999, A1, A7.

82. Martha J. Sullins et al., "Lay of the Land: Ranch Land and Ranching," in *Ranching West of the 100th Meridian*, ed. Richard L. Knight, Wendell C. Gilgert, and Ed Marston (Washington, D.C.: Island Press, 2002), 25–32.

83. Booth, *Searching for Paradise*, 112–20.

84. Eric A. Odell and Richard L. Knight, "Songbird and Medium-Sized Mammal Community Associated with Exurban Development in Pitkin County, Colorado," *Conservation Biology* 15 (2001): 1143–50.

85. William O. Vogel, "Response of Deer to Density and Distribution of Housing in Montana," *Wildlife Society Bulletin* 17 (1989): 406–13.

86. Jodie E. Canfield et al., "Ungulates," in *The Effects of Recreation on Rocky Mountain Wildlife Rocky Mountain Wildlife: A Review for Montana*, coord. Gayle Joslin and Heidi Youmans (Committee on Effects of Recreation on Wildlife, Montana Chapter of the Wildlife Society, 1999), 6.1–6.25. In both Colorado and Montana a number conservation land trusts view the preservation of elk wintering and calving grounds as an important goal. See Booth, *Searching for Paradise*, 173–96.

87. Hal Herring, "Strangling the Last Best River," *High Country News* 31–37 (April 12, 1999): 6; and American Rivers, "Yellowstone River Named One of Nation's Most Endangered Rivers," http://www.amrivers.org/pressrelease/pressmeryellowstone1999.htm, 1999 (accessed January 12, 2002).

88. Robert L. Harrison, "A Comparison of Gray Fox Ecology between Residential and Undeveloped Rural Landscapes," *Journal of Wildlife Management* 61 (1997): 112–22.

89. U.S. Executive Office of the President, Council of Economic Advisors, *Economic Report of the President: Transmitted to the Congress, February 2002* (Washington, D.C.: U.S. Government Printing Office, 2002), Table B1. A strong value of the dollar in foreign currency markets contributed in recent years to the growing gap between imports and exports. A strong dollar makes U.S. goods more costly overseas and U.S. imports cheaper.

90. Jason Van Driesche and Roy Van Driesche, *Nature Out Place: Biological Invasions in the Global Age* (Washington, D.C.: Island Press, 2000), 57–66.

91. Chris Bright, *Life Out of Bounds: Bioinvasions in a Borderless World* (New York: W. W. Norton, 1998), 16–31.

92. Van Driesche and Van Driesche, *Nature Out Place*, 38–41.

93. Peter M. Vitousek et al., "Biological Invasions as Global Environmental Change," *American Scientist* 84 (1996): 468–78.

94. U.S. Congress, Office of Technology Assessment, *Harmful Non-Indigenous Species in the United States*, OTA-F-565 (Washington, D.C.: U.S. Government Printing Office, 1993), 79–85.

95. Van Driesche and Van Driesche, *Nature Out Place*, 59.

96. Cynthia S. Kolar and David M. Lodge, "Freshwater Nonindigenous Species: Interactions with Other Global Changes," in *Invasive Species in a Changing World*, ed. Harold A. Mooney and Richard J. Hobbs (Washington, D.C.: Island Press, 2000), 79–82.

97. U.S. Congress, Office of Technology Assessment, *Harmful Non-Indigenous Species in the United States*, 91–106.

98. David Pimentel et al., "Environmental and Economic Costs of Nonindigenous Species in the United States," *Bioscience* 50 (2000): 53–65.

99. Kolar and Lodge, "Freshwater Nonindigenous Species," 3–30.

100. Kolar and Lodge, "Freshwater Nonindigenous Species," 8–9.

101. Ship ballast water has brought other species with it as well including fish such as gobies and ruffe and the spiny water flea. See Kolar and Lodge, "Freshwater Nonindigenous Species," 8–9; U.S. Congress, Office of Technology Assessment, *Harmful Non-Indigenous Species in the United States*, 73; Van Driesche and Van Driesche, *Nature Out Place*, 74–76.

102. The best single source on the topic is U.S. Congress, Office of Technology Assessment, *Harmful Non-Indigenous Species in the United States*.

103. Brian Czech, Paul R. Krausman, and Patrick K. Devers, "Economic Associations among Causes of Species Endangerment in the United States," *Bioscience* 50 (2000): 593–601.

104. Jeffrey S. Dukes and Harold A. Mooney, "Does Global Change Increase the Success of Biological Invaders?" *Trends in Ecology and Evolution* 14 (1999): 135–39; Richard J. Hobbs, "Land-Use Changes and Invasions," in *Invasive Species in a Changing World*, ed. Harold A. Mooney and Richard J. Hobbs (Washington, D.C.: Island Press, 2000), 55–64.

6

Conventional and Ecological Economics: Adjusting the Environment to the Economy versus Adjusting the Economy to the Environment

Two strategies are available for dealing with the problem of environmental decline. One uses the approach of conventional economics and calls for adjusting the environment to the economy. The other uses the approach of ecological economics and calls for adjusting the economy to the environment. The first gives the economy priority; the second gives the environment priority. The conventional approach doesn't really call for much in the way of environmental improvement, as we will see. If we are serious about bringing environmental decline to a halt, then it is the approach of ecological economics we want. To make a reasonable judgment about whether this is the right way to go, we do need to know what giving the environment priority will do to the economy and our patterns of everyday life. This will be done in the context of the three critical environmental problems discussed in the last chapter—greenhouse warming, population spreading, and the invasion of exotics.

A serious effort to reverse environmental decline, global warming especially, will result in a new macroeconomic world where the question of "environmental productivity" will rival the notion of "labor productivity" as the essential element determining the maximum feasible pace of economic growth. If the end result of bringing environmental decline to a halt is a reduction in the maximum feasible pace of growth, then the

whole question of being "hooked on growth" will emerge as a critical issue. Solving the environmental problem will require getting unhooked
from growth. How to do this is a serious challenge, one that will be taken
up in the final pages of this chapter.

CONVENTIONAL ENVIRONMENTAL ECONOMICS

Adjusting the environment to the economy is the central message of standard environmental economics. Greenhouse warming will be used as a
example to illustrate the inner workings of the standard view. Economists
of a conventional persuasion argue that greenhouse gas emissions should
be controlled up to the point where the net benefits (benefits minus costs)
are maximized but no further. Beyond this point additions to cost from
emissions reductions exceed additions to benefits.[1] To do more makes no
economic sense.

The benefit-cost approach requires considerable data on both the benefit and the cost side of the equation and a huge amount of number crunch-
ing to come up with an answer on exactly how much emissions should be
controlled.[2] As emissions are reduced, the cost of removing more is likely
to go up, but this may not happen right away. Surprisingly, emissions reduction may initially generate net cost savings. For example, the replacement of a regular 90-watt light bulb with a compact fluorescent results in
both energy savings and a net cost savings. The compact fluorescent lasts
ten times as long as a regular bulb and uses one-fourth the energy. The resulting cost savings much more than offset the higher initial cost of the
compact fluorescent. The reduction in CO_2 emissions from switching to
compact fluorescent bulbs will be proportionate to the resulting reduction
in fossil-fuel energy requirements for electricity production. Various studies suggest that up to 30 percent of carbon emissions can be removed at a
zero cost because of the net cost savings associated with improvements in
energy efficiency of the kind offered by compact fluorescent bulbs.[3] Carbon emissions reductions of this variety are referred to as the "no regrets"
alternative for limiting global warming. If emissions are reduced by up to
30 percent, we won't regret it whether or not global warming really is a
problem, because of the net cost savings from energy efficiencies. Beyond
this point, the net added costs of emissions reductions turn positive and
need to be balanced against any resulting additions to benefits.

While calculating the costs of reducing emissions is an inexact science,
estimating the social benefits of reducing emissions is even more troublesome. The benefits of emissions reduction are equivalent to the social
costs of avoided global warming. Emissions reductions are a bit like having to jump into the frying pan or the fire. Reducing emissions is costly,

but if emissions are not reduced, the social costs of global warming will be incurred, including the costs of rising sea levels, storm damage from more frequent and extreme weather events, crop losses, damage to forests, heat-related human health problems, and lost ecosystem services. Two major studies independently agree that damage costs from a doubling of CO_2 by the end of the century will amount to 2 percent of global GDP for a warming of 2.5 degrees centigrade.[4] This figure could rise to as much as 4 percent if warming amounts to 4.5 degrees centigrade by the end of the century. In the very long term, William R. Cline suggests that warming could rise to 10 to 18 degrees centigrade, with corresponding damage costs rising to 12 to 26 percent of global GDP in 2275.[5]

Perhaps the most interesting feature of an environmental problem like global warming is that the costs of controlling emissions begin immediately while the benefits of avoiding damages from warming will come in the future. This means that the practice of discounting plays a huge role in the calculation of benefits. The value of a dollar of benefits received today is substantially different from the value of a dollar of benefits received in a hundred years. If the interest rate that can be earned from savings and capital investment is 3 percent, then a dollar of benefits received a hundred years from now is only worth \$.05 ($\$1/1.03^{100}$) today. With costs and benefits evaluated in discounted terms, reducing emissions very much (beyond the "no regrets" amount) may not pay. Suppose reducing CO_2 emissions another 10 percent beyond the no-regrets 30 percent costs \$300 per ton of carbon.[6] Suppose further that the benefit of emissions reduction is equal to \$5,000 per ton, but the benefit is not received for another century. Because of this delay, the benefit per ton today in discounted terms is only \$260 at a 3 percent discount rate. According to the benefit-cost approach, the additional 10 percent of emissions reductions should not be undertaken. The added costs of doing so exceed the added benefits.

Some would challenge this conclusion on ethical grounds. Discounting appears to be ethically inappropriate because it devalues the costs of global warming faced by future generations and in the process shifts the burden to them. Current generations can weasel out of having to do anything more about global warming by simply claiming that benefits of controlling greenhouse emissions fail to exceed costs. If current generations instead choose to live up to their responsibilities for the social costs of global warming, controlling emissions further will still not be the best thing to do. The reason is simple. Current generations can put \$260 per ton of emissions in the bank today at 3 percent interest and through the magic of compounding in a hundred years it will be worth about \$5,000, an amount that is sufficient to compensate future generations for the costs of global warming associated with the next 10 percent of uncontrolled

emissions. Current generations would find compensating future generations cheaper ($260 per ton) than further controlling greenhouse emis-
sions ($300 per ton) to the tune of $40 per ton. This example is hypotheti-
cal, but the numbers involved are not unreasonable. Given acceptance of
the benefit-cost approach to establishing the amount of greenhouse emissions reductions, and given that benefits are heavily concentrated in the
future, chances are that the amount of control called for by benefit-cost
calculations will be fairly modest.

This is exactly the case for one of the leading benefit-cost studies of
global warming. In their study, Nordhaus and Boyer call for very modest
reductions in greenhouse emissions. According to their net benefits maximizing solution, by the year 2105 worldwide carbon emissions should be
reduced by 1.5 gigatons below a baseline amount of 13.3 gigatons pre-
dicted to otherwise occur in the absence of reductions.[7] This will result in
a slight lowering of the projected increase in the average global temperature due to greenhouse warming from 2.5 degrees centigrade to 2.44 degrees centigrade. Clearly, this isn't much of a change.

William Cline in his widely quoted study of global warming takes a
rather different approach. He considers aggressively reducing global carbon emissions to a ceiling of 4 gigatons per year and then estimates the
benefits and costs of doing so. His baseline projection for emissions is a
much higher 21.6 gigatons carbon by the year 2100, and his proposed
emissions ceiling means a reduction of 17.6 gigatons below the baseline in
2100. Under his approach, the amount of CO_2 in the earth's atmosphere
still doubles relative to preindustrial levels and a 2.5 degree centigrade
warming still occurs, but long-term warming beyond this amount is
avoided. His main concern is the 6-to-18 degree warming that could occur by the year 2275 in the absence of emission limits and the resulting
damage costs that could rise to as much as 13 to 26 percent of global GDP.
Cline is not interested in maximizing net benefits but is concerned about
the ratio of total benefits to costs. He shows that for a time horizon extending to the year 2275 the ratio of benefits to costs for the "best-guess,"
"lower bound," and "upper-bound" scenarios for global warming are respectively .74, .41, and 1.52. For two out of three of the cases, benefits
don't exceed costs. A key reason for this is the timing of benefits and costs.
Costs come well before benefits. As a consequence, benefits are more
heavily discounted than costs. For Cline's upper-bound high-damage
case, the benefits of limiting greenhouse gas emissions don't exceed costs
until after the year 2070. Cline argues that if we are risk averse and weight
the "upper-bound" possibility more heavily, then the aggressive action to
curb global warming he suggests may be warranted even though two of
the scenarios have costs that exceed benefits. Still, it looks likes benefits
are in fact unlikely to exceed costs according to Cline's own calculations.

Both present and future generations are likely to be better served by present generations simply saving and investing in order to compensate future generations instead of strictly limiting greenhouse gas emissions.

What can be concluded about the conventional approach to making judgments on the extent of environmental regulation? Certainly the end results of benefit-cost analysis can differ substantially, depending on the assumptions made and the data employed.[8] Even if Cline's strategy to limit CO_2 emissions to 4 gigatons of carbon annually is accepted on benefit-cost grounds, global society will still face the consequences discussed in chapter 5 because atmospheric CO_2 will still double. If the Nordhaus-Boyer recommendations for fairly modest cuts in emissions are accepted instead, long-term warming could lead to even more serious problems. In short, species extinctions, increased human death rates, and disrupted ecosystems are perfectly consistent with the benefits-cost approach to adjusting the environment to the economy.

ECOLOGICAL ECONOMICS
AND SUSTAINABLE DEVELOPMENT

To repeat, using benefit-cost analysis to adjust the environment to the economy in the case of global warming is unlikely to avoid substantial harm to the global environment. Ecological economics and the idea of sustainable development provide an alternative to benefit-cost analysis, one that gives much more weight to environmental concerns and emphasizes adjusting the economy to the environment.

Since the rather appealing term, "sustainable development," was offered by the Brundtland Commission in their 1987 report, *Our Common Future*, people have been trying to figure out exactly what it means. The definition offered by the commission has a certain superficial attraction— "development which meets the needs of the present without sacrificing the ability of the future to meet its needs."[9] The problem with this definition is a lack of sufficient concreteness for practical applications. In response, three additional definitions of sustainable development have emerged in the economics literature. These include weak sustainability, strong sustainability, and environmental (or ecological) sustainability.[10]

For weak sustainability, the central goal is to sustain society's total capital stock. The total capital stock is composed of human-produced physical capital and natural capital, and, under weak sustainability, natural and physical capital can be substituted for one another. If the value of the total capital stock is, say, $200,000 per capita, and if the annual return is 10 percent, then no more than $20,000 per capita can be consumed annually without drawing down the total capital stock and reducing the amount available to future generations. If the value of standing forests grows at, say, 5 percent a year and if the rate of return on physical capital is 10 percent, then it makes sense to harvest and sell forests to consumers and invest the proceeds in physical capital. In this instance, natural and physical capital are substitutes. Adjusting the environment to suit the economy is still the standard operating procedure in the case of "weak sustainability."

In practice, substitutability between physical and natural capital may be quite limited. Old-growth forests, for example, may be irreplaceable as suppliers of certain ecosystem services. There may be no practical way to invest in a form of physical capital that replaces the habitat old growth provides for certain rare species of benefit to humankind. The shaded pool and riffle habitat found in streams running through old-growth forests essential for the reproduction of wild salmon cannot be easily created artificially, for instance. The physical capital of the wild salmon fishing industry, such as fishing boats and gear, and the natural capital in the form of habitat required for salmon are complements, not substitutes. The limiting factor in the harvesting of salmon is not the industry's physical capital but its natural capital. To protect the ability of the industry to harvest salmon in perpetuity, its natural capital must be preserved.

The goal of preserving natural capital is referred to as "strong sustainability." Under strong sustainability, human-made and natural capital are treated separately and one cannot be substituted for the other. Natural capital cannot be drawn down in order to augment human-made capital. To this extent, the economy must now be adjusted to the environment. Habitat must be preserved, for example, to ensure the presence of future salmon populations. Habitat reduction from clear-cutting old-growth forests would amount to a decline in natural capital and a decrease in future salmon populations.[11] Under strong sustainability this would not be acceptable.

A stock of natural capital has two components, renewable and nonrenewable resources. A salmon stock can be renewed by allowing a sufficient number of spawners to reach their spawning grounds and by protecting the migration routes and the quality of the spawning habitat. Petroleum reserves, however, are not renewable. Obviously, using nonrenewable natural capital precludes sustainability, at least directly. Achieving sustainability indirectly for nonrenewables nonetheless is a possibility. By investing the proceeds of selling off nonrenewable natural capital (i.e., petroleum reserves) into renewable substitutes (i.e., solar energy), sustainability can be indirectly achieved.[12]

A close cousin to strong sustainability is the concept of "environmental" or "ecological sustainability." Under this standard, specific environmental resources are to be preserved, not just a total stock of natural capital. The value of particular ecosystems or species to future generations cannot be known for sure. The current generation can, however, do its best to preserve all remaining existing species and natural ecosystems. Economic valuation doesn't enter at all in such conservation decisions. The resource is preserved irrespective of the economic consequences. The economy in such cases will be adjusted to the environment. Under strong sustainability, natural capital cannot be replaced by human-produced physical capital; under environmental sustainability, one ecosystem cannot be substituted for another.

GLOBAL WARMING AND ENVIRONMENTAL SUSTAINABILITY

What does sustainability theory have to say about the extent of global warming that ought to be allowed? Weak sustainability doesn't go much beyond the approach of benefits-cost analysis except to suggest that delivery to future generations of a total capital stock sufficient to produce at least as much income as today should be the central goal. So long as an increase in the stock of physical capital is sufficient to compensate for any damage from global warming remaining after control efforts have been instituted, a benefit-cost approach to determining the amount of emissions reductions is acceptable in the case of weak sustainability. Preserving the natural environment is not necessary if doing so is too costly and if compensation for environmental deterioration is cheaper.

Environmental Sustainability

Suppose instead that environmental sustainability is adopted as the standard for establishing global warming policy. This means that emissions ought to be reduced enough to prevent further global warming if it is at all possible to do so. Because some global warming is already in the pipeline because of historical accumulations of greenhouse gases, to completely prevent all warming is impossible. For purposes of discussion, let's consider the most aggressive strategy evaluated by the Intergovernmental Panel on Climate Change. This strategy calls for limiting the atmospheric concentration of CO_2 to 450 parts per million (ppm). The current concentration is about 370 ppm and the concentration prior to industrialization was about 280 ppm.[13] A 450 ppm limit is slightly more aggressive than the strategy adopted by Cline in his study and limits the temperature increase to about 1.7 degrees centigrade rather than 2.5 degrees.[14] Again, the goal according to environmental sustainability is to limit global warming as much as is reasonably feasible for the purpose of preventing harm to future generations and to the world's natural ecosystems and nonhuman species. Why one would want to do this is ultimately an ethical question, one that will be taken up in the next chapter.

Whatever the rationale for bringing global warming to a halt, the economic consequences of doing so and the consequences for everyday life need to be fully understood. Emissions will have to be substantially reduced, and this will be costly. Cost estimates for limiting CO_2 concentrations to 450 ppm range from a low of 1 percent to a high of 4 percent of global GDP in 2050, with most estimates falling in the 2 to 4 percent range.[15] Emissions will have to be reduced from the current annual global rate of around 7 gigatons of carbon to around 5 gigatons by 2050 and 2 gigatons by 2100.

Emissions Caps and Marketable Emissions Allowances

An obvious point that conventional and ecological economists can agree on is that reductions in pollution emissions ought to be accomplished at the lowest possible cost. Conventional environmental economists, such as Tom Tietenberg, and ecological economists, such as Herman Daly, are also able to find common ground on the method for minimizing the costs of emissions control—place an annual cap on emissions and sell or give away marketable emissions allowances equal to the amount of the cap.[16] To allow sufficient time for an efficient implementation of reduced emissions levels, the caps can start well above the target and be reduced over time until the target is achieved.[17] Since CO_2 emissions are cumulative, a longer adjustment period will mean a lower ultimate cap to avoid exceeding the 450 ppm target for ambient CO_2. Any emitter of CO_2 or its equivalents will be required to already possess or purchase the requisite emission allowances.

To show that emission allowances indeed result in the lowest-cost solution to limiting emissions, let's consider a very simple example. Suppose there are two firms that each emit five tons of carbon emissions daily in the absence of any restrictions. Assume that the marginal costs (the added cost of another ton of emissions reduction) of control for firm 1 starts at $100 per ton for a one ton reduction and rises to $200, $300, $400, and $500 for the second through fifth ton of emissions reduced. Suppose the emission control costs for firm 2 are exactly twice as much (i.e., $200, $400 $600, $800, and $1,000, respectively, for the first through fifth ton of emissions reduction). If limiting global warming to, say, 1.7 degrees centigrade requires these two firms to cut their emissions from ten tons to four tons, then one way of accomplishing this goal would be to simply give each firm marketable emission allowances for two tons per day. Both firms together could emit no more than four tons in total. If each firm reduced emissions by three tons, then the total cost for firm 1 would be $600 ($100 + $200 + $300) and total cost for firm 2 would be $1,200 ($200 + $400 + $600), for a grand total of $1,800. Because the emissions allowances are marketable, firm 1 can control more than it needs in order to sell surplus allowances to firm 2, permitting it to increase its emissions. A deal between firm 1 and 2 can be cut that reduces total emissions costs. Firm 1 can reduce its emissions further by a ton at a cost of $400, while firm 2 can increase its emissions by a ton and save $600. Hence, firm 1 can sell an allowance to firm 2 for something between $400 and $600 to the advantage of both. If they settle on $500, both will benefit to the tune of $100 and the total control costs will be reduced to $1,600. The same result would occur if emission allowances were auctioned off by the government and if the market price for allowances settled between $400 and $600. Firm 1 would then reduce its emissions by four tons and buy one allowance while firm 2 would reduce its emissions by two tons and buy three allowances in order to minimize the costs of emissions reductions plus allowance purchases. Marketable emissions allowances, however distributed, will do the job of minimizing pollution control costs by assuring that businesses with lower emissions control costs would do more of the work of limiting emissions. This idea originated with conventional environmental economists but is attractive to ecological economists as an effective tool for achieving caps on emissions.[18]

The marketable emissions allowance strategy has proven its worth in practice for the control of sulfur dioxide emissions. The 1990 Clean Air Act Amendments required a reduction in sulfur emissions of ten million tons below the 1980 level for coal-fired power plants. To achieve this result, a system of transferable emission allowances was established along with an auction market where allowances can be bought and sold. The marginal cost at a ten-million-ton reduction was originally projected to be around $360, but the price for allowances has dropped to about $66 per ton, indicating that the cost of controlling emissions in practice is much less than originally anticipated.[19]

A global system of carbon emissions allowances would work in essentially the same way as for sulfur emissions. Consumers of energy products containing carbon that is emitted into the environment when combustion occurs would be required to have emissions allowances equal to the volume of emissions caused by the products they sell. Under a global system of emissions trading, countries with low cost options for reducing emissions could control more than required and sell the surplus to countries faced with high cost options. Less developed countries can likely replace outmoded electric generating plants having high emissions rates with modern, efficient plants or even renewable energy sources with much lower emissions rates and sell surplus allowances to developed countries. If allowances were initially distributed on a per capita basis, less developed countries could do very well financially by selling their surplus allowances to high-energy-consuming countries like the United States. Carbon allowances in this case not only serve to reduce emissions but could also be a vehicle for global income transfers to poor countries that could be used to fund environmentally friendly economic development projects.

While reducing carbon emissions is not going to be cheap for American citizens, it is going to bring benefits beyond the advantages of avoiding global warming. By the end of the century the U.S. economy would no longer depend on fossil fuels as its primary energy source under a system of carbon emission allowances sufficiently strict to bring global warming to a halt. This means that conventional air pollution and acid rain would virtually disappear as major problems, since they originate from fossil-fuel use. If, at the same time, Americans shift away from the automobile as their principal means of transportation and toward mass transit and European-like urban population densities, urban nonpoint water pollution should also decline significantly. With less land area devoted to highways and parking lots and fewer motor vehicles in use, runoff will be reduced and contamination of rainwater by metals and oils from cars will be less. Restrictions on greenhouse gas emissions serve as a kind of "umbrella" for other environmental problems. Finally, oil would no longer constitute a major global political issue and source of military conflict as it does today.

ADJUSTING THE ENVIRONMENT TO THE ECONOMY AND GETTING UNHOOKED FROM GROWTH

Ecological economics is potentially more restrictive for economic activity than conventional environmental economics. For ecological economics, the environment comes first. If this means a sacrifice of significant economic growth, then so be it. For conventional environmental economics and its strategy of adjusting the environment to the economy, environmental quality is more likely to be sacrificed to the needs of economic growth. Getting unhooked from growth will be a problem for ecological economics but not necessarily for conventional economics.

During the "no regrets" period, in which energy conservation yields net cost savings on the way to limiting global warming, economic growth is unlikely to be hindered by the stringent carbon emissions restrictions of ecological economics. As already noted, as much as 30 percent of our energy consumption can be reduced without any net cost because of the initial "negative" added costs of energy savings. While further energy conservation beyond this point will no doubt be possible, eventually, diminishing returns to energy conservation will intensify and substantial further improvements in energy productivity will become prohibitively expensive. Once the opportunities for energy conservation have been fully exploited, a shift to renewable energy sources will be required to cut greenhouse gas emissions further. While there is much room for expansion of such renewable sources as solar and wind power, ultimately these will be limited by site availability.[20] At some point, the amount of energy production possible will reach an upper limit, placing a constraint on economic growth. The efficiency of energy use will now establish the amount of economic growth possible. The more efficiently we use energy, the more goods we can produce under the constraint of a fixed total supply of energy. If the amount of GDP per unit of energy (energy productivity) can be increased at 2 percent a year, then GDP can grow at 2 percent a year within the renewable energy supply limit. If, however, only a 1 percent growth in energy productivity is feasible, than GDP can grow only by 1 percent. Of course, the economy could temporarily grow more by returning to fossil fuel consumption, but this would violate greenhouse gas emission limits.

The energy crisis in the mid-1970s and early 1980s provides some insight into the possibilities for energy conservation and improvements in energy productivity. This was a period of rapidly rising energy prices and substantial attention to energy conservation. Between 1975 and 1981, energy prices increased 37 percent more rapidly than consumer prices in general. For the first time in the United States, small cars gained in popularity. Inflation-adjusted energy prices peaked in 1981, returned to their 1975 level in 1987, and declined thereafter through 1999.[21] During the period of relatively high energy prices from 1975 to 1986, energy productivity (GDP per unit of energy) increased at a rate of 2.8 percent per year. Again, this was a period of time during which the public was adjusting to higher energy prices by purchasing more fuel-efficient cars, insulating homes and commercial buildings, and undertaking other measures to improve energy efficiency. In the subsequent period of declining energy prices, energy productivity increased by only 1.5 percent per year. This was a time of cheaper gasoline and rising popularity for the gas-guzzling sport utility vehicle (SUV). The period of high energy prices (1975–1986) most likely involved "no regrets" improvements in energy efficiency that brought net cost savings and is probably fairly representative of what would happen initially as a consequence of a planned reduction in greenhouse-gas emissions to avoid further global warming.

The discussion of unemployment and inflation in chapter 3 introduced the notion of an economic-growth speed limit. The most a macroeconomy can grow in the long run is equal to the growth rate of the labor force plus the growth rate in labor productivity (real GDP per unit labor). This is the economic-growth speed limit. If the economy expands more rapidly than this, the ultimate result is inflation. If the economy persistently grows more slowly than this, unemployment rises. The fundamental goal of macroeconomic policy is to achieve a growth rate exactly equal to the economic-growth speed limit in order to avoid both excessive unemployment and inflation.

If caps are placed on the exploitation of environmental resources, then the only way the economy can grow is through improvements in environmental productivity (real GDP per unit of environmental resource consumption). Environmental productivity defines an environmental speed limit that overrides the economic speed limit. Because the key limiting environmental resource is energy, energy-productivity growth will most likely determine the environmental growth speed limit.

History suggests that about the best we can expect for energy productivity in the early phase of greenhouse gas emissions reductions is around 3 percent growth per year, based on the experience with high energy prices in the late 1970s and early 1980s. Once no regrets measures have been exhausted, energy costs will rise and energy-productivity growth will likely be dampened to something less than 3 percent, perhaps 1 to 2 percent. The growth potential or speed limit for the U.S. economy currently is somewhere in the 3-to-4-percent range, as outlined in chapter 3. If this figure persists in the future and if energy-productivity growth is no more than 1 to 2 percent in a world of absolute renewable-energy supply limits, then energy-productivity growth will establish an environmental-growth speed limit that is below the economic-growth speed limit. If society abides by the environmental speed limit, then the end result will be rising unemployment because of growth in the labor force and labor productivity that together exceed the actual growth of the economy. If growth in potential GDP is 4 percent a year and the environmental growth speed limit is 2 percent a year, then the actual growth rate for the economy will be held to 2 percent to stay within the environmental speed limit. GDP could be increased by 4 percent if labor hours available were fully utilized, but under the environmental speed limit the increase will be only 2 percent and the actual labor hours used will be less than the total available.[22] In such a world, the supply of labor is expanding by more than the demand for labor. If the environmental speed limit were violated, the end result would be a return to a world of rising temperatures and ecological decline. In the presence of limited environmental resources, environmental productivity growth becomes the critical variable establishing the maximum growth rate for the economy. Labor productivity is supplanted by environmental productivity as the key macroeconomic variable establishing how fast the economy can expand.

If environmental limits indeed establish the actual growth rate for GDP, and if the potential growth rate for GDP (the economic-growth speed limit) is higher than this, then unemployment is bound to rise. Under existing macroeconomic arrangements, growth is the only real answer to unemployment—society is hooked on growth. The question is how to get unhooked. To do so, the withdrawal pains of unemployment somehow need to be avoided. This will require a new kind of macroeconomic policy, and perhaps even reforms in the motivations and structure of business institutions. Briefly, the work of producing output that is limited by environmental constraints will somehow have to be spread over more people as the labor force expands and as each worker becomes more productive. Before looking into the kinds of economic strategies required to get unhooked from growth, let's consider what life in an environmentally friendly world would be like, where climate change is brought to a halt, rural landscapes are protected from population spreading, and invasions of exotic species are significantly reduced.

EVERYDAY LIFE IN AN
ENVIRONMENTALLY FRIENDLY WORLD

Reducing Global Warming

Predicting the future is always dangerous, but some very general conclusions can be drawn from the necessity of cutting annual carbon emissions from their current seven gigatons to around two gigatons by the end of the century. Since fossil fuels are responsible for most carbon emissions, this will mean roughly a 71 percent reduction in the use of such fuels.[23] Perhaps 35 or 40 percent of this reduction can be accomplished through increases in energy efficiency and the rest through expansion of emissions-free, renewable energy sources such as solar and wind. At the end of the century, under this scenario Americans would be living in a world where energy efficiency is much higher, fossil fuels play a relatively minor role in energy supply, and renewable sources of energy are much more prominent in daily life. Presuming the use of carbon emissions allowances to achieve emissions reductions, the price of allowances and fossil-fuel energy will rise over time as a consequence of a declining supply of such allowances to stay within emissions caps. Under such an arrangement, fossil-fuel energy users will have to purchase allowances and cover their costs in the prices they charge for the products they sell if they are businesses or in their personal budgets if they are final consumers. In response to rising energy prices, consumption patterns and the patterns of daily life will change.

For starters, the homes we live in will be much more energy efficient. Integrated building design involving the intensive use of insulation and energy-efficient windows can realize energy savings of anywhere from 30 to 60 percent. Similarly, the appliances we use will require 30 to 40 percent less energy. Compact fluorescent lighting as well as built-in passive and photovoltaic energy systems will further reduce the need for fossil fuels to run our homes. All this can probably be done at a net cost savings. The commercial buildings we shop and work in will take advantage of the same kinds of technologies and will also be much more energy efficient than they are today.[24]

Possibly the most profound changes will come in the way we get around. A really interesting question is whether Americans will stick to low-density development in the classic suburban pattern or whether over the next hundred years they will change to a more European style of urban living, with higher land-use densities and greater use of public transportation. Shifting to the European mold could generate significant energy savings. For major cities, average metropolitan population density in Europe as of 1990 was 49.9 persons per hectare, while the same figure in the United States was 14.2. Europeans clearly live at much higher densities. City-dwelling Europeans also make much greater use of mass transit than their American counterparts. Europeans travel an average of 1,895 kilometers per capita annually on mass transit while urban-dwelling Americans manage to travel an average of only 474 kilometers. Conversely, Americans travel 16,045 kilometers per capita by motor vehicle each year, while Europeans only manage 6,601 kilometers. Living at higher densities, Europeans find mass transit much more convenient and don't have to commute as far as Americans (ten vs. fifteen kilometers on average).[25] Europeans use only 40 percent as much energy in public and private transportation as Americans do. This difference in energy use is only partly attributable to Europeans driving automobiles with greater fuel efficiencies. The typical European car uses 74 percent of the fuel required by an American car to drive a kilometer. Since European energy consumption in transportation is only 40 percent as much as American, higher motor-vehicle fuel efficiency can't be the only explanation for energy consumption differences. Less driving, shorter commutes, and greater use of mass transit must be a big part of the story behind lower European transportation energy consumption. Income, price, and fuel efficiency differences across global cities explain only half of the difference in gasoline consumption, providing further evidence that differences in urban densities and mass transit availability are an essential part of the explanation for differences in energy consumption.[26] While higher energy prices stimulate energy conservation, high-density living in and of itself is an important source of energy efficiency in transportation.

If the United States goes beyond simple increases in fossil-fuel energy prices and moves explicitly to raise urban population densities through land use planning measures and to expand the availability of mass transit through public sector investment, then greater fossil fuel energy savings will occur than otherwise. If this happens, Americans will end up living at higher densities in urban areas where mass transit is readily available. In such a setting, the typical amount of space in a new home will probably be closer to current European levels (England: 818; France: 1,183; Germany: 1,096 square feet) than the American figure (2,225 square feet).[27]

While many Americans would have to give up the conventional suburban dream, the quality of life in urban America could actually improve as the result of a shift to high-density, pedestrian-friendly cities and suburbs. In her classic work, *The Death and Life of Great American Cities*, Jane Jacobs offers powerful arguments for high-density cities. Her emphasis is on the importance of vibrant neighborhoods. According to Jacobs: (1) A city's neighborhoods should serve more than one primary function, ideally more than two; (2) most blocks should be short—the opportunity to turn corners should be frequent; (3) neighborhoods should mingle buildings that vary in age and condition and should include older buildings; and (4) the density of population must be sufficient to support the purposes for which people are attracted to a neighborhood.

For streets to be successful and offer a sense of security and safety, people must appear at different times of the day. This is fostered by different primary uses. Neighborhood streets are active throughout the day, for example, if people come to work in the neighborhood in the morning, spill out on the streets for lunch, and go home again at night. In between, neighborhood residents come out to shop. Perhaps in the evening, people are attracted to the area for the restaurants or entertainment. Streets that are used steadily are safe, can be used by children safely, and are attractive as a place to engage in casual social contacts. Short blocks create a variety of paths through a neighborhood. Long blocks are isolating and are used less by neighborhood residents. A city needs a variety of older buildings to attract a variety of new businesses that can't afford very high rents. Older buildings with low rents often serve as incubators for new businesses. A variety of old and new buildings brings a variety of building uses to a neighborhood. Older buildings can often be cleverly adapted to new uses. These are the features Jacobs envisions for a socially successful city, and they rely on increased urban densities.[28]

Although it would help, simply raising the cost of driving is unlikely to stimulate the development of more high-quality, pedestrian-friendly urban environments. The creation of such settings requires the expansion and improvement of public transportation in most cities as well as substantial changes in land-use practices. Development in pedestrian-friendly cities should be clustered at higher densities along public transit routes, and the long-established practice of segregated zoning by use should be abandoned. Automobiles can still be an important part of the urban matrix, but their needs must be balanced against the needs of pedestrians and bicyclists. One means for doing this is traffic calming, something that can be accomplished with wider sidewalks, center islands on streets and boulevards, and traffic circles. Traffic calming can be combined with landscaping on the widened sidewalks, center islands, and traffic circles to make streets increasingly attractive to pedestrians. One reason people have left increasingly auto-dominated central cities for the suburbs is that city life has often been given over to the automobile. Long unbroken streets with high-speed traffic, narrow sidewalks, and a lack of landscaping are unappealing to pedestrians, as are acres of parking lots or large, noisy freeway structures. Conversely, high-density, pedestrian-friendly cities combined with convenient public transportation are likely to win converts back to a less auto-oriented way of life. This doesn't mean giving up cars completely; it just means depending on them less for urban transportation.[29]

Irrespective of whether Americans go so far as to adopt higher-density living patterns, the cars they drive will indeed be different in a world of limits on carbon emissions. Cars will most likely be lighter and smaller, powered differently, and much more fuel efficient than they are today. Hybrid electric-powered vehicles that combine an internal combustion engine with an electric drive train and battery are already available and roughly double the efficiency of conventional vehicles in stop-and-go driving conditions. Hydrogen-powered fuel cells that produce electric power are likely to become available for motor vehicles within the next decade or two and can achieve even greater efficiencies. Hydrogen is a clean fuel that results in zero emissions when combusted and could be produced by solar energy. A combination of fuel-cell-powered vehicles and hydrogen produced from solar energy would result in very little greenhouse gas emissions.[30]

Other less apparent changes will occur in a world with serious limitations on greenhouse-gas emissions. A variety of changes in industrial processes can yield significant energy efficiencies at fairly reasonable costs. Examples include cogeneration of heat and power, use of high-efficiency electric motors, incineration of industrial residues for power generation, and efficient building design. In the past, the central goal of investment in manufacturing has been to increase the productivity of labor; now it will be to increase the productivity of energy consumption as well.[31] Significant opportunities exist for the reduction of non-CO_2 emissions, such as nitrous oxides, in agriculture. Nitrous oxide emissions can be reduced in the agricultural sector, for instance, through a reduction in the application of nitrogen fertilizers. Careful measurement of crop nitrogen requirements and limiting applications to need can result in significant reductions of nitrogen fertilizer use and subsequent nitrous oxide emissions. At the same time, fertilizer costs can be cut as well. Attention to greenhouse gas emissions in both industry and agriculture will become a significant part of daily life for workers, managers, and farmers under a regime of carbon emission reductions.

Finally, the way that energy is produced a century from now will differ substantially from the present if the limiting of greenhouse gas emissions is taken seriously. Many options exist for increasing the efficiency of energy production, such as increased electric power plant efficiency, expanded use of improved gas turbine generators, and the introduction of hydrogen powered fuel cells. Substantial new sources of carbon-free energy will be needed, however, in order to replace fossil-fuel energy and the carbon emissions it inevitably produces. Possible sources include nuclear, hydroelectric, biomass, wind, and solar energy. For the moment, expansion of nuclear energy production is probably not politically feasible in the United States because of the spent-fuel disposal problem and concerns about possible radiation releases from accidents. Hydroelectric power sites in this country have been largely exploited, and the environmental opposition to dam construction is substantial. This leaves biomass, wind, and solar. While waste products from forestry and agriculture are obvious sources of biomass energy along with municipal wastes, the production of crops for energy production conflicts directly with crop production for food. For this reason, biomass as a source of energy is likely to be limited.

The production of electricity from wind generators is growing rapidly and its cost per kilowatt hour is currently competitive with conventional power sources. Many potential sites for wind-energy production remain unexploited. One can imagine extensive wind farms on the Great Plains in the United States, an area currently suffering economic and population decline. Wind generators are not totally environmentally benign. Many see them as a visual blight on the landscape, and they pose a threat to bird life. Nonetheless, wind generators could easily provide as much as 10 percent of global electricity generation by 2020.[32]

The most promising source of renewable, pollution-free energy is solar. At high noon on a cloudless day as much as 1 kilowatt (1000 watts) of power hits a square meter of the earth's surface. This translates into an average of anywhere from 5 to 9 kilowatt hours of energy each day per square meter, depending on the amount of cloudiness. Sunny Phoenix will have a higher amount of average solar energy than cloudy Seattle. For the United States as a whole, there is on average somewhere between 2 and 3 megawatt-hours (million watt-hours) hitting a square meter of land surface each year.[33] The total amount of energy striking the total surface area in the lower forty-eight states is roughly 555 times the total amount of energy consumed.[34]

The point is simple; an abundance of unexploited solar energy hits the earth's surface each day. The trick is converting it to a usable form. The efficiency of solar photovoltaics currently on the market ranges from 12 to 17 percent, meaning that, theoretically, if all solar energy were captured at the least efficient rate, 67 times current energy consumption could be produced in the United States.[35] This means its current energy consumption could be met on roughly 1.5 percent of the country's surface area.

Solar energy is not uniformly available over time and space, since the sun is periodically covered by clouds and solar radiance is higher near the equator. Technologies for storing and transporting solar energy will be needed. Hydrogen production is one option for a storable and transportable form of energy from solar.[36] A solar-hydrogen system is by no means a "pie-in-the-sky" alternative. Honda R&D America has an operating hydrogen production facility in Torrance, California, that converts solar energy and water into hydrogen for fueling its experimental fuel-cell-powered Honda FCX automobile.[37] Production estimates based on solar radiance alone fail to account for energy losses from converting solar to hydrogen, transporting hydrogen, or distributing solar to final users. Since the best solar sites on unused land are probably fairly remote, such losses are unlikely to be trivial.

The key problem currently with solar produced from photovoltaics is its relatively high generating costs of twenty to forty cents per kilowatt hour. Costs for photovoltaics run about four to eight times the costs for producing electrical energy from fossil fuels. As the volume of solar cell production increases, costs per unit will fall because of scale economies. One study suggests that a $660 million investment in a single plant producing five million solar panels a year (400 megawatts) combined with a $100 billion investment in panels would drive the generating costs down to five cents a kilowatt hour. Rising costs of producing energy from fossil fuels under a scheme of carbon emissions allowances will make this kind of investment increasingly attractive.[38]

The truly binding constraint on renewable pollution-free energy production will be the availability of sites for solar and wind energy facilities. Land area used for solar energy production will be unavailable for other uses. Lands currently unused by humans are, with few exceptions, used by other species. The human species already appropriates a significant proportion of the earth's resources for its own purposes.[39] Both the conversion of land to energy production and the spreading of human population over the globe reduces the chances for the survival of numerous nonhuman species. Solar energy production and biodiversity conservation will be in direct conflict.

The question of limits on the availability of land in a world of solar energy production is worth pursuing a little further. Eventually, fossil-fuel energy will have to be replaced by nonpolluting renewable sources such as solar to avoid global warming. If the U.S. economy grows at 3 percent per year over the next century and if energy productivity can grow at 2 percent per year under business-as-usual arrangements, then energy consumption would increase by 170 percent or 1 percent per year in order to meeting the needs of a 3 percent GDP growth.[40] This means that energy consumption in 2100 will be 2.7 times the current level. With strict limits on carbon emissions in place, energy consumption can probably be cut by 35 percent through improvements in energy productivity without putting a major dent in economic growth.[41] This would leave us with the need to supply 1.76 times current energy use (0.65 × 2.70). As noted above, fossil-fuel energy consumption needs to be reduced to 29 percent of current use by 2100 to insure that carbon emissions are decreased from seven to two gigatons per year on a global basis. Since fossil fuels currently equal about 85 percent of U.S. energy consumption, this means that fossil fuels can take up no more than about 25 percent of current energy consumption (85 percent × 0.29).[42] Assuming that 25 percent of current energy consumption can be supplied from wind and other nonpolluting sources, then the United States would have to use solar for 1.76 − 0.25 − 0.25 = 1.26 times current energy use by 2100. Given a conservative 12 percent conversion efficiency for photovoltaics and 2 megawatt hours per square meter annual energy availability, roughly 15 million hectares (37 million acres) would be required to produce 1.26 times current use.[43] This would amount to about a 38 percent increase in developed land in the lower forty-eight states for the United States, or around fifteen thousand square feet per household. While perhaps 10 percent of this need could in theory be met within existing urban areas by utilizing rooftops, this wouldn't be easy in residential areas because of current roof designs with surfaces facing away from the sun.[44] In any case, substantial additions to developed land would be needed to meet energy requirements, taking land away from other uses, such as agriculture, forestry, or natural habitat. At some point, the development of solar energy will bump up against a land-supply constraint. The need for energy will come into conflict with demands for housing space and food and fiber and desires to conserve biological diversity. Once the land constraint is reached, further economic growth can be accommodated only by increasing the productivity of energy, that is, the amount of GDP that can be produced per unit of energy. In an environmentally friendly future, the key resource that will most require conserving is likely to be land, bringing us to the other major social trend placing pressure on land supplies—the spreading of human population over the landscape.

The Design of Cities and Limiting Population Spreading

The inexorable outward spreading of population in the United States takes form as both an outward movement of population around existing metropolitan areas as well as a movement to scenic rural areas with appealing natural amenities. The consequences of this outward spreading include an increase in impervious surfaces and associated flooding and runoff pollution, a loss of open space and scenic views, a decline in productive farmland, a reduction in wetland and riparian habitats, a loss of forest, prairie, and grassland habitat, and a decline in populations of species that have difficulty adapting to significant human presence.[45]

An important option for limiting human spreading and in the process conserving natural landscapes is the creation of pedestrian-friendly, high-density urban areas. Such areas can be highly attractive places to live, helping to reverse the outward flow of human population to suburban and rural areas and thereby serving to improve energy efficiency and reduce global warming. Reducing global warming and limiting the continuing spreading of population over the landscape will be big pluses for the conservation of biological diversity. The role of high-density cities in the conserving of biodiversity is a topic that clearly deserves further attention.

Landscapes fall on a spectrum of human use with wildlands at one end, where human influence is minimal, and cities on the other, where human use predominates. While humans in the larger sense are necessarily a part of nature—we rely for our sustenance on the resources and services of the natural world—the spectrum of land use reflects a divide between cultural and biological evolution. Human beings are subject to urban-oriented forces of cultural evolution; so are other species who occupy the human end of the landscape spectrum (i.e., domesticated animals and urban wildlife such as crows or squirrels). Species who inhabit landscapes at the wildlands end of the spectrum are more likely to be subject to the forces of biological evolution (i.e., grizzly bears).[46]

To conserve biodiversity and the processes of biological evolution, conservation biologists argue that immense, relatively wild core areas, where human impacts are largely absent, need to be preserved. In addition, core reserves should be protected by surrounding buffer zones, where human activity is limited in scope, and linked together by relatively natural corridors. This form of habitat protection, conservation biologists argue, is essential for limiting further declines in biodiversity. Noss and Cooperrider[47] argue that four fundamental objectives need to be pursued in order to protect biodiversity at a regional level:

1. Represent in a system of protected areas, all native ecosystem types and seral[48] stages across their natural range of variation.

2. Maintain viable populations of all native species in natural patterns of abundance and distribution.
3. Maintain ecological and evolutionary processes, such as disturbance regimes, hydrological processes, nutrient cycles, and biotic interactions.
4. Manage landscapes and communities to be responsive to short-term and long-term environmental change and to maintain the evolutionary potential of the biota.

These goals are best accomplished with a system of core reserves that include all native ecosystem types and provide adequate habitat for all native species unable to survive in the interstices of human-dominated landscapes. A core reserve is to be maintained in a natural state, and within the reserve natural disturbance events, such as fire, are either "allowed to proceed without interference or are mimicked through management."[49] Ideally, reserves should be big enough to accommodate recovery from disturbance events. A reserve that is too small, for example, may lack a sufficient undisturbed seed stock of native plants to recover from a catastrophic fire. Also, reserves should be of sufficient size or configured in such a way as to allow adaptation to long-term changes, such as the northerly movement of habitat range boundaries for species from climatic warming.[50]

Multiple-use buffer zones surrounding core reserves serve several purposes, including the amelioration of edge effects, enlargement of the effective size of the reserve for mobile species, and connectivity to other reserves. Buffer zone activities compatible with conserving native biodiversity could include nonmotorized recreation, selection forestry, light grazing, and small-scale agriculture. The subject of biological connectivity is complex and controversial. Basically, suitable landscapes or corridors are needed for seasonal migrations, dispersal to new habitat ranges, extension of the effective habitat area of core reserves for wide-ranging species, and for effective gene flow between subpopulations to maintain local genetic diversity. Connectivity can be served in some instances by well-placed habitat patches, landscapes with relatively low road densities, and specific habitat corridors such as riparian forests along streams and rivers. For large carnivores, such as black bears, grizzly bears, mountain lions, and wolves, home ranges are so large that no single reserve can encompass populations of sufficient size to avoid extinction in the long term. Networks of reserves are needed that are connected by regional-scale corridors.[51]

The conclusion that follows from this discussion of conservation biology is relatively simple: Some physical separation between wild nature and modern human activity—especially of the kind found in urban areas and rural landscapes devoted to an industrial-style agriculture—is essential for conserving biodiversity. While small patches of habitat within the urban and agricultural land matrix may be necessary for conserving local endemic species with relatively small-scale habitat needs, and while migratory corridors of semi-natural habitat through such areas may be important, the conservation of biodiversity requires landscapes where modern human impacts—roads, housing developments, clearcut logging, mining, and intensive agriculture—are precluded.

Although urban life is predominantly shaped by the forces of culture, it still is a part of nature. The practices of urban life occur in an ecological context and affect local and global ecological processes. Urban life draws on local and global supplies of energy, water, and materials and emits waste products into the local and global environment, affecting nutrient, carbon, and hydrological cycles. Urban settlement has spread out over the global landscape, taking over relatively wild landscapes and reducing the habitat of species intolerant of intense human activity.

And yet the design of urban landscapes and the health of city economies are of central importance for the protection of the environment and the conservation of biodiversity, for three fundamental reasons: (1) attractive cities where decent living standards can be obtained are needed to limit the spreading of population into rural core habitat reserves, buffer areas, and natural corridors; (2) urban areas as currently constituted use the resources of nature unsustainably and place too large an environmental footprint on the world, one that can only be shrunk through environmentally sensitive urban design and consumption patterns; (3) environmental values and the political will to conserve critical habitats needed for biodiversity conservation are more likely in a society engaged in the practice of applying ecological principles to everyday urban life. If the bulk of the world's human population lives in cities lacking in natural amenities and devoid of opportunities for contact with elements of non-human nature, adequate political support for the conservation of biodiversity, much less halting global warming, seems unlikely. High-density urban living is necessary to help solve the problem of global warming and conserve nature's resources, but it needs to be combined with the protection of natural amenities within urban areas in order for the public to be familiar enough with the world of nature to be willing to support its conservation outside the urban setting.

Jane Jacobs sees the city as essentially a human artifact, one that ought to be shaped in such a way as to satisfy human social needs. While the human species is ultimately a natural being, according to Ian McHarg, a well-known environmentally oriented landscape architect, the city in which human beings reside cannot contain internally all the processes of nature:

The modern city is, in this respect, profoundly different in that major natural processes which sustain the city, provide food, raw materials for industry, commerce, and construction, resources of water, and pure air are drawn not from the city or even its metropolitan area but from a national and even international hinterland. The major natural processes are not intrinsic to the locus of the city and cannot be.[52]

Still, in McHarg's view, human beings should not live in a totally artificial environment. Nature in cities not only offers tangible values, such as wooded slopes that absorb moisture and prevent flooding and erosion, but also a variety of intangible values that include stimulation of reflection on the source of human meaning:

> Clearly the problem of man and nature is not one of providing a decorative background for the human play, or even ameliorating the grim city: it is the necessity of sustaining nature as source of life, milieu, teacher, sanctum, challenge, and, most of all, of rediscovering nature's corollary of the unknown in the self, the source of meaning.[53]

While urbanization as it is currently proceeding is typically unresponsive to its natural setting, it need not be this way. McHarg argues for the preservation of natural processes in open spaces interfused with urban development. McHarg's vision is captured in the following quote:

> Indeed, in several cities, the fairest image of nature exists in these rare occasions where river, flood plain, steep slopes and woodlands have been retained in their natural condition. . . . If rivers, flood plains, marshes, steep slopes, and woodlands in the city were accorded protection to remain in their natural conditions or were retrieved and returned to such a condition where possible, this single device, as an aspect of water quality, quantity, flood and drought control, would ensure for many cities an immeasurable improvement in the aspect of nature in the city, in addition to the specific benefits of a planned watershed.[54]

While cities themselves cannot fully embody their connections to nature within their boundaries, they can be designed so as to preserve critical elements of nature and natural processes.

A socially and environmentally attractive city of the kind described by Jacobs and McHarg will take us at least part way toward reducing the city's ecological footprint by using the resources of nature more efficiently. The relatively high population densities envisioned by Jacobs will reduce the consumption of energy for both transportation and space heating and the volume of materials required for housing construction. In densely populated cities, reliance on the automobile can be reduced and alternative, more energy-efficient forms of transportation can be utilized, such as light rail or subway systems or even bicycles. In the mixed-use neighborhoods described by Jacobs, moving around on foot to satisfy daily needs becomes a real alternative. In short, getting unhooked from the automobile, a source of many of our environmental problems, becomes a distinct possibility.[55] These same high population densities will support the preservation of local open space and natural processes that McHarg advocates by limiting the spread of population into local natural habitats with significant natural value. Habitat patches and natural corridors in cities contribute to the conservation of local biodiversity and offer opportunities for human contact with natural ecological processes and wild species. This in turn increases public support for the preservation of biodiversity in more remote, large-scale reserves for those species adverse to substantial human contact. A public exposed to the beauties and wonders of nature in and around their own communities will probably be much more disposed to support landscape protection on a global scale in order to reverse current patterns of ecological decline and species extinctions.

Conservation Land Trusts and Limiting Rural Population Spreading

Dealing with the problem of global warming and population spreading potentially has the side effect of improving the quality of urban life and making cities more attractive places to live. Increasing the attraction of existing urban centers will likely slow the flow of population to places of natural beauty in rural areas, but it is unlikely to bring it to a halt. Strategies to mitigate the effects of population growth and development within rural landscapes themselves are also needed, especially in the mountain West, where rural growth has been particularly rapid.[56] While management issues on public lands concerning biodiversity conservation continue, the main problem associated with population spreading is the loss and fragmentation of natural habitat on private lands, and the key question is how habitat and species can be protected with land under private ownership.

One vehicle for preserving open space and natural habitat on private lands is the conservation land trust. Land trusts are nonprofit voluntary organizations that accept donations of property or easements or raise funds to purchase property or easements for purposes of land conservation. A conservation easement is a legally binding agreement between a property owner and a land trust that restricts property development rights but allows the landowner to retain ownership. These rights are essentially donated to the land trust, and, if the land trust qualifies as a nonprofit in the eyes of the IRS, the donor can take a tax deduction for the appraised value of the rights. In addition, to qualify for a tax deduction, restrictions of development rights must have a public benefit, such as the preservation of open space or natural habitat. The easement agreement is recorded as part of the deed and applies in perpetuity to all future owners of the property. The role of the land trust is to monitor and enforce the easement agreement. A land trust is in essence a vehicle for voluntary action to limit development for the purpose of preserving open space, natural areas, and traditional land uses, such as ranching and farming.[57] While land trusts have been quite successful increasing the amount of land protected from development, they do face significant challenges.

In terms of the language of conservation biology, land trusts operate mainly in the working landscapes of buffer areas and connecting corridors as opposed to core reserves. The challenge faced by land trusts is to prevent high-density development on agricultural landscapes that still retain habitats for native plant and animal species. A second challenge is to promote agricultural practices consistent with maintaining these habitats. The tools available to these voluntary organizations are clearly limited. Land trusts can offer the opportunity to landowners to take charitable deduction tax breaks, reduce inheritance taxes, and, in some cases, lower local property taxes in exchange for conservation easements. Easements can reduce the market value of agricultural land and make it easier for younger farmers and ranchers to enter into the business, although easements can have a negative effect on agricultural loan collateral by reducing the value of property that can be used to back up a loan. In some cases land trusts are able to raise funds from public and private sources to purchase conservation easements.

While tools used by land trusts are effective in slowing development, they probably are insufficient to bring rural residential sprawl and population spreading to a halt. Obviously, greater public-sector funding from such sources as federal offshore oil lease revenues or from the sale of carbon emissions allowances could significantly increase the capacity of land trusts to use their tools to forestall development pressures. Using carbon allowance revenues for funding easements or land purchases to preserve habitat would kill two environmental problems with one stone. With increased funding, land trusts would no longer be limited to accepting donations of easements and could purchase more easements.

The critical problem now facing land trusts is the requirement of either voluntary fund raising for easement and property purchases or voluntary landowner contributions of easements or properties. Not all land trusts can raise enough funds to compete with developers in the local property market, and not all owners of critical natural habitat are willing to contribute easements or land. Development will be diverted to lands outside the sphere of land trust influence. While land trusts may be able to help limit sprawl beyond urban boundaries, they are not by any means the only and final answer to the spreading of human population over the landscape. Ultimately, this will require more substantial measures. To a discussion of such measures we now turn.[58]

Further Measures for Limiting Rural Population Spreading

In rural areas, a relatively conventional vehicle for protecting open space and natural habitat is land-use planning and zoning at the county level. Through land-use planning, sensitive landscapes can be identified and mapped, and through zoning the density of development can be limited on such sites. As an alternative, the density of development can be limited for all existing agricultural and undeveloped lands. Custer County in Colorado, for example, took this approach by limiting development to one house per eighty acres for valley-bottom ranch land, higher than the state restriction of one per thirty-five acres. County-level zoning is unfortunately not always acceptable to local landowners, who fear restrictions that impinge on current uses of the land or reduce its market value. Ranchers and farmers who are land rich but cash poor in rural areas are not going to give up the right to develop their land very easily.

An alternative approach likely to be more acceptable to landowners is a scheme of zoning regulations that allows residential construction at higher densities in exchange for the clustering of development and the preservation of a certain amount of open space.[59] For example, the owner of a hundred-acre parcel, normally restricted to the construction of a single dwelling by zoning regulations, might be allowed to build more units if development is concentrated on, say, a twenty-acre site and the remaining eighty acres are left as open space. This arrangement would be more attractive to landowners concerned with the market value of their property. Routt County in Colorado, the location of the skiing and resort community of Steamboat Springs, has a provision for conservation subdivisions that allows development in exchange for open-space conservation. In practice, however, this provision acts like a normal subdivision law and has been a vehicle for facilitating development in the Steamboat Springs area.[60]

Zoning becomes much more acceptable to landowners if used in combination with transferable development rights (TDRs). TDRs are essentially a first cousin to marketable emissions allowances and permit flexibility in meeting habitat conservation goals. Under a TDR program, landowners can transfer development rights from areas where development is restricted to areas where development is permitted. For example, suppose the normal density limit in the zoning law is one dwelling per twenty acres and that all landowners are allocated one development right per twenty acres. Under a TDR scheme, development is restricted in some areas of a county while, in other areas, the development can be increased by purchasing development rights from landowners in the restricted area. The restricted locations are sending areas for development rights while the unrestricted locations are receiving areas. TDRs can be purchased in the sending areas and used for increasing the density of development in the receiving areas.[61] While land in sending areas cannot be developed, landowners can nonetheless realize economic value from their land by selling their development rights. The net result is the concentration of development in less environmentally sensitive locations. Such a scheme should reduce landowner opposition to zoning restrictions because all landowners can benefit from development even though it cannot occur everywhere.

While county-wide zoning is not very popular in rural areas, at least one state has come up with an appealing voluntary option for local zoning to achieve land conservation goals. Montana state law permits the formation of zoning districts at a sub-county level. A zoning district can be established if at least 60 percent of the landowners sign a petition for such a district and if fewer than 40 percent of the landowners who in total own less than 50 percent of the land enter written protests against the district. An advisory committee of landowners then works with the local county planning board and commission to prepare a draft zoning regulation for adoption by the county commission after public hearings.[62] In Gallatin County sixteen of these zoning districts are currently in existence.

One of the more interesting examples is the Springhill Zoning District, located just north of Bozeman, Montana, near the Bridger Mountain Range in Gallatin County. The community is composed of around 140 individuals equally split among ranchers, retirees, and people who work at home or else commute to Bozeman for employment. The Springhill Community includes approximately nineteen thousand acres, of which eleven thousand are national forest land. The area includes eighty-eight parcels of land with fifty-one residential dwellings. In 1989 a petition was successfully circulated for the establishment of a zoning district with the same boundaries as the local elementary school district. Seventy percent of the landowners supported formation of the district. Landowners were concerned with a residential subdivision constructed in the area in 1989, and local residents wanted to maintain the character of the existing landscape and limit the extent of new residential development. By 1992 a land-use plan and zoning regulations were established.

The goals of the Springhill land-use plan include preserving the existing rural agricultural community, protecting riparian areas, preventing development on steep slopes and in wetlands, preserving the natural vegetation, and conserving wildlife habitat. The principal means for accomplishing these goals are to limit residential development and to cluster it

on a limited amount of land. The primary vehicle in the zoning regulations for limiting and clustering residential development is a system of
transferable development rights (TDRs). In the Springhill Zoning District,
one residential dwelling unit is allowed as a matter of right per 160 acres
or per parcel existing at the time the zoning law was adopted in 1992. In
addition, landowners are allowed one additional development right for
every eighty acres within an original parcel subject to obtaining a conditional use permit. The owner of a two-hundred-acre parcel, for example,
would have a total of three development rights, two of which would require a conditional use permit. These could be used to construct three
dwellings, or the development rights could be sold. Any development
right can be transferred through sale to any other parcel within the zoning district. Transferable development rights are a marketable entity that
can be separated from the original property. Transferable development
rights as well as development rights arising from the eighty-acre provision, however, can be used on only 15 percent of the original parcel area.
The remaining 85 percent must be permanently preserved as open space.
In this way, development will be limited and much of the district will be
preserved in its current open-space status. For example, an owner of a
two-hundred-acre parcel with one dwelling on the property could purchase an additional three development rights for a total of five, subject to
conditional use (two development rights are from the eighty-acre provision), but development of the five units would have to be confined to subdivided parcels totaling no more than thirty acres.[63] The primary limitation of zoning districts is that they cover only a part of the county. Because
much of Gallatin County, the home of Spring Hill as well as other zoning
districts, remains unzoned, development is readily diverted to those areas
not covered by zoning laws.

All these measures are local in focus and don't really speak to larger national goals of protecting species and natural habitats. Such local measures can be folded into national goals, however, through various funding
schemes using revenues from greenhouse gas emission allowances auctioned off by the federal government. Funds can be provided to land
trusts who conserve critical habitats through easements or land purchases, to counties that institute zoning and land-use planning that pro-
tects natural areas, to localities that institute systems of transferable development rights, and to states that pass comprehensive planning laws
requiring localities to institute environmentally sensitive land-use plans
and zoning.

All this boils down to a rather simple point: to conserve naturally occurring flora and fauna in the rural landscapes, the density of development
needs to be increased in both urban and rural areas. Denser, pedestrian-
oriented cities are more attractive than low-density, auto-oriented cities,

and more attractive cities will entice population and limit outward spreading to rural areas. A similar dynamic may be at work in rural areas as well. Residents of such towns as Bozeman, Montana, may have the best of two worlds. They live in an attractive community with a vibrant street life and a system of trails connected to wilderness in the mountains beyond. In the Bozeman area, one doesn't need to live on a large piece of land outside city boundaries to enjoy the beauties of the natural landscape. Living at higher densities in towns like Bozeman yields the added benefit of leaving more habitat available for nonhuman species. Finally, living at relatively high densities in attractive cities that limit sprawl and provide decent public transportation, such as Portland, Oregon, serves to limit the human ecological footprint on the global environment and, in the process, helps to conserve biodiversity on a global scale. If we take seriously the problems posed by population spreading, then the essential change is that we will be living at higher densities, but chances are that life will be more pleasant as a consequence.

Addressing the Problem of Invasive, Exotic Species

The global movement of goods and people, driven in part by the business quest for ever larger markets, has created broad pathways between continents and islands that were once biologically isolated from one another. In response, the flora and fauna of different continents are increasingly coming into contact with each other. Because of the absence of built-in ecological constraints on the predatory and competitive capabilities of many exotics invading new territories, the consequences of increased contact unfortunately are often devastating for native species and ecosystems.[64] Rolling back the flood of invasive species is a huge challenge for those concerned with protecting native plants and animals.[65]

The growth of international trade is undoubtedly the primary source of expanded exotic species invasions throughout the world. As trade continues to expand, so will the global movement of species from one continent to another.[66] Short of bringing trade to a standstill, limiting the global flow of exotics will be extremely difficult. Once exotics are loose, they are tough to eradicate or control. For this reason, the most effective option for reducing exotic invasions is prevention. The federal government and some state governments already have legislation on the books and regulatory systems in place to limit the inflow of exotic species into the United States. The problem is that existing regulatory efforts are oriented primarily to the protection of agriculture. The single biggest U.S. agency focused on restricting the importation of exotics is the Animal and Plant Health Inspection Service (APHIS). This agency runs an extensive system of quarantine operations and inspections at points of entry into the

United States, including baggage inspections at international airports. The focus of these efforts is on agricultural pests, such as weeds and pathogens, not species that are a threat to natural areas alone. The U.S. Fish and Wildlife Service has a much smaller program of inspection for banned wildlife species. The Nonindigenous Aquatic Nuisance Prevention and Control Act was passed in 1990 in response to the growing zebra mussel problem in the Great Lakes and could be a major force in stanching the flow of harmful aquatic species into the United States if key features of the act are funded and implemented. Provisions to regulate ballast water in ships, a key path for entry of invasive aquatic species, have been instituted under the 1996 National Invasive Species Control Act. Not all invasive species are covered by inspections, and the inspection process is overwhelmed by the volume of international trade and travel. Simply put, the scope and scale of existing inspection efforts is insufficient to put a major dent in the flow of exotics across U.S. borders.[67]

A part of the problem is the inherent tension between the expansion of trade and restraints on the flow of exotic species. The political interests favoring trade are powerful, while concern for invasive species is limited. One of the most effective arrangements for addressing exotic invasions is the International Plant Protection Convention (IPPC). The IPPC is an international agreement among ninety-eight signatories to protect agriculture from pests that could spread through international trade in plant products. Parties to the convention agree to prevent pests from getting outside their own countries through inspection of exports and through eradication and control of pest outbreaks in exported agricultural products. As Chris Bright notes, the coverage of the IPPC could be easily extended from pests that cause damage in agriculture to pests and exotics with the potential to harm natural ecosystems. The plant protection offices already in place, such as APHIS in the United States, have the expertise to go beyond their current focus on exotics that do economic harm and to take on the larger problem of invasive exotic pathogens, plants, and animals damaging to all ecosystems, whether human-created or natural.[68]

Expansion of efforts to limit the flow of exotic species, however, is bound to run up against efforts of the World Trade Organization (WTO) to increase trade and override environmental restrictions that would limit trade volumes. The job of the WTO is to write the rules for the global trading system and to eliminate as many barriers to trade as possible. The WTO prefers to see a harmonization of global environmental standards rather than any single country restricting imports on its own for environmental reasons. Such restrictions are often construed as barriers to trade, inimical to the goal of an expanding global economy. Recent amendments to the IPPC to bring it into conformity with WTO efforts to harmonize environmental standards have basically gutted the IPPC's power to halt incoming pests by requiring a risk assessment to be done first. In the meantime, while the risk assessment is under way, pests can flow freely, according to Bright.[69] In the world of pest management, rapid reaction is essential. Action is needed before analysis, not the reverse. The political pressure to keep goods moving in the trade pipeline in the modern global economy is tremendous. To institute a regulatory system to protect against exotic invasives means breaching critical political barriers. The WTO, it must be remembered, is devoted to trade expansion, not protecting the global environment. In its rule making, it is going to be more responsive to political pressures from global corporations demanding the removal of trade barriers than it is to environmental groups desiring to protect the global environment. The WTO has expressed little interest in establishing truly rigorous environmental standards for traded goods, much less in seriously addressing the problem of invasive exotics. A workable system to limit invasives is going to be costly and will no doubt have a dampening effect on trade at the margin. Some goods, such as Siberian raw logs, may even have to be excluded from U.S. imports simply because the potential for pest introductions is just too great.[70] Free trade can no longer be put on a pedestal in a world of environmental threats. Rather than adopting the environment to the needs of trade, trade needs to be adjusted to the needs of the environment in accordance with the principles of ecological economics if the problem of exotics is to be brought under control.

Once invasions of exotics have occurred, limiting the damage they cause becomes extremely difficult, although not impossible. The sea lamprey in the Great Lakes has been effectively controlled with the application of a chemical to lamprey spawning sites that selectively kills lamprey larvae. Ironically, the chemical used is due for reregistration under U.S. pesticide control laws, and the suppliers are unwilling to bear the $8 million cost. To continue control, either pesticide regulators will have to make an exception on registration or else the Great Lakes Fishery Commission, the agency in charge of controlling sea lamprey, will have to bear the cost.[71]

As an alternative to pesticides, another method of control is to introduce species that prey on exotics. In the Great Lakes, various species of nonnative salmon have been introduced to prey on the alewife, an alien fish species that has become a nuisance because of spring die-offs, as noted in the previous chapter.[72] While salmon introductions have been quite successful in the Great Lakes as a biological control and created a popular sport fishery in the process, introductions of this kind can backfire. Mongooses, for example, were imported into Hawaii to control rats, but also preyed upon native birds.[73]

Figuring out the best method to eradicate or control exotics is not easy. Controlling some species, such as the prolific zebra mussel in the Great Lakes, is extremely difficult if not impossible. Nonetheless, progress has been made in the eradication and control of some exotics.[74] The work tends to be labor intensive and requires significant increases in funding. A potential source for such funding could be revenues generated by the sale of carbon emission allowances or user fees charged on the international shipment of goods and on global travel. Controlling exotics is an environmental problem not amenable to conceptually simple solutions such as marketable emissions allowances and transferable development rights. Tackling the problem of exotic invasions requires the expansion or creation of public agencies to do the challenging work of monitoring, controlling, and restricting the global flow of exotics.

Addressing the problem of exotics in a serious way will no doubt alter the daily patterns of life, although not in ways that are especially obvious. Some imported items may disappear from stores (e.g., lumber from imported logs) and most imports will cost more under serious monitoring of international shipping to prevent exotic species from hitching rides. International travel will also be more costly and inconvenient if inspections are expanded enough to significantly limit travel-related plant and animal invasions. For Americans a price will be paid for such efforts, but no doubt it will be less than the $137 billion annual cost of damages from exotic species.[75] Increased public awareness of the importance of the issue could result in the mobilization of local community efforts to eradicate exotics. Attention to exotics in one's immediate environment is a good way to get to know the local landscape.[76]

GETTING UNHOOKED FROM GROWTH

All this offers a vision of what life would be like in an environmentally friendly world with such key environmental problems as global warming, habitat decline for native species, and the invasion of exotic organisms under control. Life would clearly be different, and in many ways maybe even improved, but emphasis on the business pursuit of profits through the introduction of new and novel products and the individual pursuit of new and novel consumer goods would certainly be less. This is not to say that seeking stimulation or the demonstration of status through consumption will disappear or that Schumpeter's forces of creative destruction will die, but these features of economic life would likely lose some of their prominence in an environmentally friendly world. Since researchers have found that a connection between aggregate economic growth and expressed happiness is absent in all but the poorest societies, a slower pace of growth in the availability of consumer novelties and status goods is unlikely to reduce subjective well-being very much.[77] Recalling that the pursuit of status goods is akin to an arms race from which no one benefits and that the pleasure derived from consumer novelties tends to be transitory, the failure of growth to bring forth more happiness is unsurprising.[78]

A critical problem that an affluent society would have to face in such a world is the generating of enough jobs to employ everyone who wants to work. The maximum growth rate for the economy would no longer be the sum of the growth rates of the labor force and labor productivity but would now be the growth rate of environmental productivity. In a world with caps in place on the use of limited environmental resources, growth can only occur if those resources can be used more productively, or, to put it slightly differently, if the amount of GDP that can be produced from a fixed volume of environmental resources rises over time. If energy is fixed in supply, then the only way GDP can grow is if GDP per unit of energy consumed rises (i.e., if the productivity of energy increases). The problem is, if labor productivity and the labor force together grow more quickly than the economy is allowed, not all the labor available will be needed to produce the economy's output. The environmental speed limit will be less than the economic speed limit and, as a consequence, the unemployment rate will rise, at least under current economic arrangements. So the question is, What kind of reforms will get us unhooked from the need for growth to keep unemployment from rising?

The essence of the problem is in the nature of the reaction by businesses to a decline in their need for labor hours, either because of a decline in product demand or growth in labor productivity outpacing product-demand expansion. If workers increase their output per hour and the added output is not fully absorbed by consumers, then employer demand for labor hours will fall. The usual reaction is to lay off workers, not to reduce the hours of all workers. The end result, of course, is rising unemployment.

Why not cut labor hours for everyone instead and avoid the unemployment problem? The trouble with this approach is that not all labor costs are associated with hours worked; some are associated with the number of workers employed. More costs can be cut by reducing the number of workers employed than by reducing hours alone. Letting a worker go not only means avoiding the hourly pay and employment taxes associated with hours worked, but also the costs of having a worker on the payroll, such as the expenses of health and other types of insurance, defined benefit retirement programs, and on-the-job training. Also, across-the-board hours reductions instead of layoffs can weaken the employee's bond to the job. With fewer hours, those who most intensely miss the income may look elsewhere for work, and they could well be the most experienced and productive employees, who would normally be kept on under a regime of layoffs. Also, getting fired will be less costly with fewer hours being worked, and as a result the price of shirking work and taking a chance at being fired will be lessened. This will in turn put a dent in labor productivity and dampen profits for the employer. Other things being equal, employers prefer more hours per worker to limit employment costs, maintain the employment bond, prevent the loss of experienced employees, and limit the incentive for shirking of work.

Given such employer preferences, then unemployment will rise as labor hours supplied rise by more than labor hours demanded whenever the economic speed limit (the sum of labor force and labor productivity growth) exceeds the environmental speed limit (environmental productivity growth). Suppose the environmental speed limit is 2 percent a year and the economic speed limit is 3 percent a year. If economic growth obeys the environmental speed limit, then the unemployment rate will move ever upward. If, for example, the labor force grows by 1 percent a year and labor productivity grows by 2 percent a year, the economy would have to grow at 3 percent a year to absorb added product from new members of the labor force and increased worker productivity. Only growth at the economic speed limit, in this case 3 percent per year, will prevent rising unemployment. The choice is not a pretty one. Either unemployment is avoided through economic expansion at the cost of a deteriorating environment, or the environment is preserved at the cost of rising unemployment. Given these possibilities, society indeed appears to be hooked on growth.

A conceptually simple reform in employee relations could avoid this outcome. Suppose productivity growth is running 2 percent and labor force growth 1 percent a year for a total of 3 percent potential GDP growth. Suppose also that the environmental growth speed limit for GDP is 2 percent a year. Without any per-worker hours reductions, GDP would have to grow at 3 percent a year to absorb the product of all workers at full employment. If workers instead take their share of the productivity increase as a 1 percent pay increase and a 1 percent hours reduction spread equally across all, then the economic speed limit will be brought into alignment with the environmental speed limit. A 2 percent annual growth in GDP is now sufficient to absorb the product of all workers under full employment since all workers agree to reduce the hours of labor they are supplying by 1 percent.[79] Workers will essentially take a part of their pay increase as an increase of leisure. The reduction in hours will be spread over all workers, avoiding the problem of rising unemployment. Through this simple measure the economy can unhook itself from environmentally damaging excess growth. For the success of such an approach, employees need to accept it and employers need to abide by it.

Surprisingly, Americans who work full-time appear to be working more hours per year than in the past. The long-term trend of declining per-person working hours appears to have been reversed in the United States. While this conclusion is hotly debated for individual workers because of measurement issues, it is clear that families, husbands and wives together, have significantly increased their working hours in recent years.[80] Also, the share of workers putting in more than fifty hours a week has risen significantly. Survey research suggests that many full-time workers in the United States would be happy to work less. Part-time workers are typically underemployed and would like to work more, but those who work more than forty hours a week want to work less.[81] Many workers are also willing to give up wage increases in order to have more free time.[82] Despite powerful drives to expand consumption in modern society, workers are willing to take at least some of their future pay increases in the form of leisure. Shortening labor time is not only a measure to keep the economy within the environmental speed limit, but it is also desired for its own sake.

Workers are not getting the shorter hours they want, suggesting that employers are unwilling to reduce working time. As already noted, labor costs are cheaper for a given amount of hours if accomplished by employing fewer workers and reducing costs associated with the number of workers on the payroll. This is often the case even if overtime hours are paid at a higher rate. In order for employers to buy into work-time reductions, costs related to hiring another worker need to be reduced or even eliminated. Employer-funded health insurance is the single biggest cost associated with additions of workers to the payroll. Because of publicly funded health insurance, Europeans don't face this issue. The obvious answer for Americans is health-care funding reform that eliminates employer financing of health insurances. This is a huge issue in its own right that goes well beyond our immediate concerns here. The point is simple—universal health insurance is needed, not only for its own sake, but to make desired reductions in working time possible. Since defined benefit retirement plans are fast disappearing anyway in favor of defined contribution, retirement funding in the future is likely to be associated with hours as opposed to number of employees. The training-cost barrier to added hiring could be overcome through lifetime government-subsidized training accounts. On-the-job training could be partially funded by the drawing down of such accounts. Under such arrangements, new hires would have the attraction of subsidized training costs. Alternative forms of compensation, such as profit sharing based on seniority, could be used to offset the weakening of bonds to employment caused by reduced

hours. Through some simple reforms, the objections of employers to reduced hours can be largely overcome.

The actual effects of legislated or union-negotiated reductions in working hours are a subject of some controversy. A number of authors find that
reductions in standard weekly hours have no discernible impact on employment.[83] Others have found the opposite.[84] In one case during the
1980s, the Dutch successfully worked out a national agreement between
employers, government, and organized labor to shorten hours and undertake other measures for the explicit purpose of increasing employment. Evidence suggests that employment did in fact increase in response
to the agreement.[85] One author makes the important point that collective
work-time reductions will not automatically create employment. Certain
necessary conditions must be fulfilled, including "an active training policy, wage increases in line with productivity gains, the standardization of
actual hours worked, the reduction of differences in hourly rates for full-
timers and part-timers, better social security for flexible working lives, a
change in the deep-seated full-time culture in the workplace, and social
security contributions that are proportional to paid hours of work."[86] If
the desire to reduce working hours is strong, the means for doing so are
available, and in the process employment can indeed be spread over more
workers, reducing the unemployment problem. Economic growth is not
the only path to full employment. Getting unhooked from growth
through workweek reductions is an attractive alternative.

If workweek reductions are instituted and the growth of the economy
does in fact slow as a consequence, less investment spending by businesses on new plant and equipment will be required. Whenever a company adds permanently to the amount of its product sales, a one-time investment in new plant and equipment is needed, at least when excess
productive capacity does not already exist. With less growth in sales, less
investment spending will be undertaken. This creates a problem of insufficient product demand for the aggregate economy that somehow needs
to be offset.

Because of the increased emphasis in an environmentally friendly
economy on improvements in energy productivity and the productivity
of environmental resources, some investment spending will be redirected to these tasks. This could offset any decline in investment spending caused by slower growth. If the amount of this offset is insufficient,
other kinds of spending may be needed to fill in the gap and prevent unemployment. For this to happen, fiscal policy measures may be required,
such as increasing government spending on public sector capital goods
to replace private sector investment. There are plenty of possibilities for
spending that could further the cause of environmental improvement
and increased environmental productivity, including investment in so-

lar- or wind-energy research, public mass transit, energy conservation, and habitat restoration. To prevent economic decline, some Americans in this situation would have to overcome biases that they have against public sector expansion.

The funding of such spending is a critical matter. While deficit spending may be appropriate in the short term if the economy is in a slump, ultimately spending to replace private sector investment will have to be funded by taxes. Since government investment will increase environmental productivity and the potential for economic expansion in the future, such spending could be funded by taxes put in place at the time investment projects come on line. At that time, increases in environmental productivity will be noted, relaxing the limitations on growth imposed by the environmental speed limit. With improvements in energy efficiency, for instance, economic activity could be increased even though energy supplies are fixed. Tax revenue increases from increases in taxation rates and the added economic growth could then be used to repay government debt issued to fund the initial investment.

What all this amounts to is a different sort of macroeconomic policy in an environmentally friendly world. The centerpiece will be a shortening of standard working hours backed up by public investment in environmental productivity improvements. To prevent a dampening of aggregate product demand from the government sale of carbon emission allowances, something that would reduce spending power much in the same way as taxes, government spending would have to be increased or taxes reduced. Rising energy costs induced by increased requirements to purchase carbon emissions allowances could in theory induce a cost-push inflation, although such cost increases could be spread out over time, allowing for adjustments that would moderate the increases. Conventional monetary policy would likely be able to handle any stimulus to inflation from the costs of environmental improvements.[87]

CONCLUSION

The economy can be adjusted to the requirements of environmental protection, or the environment can be adjusted to the needs for economic activity. The latter ensures that priority will be given to economic concerns, while the former ensures that priority will be given to environmental concerns. Adjusting the needs of the economy to the environment will more likely than not impose limitations on economic growth, and adjusting the environment to the needs of the economy in all probability will bring forth greater economic expansion at the expense of greater present and future deterioration in environmental quality and biological diversity. Adjusting the environment to the economy with caps on the use of environmental resources is one possibility; getting unhooked from growth without causing unemployment by using measures to reduce standard working hours is another.

Limitations on growth will likely dampen the consumer quest for novelty and status. The stakes for conspicuous consumption will be lowered, but doing so will not necessarily reduce anyone's sense of well-being. The consumption arms race will simply be reduced in scale. The Joneses will spend less on status goods, reducing the need for others to spend as much. If the status associated with an individual's consumption fails to rise because of growth restraints, then others won't have to increase their consumption to keep up. Growth restraints limit the self-defeating rises in consumption undertaken to prevent status declines caused by others boosting their consumption.

While consumers may ultimately benefit from restraints on status-goods consumption imposed by growth restrictions, they will have to forgo at least some pleasure-providing consumer novelties at the margin. The stimulus of such fleeting pleasures is probably easily replaceable by other, more enduring joys in life that come from activities not requiring high levels of consumption, such as a pickup softball game, an interesting conversation at the coffee shop, an afternoon at the library reading a good book, a hike in the woods, or an afternoon spent with a loved one. With more leisure, more of such pastimes become feasible.

The stakes of the creative destruction process will also be lowered somewhat with reduced possibilities for growth and the production of consumer novelties and status goods. The markets for such goods will by no means disappear, and the process of replacing older kinds of goods with new kinds will no doubt continue. Only the amount of growth in such markets will be more limited. Of course there will be an opening up of opportunities for entrepreneurial talent in such areas as energy productivity improvements, fuel-efficient vehicles, and alternative systems of energy production. Creative destruction and technological advance will no doubt continue in an environmentally friendly world, but with a somewhat different content.

NOTES

1. Economists often look at net benefits maximization in "marginalist" terms. Suppose, for example, the added cost of controlling emissions is a constant $500 per ton of carbon. Suppose the added benefit of controlling emissions begins at $1,000 per ton for the first 10 percent of control, declines by $100 for the second 10 percent, declines by another $100 for the third, and so on. Net benefits will rise as

emissions are reduced so long as the added benefits per ton exceed the added costs per ton. A maximum of net benefits will be achieved in this example when emissions reductions reach 50 percent, and beyond 60 percent emissions reduction net benefits will decline. A maximum of net benefits will be reached when the addition to benefits (marginal benefits) equals the addition to costs (marginal costs). This example doesn't explicitly consider the timing of benefits and costs and the resulting need to apply a discount factor to future benefits and costs.

2. For a couple of detailed and sophisticated examples of this approach, see William R. Cline, *The Economics of Global Warming* (Washington, D.C.: Institute for International Economics, 1992), and William D. Nordhaus and Joseph Boyer, *Warming the World: Economic Models of Global Warming* (Cambridge, Mass.: MIT Press, 2000).

3. Cline, *The Economics of Global Warming*, 203–7.

4. Cline, *The Economics of Global Warming*, 130–33; Nordhaus and Boyer, *Warming the World*, 95–98.

5. Cline, *The Economics of Global Warming*, 130–33.

6. The added cost of removing another ton of carbon for the United States, assuming the reduction required by the Kyoto accords (5 percent below 1990 emissions), ranges from a low of $76 to a high of $410 in a series of greenhouse gas abatement cost studies. Intergovernmental Panel on Climate Change, *Climate Change 2001: Mitigation* (Cambridge: Cambridge University Press, 2001), 514.

7. One ton of carbon is equivalent to 3.67 tons of CO_2. A gigaton is billion metric tons.

8. For a more extensive critique of cost-benefits analysis in the case of global warming, see Clive L. Spash, *Greenhouse Economics: Values and Ethics* (London: Routledge, 2002), 153–83.

9. World Commission on Environment and Development, *Our Common Future* (Oxford: Oxford University Press, 1987), 43.

10. Tom Tietenberg, *Environmental and Natural Resource Economics*, 5th ed. (Reading, Pa: Addison Wesley Longman, 2000), 93–95.

11. While salmon hatcheries, an example of physical capital, have in some cases been fairly successful, they have never come close to replacing the historic salmon runs that have been lost as the result of habitat deterioration. See Bruce Brown, *Mountain in the Clouds: A Search for the Wild Salmon* (New York: Simon & Schuster, 1982), 213–39. Another possible substitute based on physical capital is pen-raised salmon, but anyone who has tasted wild and pen-raised salmon knows that they are not the same.

12. For a more extensive treatment of the notion of natural capital and the idea of strong sustainability, see Herman E. Daly, *Beyond Growth: The Economics of Sustainable Development* (Boston: Beacon Press, 1996), 75–87.

13. Intergovernmental Panel on Climate Change, *Climate Change 2001: The Scientific Basis* (Cambridge: Cambridge University Press, 2001), 38–39.

14. Cline, *The Economics of Global Warming*, 130–33.

15. Intergovernmental Panel on Climate Change, *Climate Change 2001: Mitigation*, 548.

16. Tietenberg, *Environmental and Natural Resources*, 348–49; Daly, *Beyond Growth*, 52–53.

17. For examples of possible paths for emissions, see Intergovernmental Panel on Climate Change, *Climate Change 2001: Mitigation*, 544–47.

18. For a complete explanation of the approach, see Tietenberg, *Environmental and Natural Resources*, 343–49.

19. Tietenberg, *Environmental and Natural Resources*, 389–98.

20. See the discussion of the details of solar energy production below for more on upper limits for solar energy production.

21. Inflation-adjusted energy prices are derived by dividing the energy price index by the consumer price index and multiplying by one hundred. The result is an inflation-adjusted energy price index that measures. GDP and price data were taken from U.S. Executive Office of the President, Council of Economic Advisors, *Economic Report of the President: Transmitted to the Congress, February 2002* (Washington, D.C.: U.S. Government Printing Office, 2002), Tables B-2 and B-40. Energy consumption data were taken from U.S. Bureau of the Census, *Statistical Abstract of the United States, 2001* (Washington, D.C.: U.S. Government Printing Office, 2002), 570.

22. A 2 percent reduction in GDP may not seem like much on the surface, but it actually is pretty significant. At a 4 percent growth rate, GDP doubles in only twenty years; at a 2 percent growth rate, GDP doubling takes about thirty-six years. Seemingly small growth rates have relatively substantial consequences.

23. The five-gigaton reduction required is 71 percent of the seven gigatons of emissions. The presumption is that emissions reductions are proportionate to the reductions in fossil-fuel consumption. The figure may be less because some carbon-emission reduction can be achieved by switching from fuels that emit more carbon per Btu (British thermal unit) of energy, such as coal, to fuels that emit less, such as natural gas.

24. Intergovernmental Panel on Climate Change, *Climate Change 2001: Mitigation*, 184–89.

25. Peter Newman and Jeffrey Kenworthy, *Sustainability and Cities: Overcoming Automobile Dependence* (Washington, D.C.: Island Press, 1999), 68–126.

26. Newman and Kenworthy, *Sustainability and Cities*, 78–80.

27. Ministry of the Environment Finland, *Housing Statistics in the European Union* (Helsinki: Ministry of the Environment Finland, 2001, http://www .euhousing.org), 24; U.S. Bureau of the Census, *Statistical Abstract of the United States: 2000* (Washington, D.C.: United States Government Printing Office, 2001), 714.

28. Jane Jacobs, *The Death and Life of Great American Cities* (New York: Vintage Books, 1961), 150–221.

29. See Newman and Kenworthy, *Sustainability and Cities*, chapter 4, for a more extensive discussion of reducing automobile dependence and making cities more pedestrian friendly.

30. Intergovernmental Panel on Climate Change, *Climate Change 2001: Mitigation*, 194–96.

31. Intergovernmental Panel on Climate Change, *Climate Change 2001: Mitigation*, 207–22.

32. Intergovernmental Panel on Climate Change, *Climate Change 2001: Mitigation*, 237–47.

33. Ken Zweibel, *Harnessing Solar Power: The Photovoltaics Challenge* (New York: Plenum Press, 1990), 11–13.

34. The amount of energy consumed in 1999 was 96.6 $\times$ 10^{15} Btu's. See U.S. Census Bureau, *Statistical Abstract of the United States, 2001* (U.S. Government Printing Office, 2001), 570. The amount of solar energy hitting a hectare of land each year is 20,000 megawatts or 68.2 $\times$ 10^9 Btu's. Give 786.17 $\times$ 10^6 hectares of land in the lower forty-eight states, 53,617 $\times$ 10^{15} Btu's of solar energy hit the land surface each year. For the land area, see U.S. Census Bureau, *Statistical Abstract of the United States, 2001* (U.S. Government Printing Office, 2000), 229.

35. Intergovernmental Panel on Climate Change, *Climate Change 2001: Mitigation*, 247–48.

36. Intergovernmental Panel on Climate Change, *Climate Change 2001: Mitigation*, 247–48.

37. Honda Motor Company Ltd., "Honda Starts Experiments with Hydrogen Production and Fueling for Fuel Cell Vehicles at New Station in California (U.S.)," *Honda Corporate News*, July 10, 2001, http://world.honda.com/news/2001/c010710.html: 1–2.

38. Intergovernmental Panel on Climate Change, *Climate Change 2001: Mitigation*, 247–49.

39. Peter M. Vitousek et al., "Human Domination of Earth's Ecosystems," *Science* 277 (1997): 494–99.

40. If energy productivity did not grow, then a 3 percent growth in GDP would require a 3 percent growth in energy consumption. This amount of energy growth needed will be reduced by the percent growth in energy productivity (energy productivity equals the amount of GDP per unit of energy consumed). Obviously, lower economic growth rates will reduce the amount of energy consumed relative to current levels. In the transition phase, as caps on greenhouse gas emissions are being introduced, it is unlikely that significant constraints on growth will occur. The restraints will come later once limits on renewable energy supplies are reached.

41. As noted above, the "no regrets" amount of energy conservation possible at zero net cost is around 30 percent. See Cline, *The Economics of Global Warming*, 203–207.

42. This assumes that the United States is responsible for reducing carbon emissions in proportion to global emissions reductions.

43. The amount of fossil-fuel consumption in the United States in 1999 amounted to 96.6 $\times$ 10^{15} Btu's (fn. 30). At 12 percent efficiency, 8.18 $\times$ 10^9 Btu's of solar energy can be produced per hectare of land using photovoltaics. Efficiency will no doubt be higher than that, but a lower figure accounts in part for transmission losses and losses in conversion to other forms of energy such as hydrogen.

44. Of the 15,000 square feet needed per household, 10 percent would amount to 1,500. A typical house would have to be, say, 50 by 30 feet and have a relatively flat roof to provide 10 percent of energy requirements on average. Shading by trees would reduce the usable area as well. The square footage of a median housing unit in 1999 was 1,685, which means the median footprint square footage is likely much less because of multistory dwellings. U.S. Bureau of the Census, *American Housing Survey for the United States: 1999* (Washington, D.C.: U.S. Government Printing Office, 2003, http://www.census.gov/hhes/www/housing/ahs/ahs99/tab1a3.html), Table 1A-3.

45. See chapter 5.

46. Donald M. Waller, "Getting Back to the Right Nature: A Reply to Cronon's 'The Trouble with Wilderness,'" in *The Great New Wilderness Debate*, ed. J. Baird Callicott and Michael P. Nelson (Athens, Ga.: University of Georgia Press, 1998), 541–67; Holmes Rolston III, *Genes, Genesis, and God: Values and their Origins in Natural and Human History* (Cambridge: Cambridge University Press, 1999), 108–59.

47. Reed F. Noss and Allen Y. Cooperrider, *Saving Nature's Legacy: Protecting and Restoring Biodiveristy* (Washington, D.C.: Island Press, 1994), 89–90.

48. The term "seral" refers to the steps in the growth and development of plant life in an ecosystem after a major disturbance. Ten years after a forest fire, a forest's plant life will be quite different from its plant life two hundred years later.

49. Noss and Cooperrider, *Saving Nature's Legacy*, 148.

50. Noss and Cooperrider, *Saving Nature's Legacy*, 129–77.

51. Reed F. Noss, Michael A. O'Connell, and Dennis D. Murphy, *The Science of Conservation Planning: Habitat Conservation Under the Endangered Species Act* (Washington, D.C.: Island Press, 1997), 4–5.

52. Ian L. McHarg, "The Place of Nature in the City of Man," in *Western Man and Environmental Ethics: Attitudes toward Nature and Technology*, ed. Ian G. Barbour (Reading, Mass.: Addison-Wesley Publishing Company, 1973), 180.

53. Ian L. McHarg, *Design With Nature* (Garden City, N.Y.: Natural History Press, 1969), 19.

54. McHarg, "The Place of Nature in the City of Man," 183.

55. For more on the role of the automobile in cities, see the above discussion and Newman and Kenworthy, *Sustainability and Cities*.

56. For a discussion of mountain West growth issues, see my *Searching for Paradise: Economic Development and Environmental Change in the Mountain West* (Lanham, Md.: Rowman & Littlefield, 2002).

57. Julie A. Gustanski and Roderick H. Squires, *Protecting the Land: Conservation Easements Past, Present, and Future* (Washington, D.C.: Island Press, 2000).

58. Booth, *Searching for Paradise*, 169–202.

59. Jim Howe, Ed McMahon, and Luther Propst, *Balancing Nature and Commerce in Gateway Communities* (Washington, D.C.: Island Press, 1997), 56 and 74.

60. Phone conversation with Susan Dorsey Otis, Director of the Yampa Valley Land Trust, July, 2001.

61. Howe et al., *Balancing Nature and Commerce in Gateway Communities*, 80–83.

62. Gallatin County Planning Board, *Zoning District Model* (Bozeman, Mont.: Gallatin County, 1996), 1–5.

63. Gallatin County Planning Department, *Springhill Planning and Zoning District* (Bozeman, Mont., 1992); Conversation with Jim Madden of the Gallatin Valley Land Trust, July, 2001.

64. See chapter 5.

65. Peter M. Vitousek et al., "Biological Invasions as Global Environmental Change," *American Scientist* 84 (1996): 468–78.

66. U.S. Congress, Office of Technology Assessment, *Harmful Non-Indigenous Species in the United States*, OTA-F-565 (Washington, D.C.: U.S. Government Printing Office, 1993), 287–91.

67. U.S. Congress, Office of Technology Assessment, *Harmful Non-Indigenous Species in the United States*, 137–43, 168–69, 170–77, 184–85; Chris Bright, *Life Out of Bounds: Bioinvasions in a Borderless World* (New York: W. W. Norton, 1998), 213.

68. Bright, *Life Out of Bounds*, 202.

69. Bright, *Life Out of Bounds*, 202–203.

70. Bright, *Life Out of Bounds*, 216.

71. U.S. Congress, Office of Technology Assessment, *Harmful Non-Indigenous Species in the United States*, 161.

72. See chapter 5 for a discussion of exotics in the Great Lakes.

73. Bright, *Life Out of Bounds*, 111–12.

74. See U.S. Congress, Office of Technology Assessment, *Harmful Non-Indigenous Species in the United States*, 143–62.

75. David Pimentel et al., "Environmental and Economic Costs of Nonindigenous Species in the United States," *Bioscience* 50 (2000): 53–65. APHIS spent approximately $106 million in 1992 on agricultural inspection and quarantine. U.S. Congress, Office of Technology Assessment, *Harmful Non-Indigenous Species in the United States*, 173.

76. Bright, *Life Out of Bounds*, 224–26.

77. Bruno S. Fey and Alois Stutzer, *Happiness and Economics: How the Economy and Institutions Affect Well-being* (Princeton, N.J.: Princeton University Press, 2002), 75–76.

78. Daniel Kahneman, "Objective Happiness," in *Well-Being: The Foundations of Hedonic Psychology*, ed. Daniel Kahneman, Ed Diener, and Norbert Schwartz (New York: Russell Sage Foundation: 1999), 3–25; Robert H. Frank, *Luxury Fever: Money and Happiness in an Era of Excess* (Princeton, N.J.: Princeton University Press), 1999, 159–60. See chapter 2 for a more detailed discussion of the link between economics and happiness.

79. This assumes a proportionate relationship between hours and output. A 1 percent reduction in hours leads to a 1 percent reduction in output. If there are diminishing returns to labor at the margin, then something less than a 1 percent reduction in hours would be needed to reduce output by 1 percent.

80. The classic work on this topic is Juliet B. Schor, *The Overworked American: The Unexpected Decline of Leisure* (New York: Basic Books, 1991). See also Juliet B. Schor, "Working Hours and Time Pressure: The Controversy about Trends in Time Use," in *Working Time: International Trends, Theory and Policy Perspectives*, ed. Lonnie Golden and Deborah M. Figart (London: Routledge, 2000), 73–86; Barry Bluestone and Stephen Rose, "The Enigma of Working Time," in *Working Time: International Trends, Theory and Policy Perspectives*, ed. Lonnie Golden and Deborah M. Figart (London: Routledge, 2000), 21–37; and Jerry A. Jacobs and Kathleen Gerson, "Who Are the Overworked Americans?" in *Working Time: International Trends, Theory and Policy Perspectives*, ed. Lonnie Golden and Deborah M. Figart (London: Routledge, 2000), 89–105.

81. Jacobs and Gerson, "Who Are the Overworked Americans?" 95–99.

82. Schor, *The Overworked American*, 128–32.

83. William K. Roche, Brian Fynes, and Terri Morrissey, "Working Time and Employment: A Review of International Evidence," *International Labour Review* 135 (1996): 129–57; Michael Marti, "Substitution between Working hours and

Employment: An Empirical Analysis for Switzerland," *Journal of Economics and Statistics* 136 (2000): 397–415; Christian Dreger, Olaf Fuchs, and Jurgen Kolb, "The Effection of a Reduction in Working Hours on Employment: Empirical Evidence for West-Germany," *Journal of Economics* 27 (2001): 69–81.

84. A. H. G. M. Spithoven, "The Third Way: The Dutch Experience," *Economy and Society* 31 (2002): 333–68; Petri Bockerman and Jaakko Kiander, "Has Work-Sharing Worked in Finland?" *Applied Economic Letters* 9 (2002): 39–41; Gerhard Bosch, "Working Time Reductions, Employment Consequences and Lessons from Europe: Defusing a Quasi-Religious Controversy," in *Working Time: International Trends, Theory and Policy Perspectives*, ed. Lonnie Golden and Deborah M. Figart (London: Routledge, 2000), 179–95.

85. Spithoven, "The Third Way: The Dutch Experience."

86. Bosch, "Working Time Reductions, Employment Consequences and Lessons from Europe," 192–93.

87. The focus of attention here is on environmental improvement in affluent societies. Population growth is clearly a potential source of added pressure on environmental resources and increases labor-force growth, causing expansion in the economic speed limit for the economy and the amount of growth needed to avoid unemployment. Getting unhooked from growth if population is growing rapidly is more of a challenge than if population is stable. Most affluent countries are approaching population stability because of diminishing fertility rates approaching two-plus births per couple, enough for a simple replacement of population in the long term. Population growth in affluent countries for this reason is not a major issue. It is a huge issue in less affluent countries where fertility rates are quite high, and such rapid population expansion can affect population growth in affluent countries by stimulating migration. See the World Resources Institute, *World Resources: 1998–99* (Oxford University Press, 1998) for global population data.

7

Environmental Values
and Getting Unhooked
from Growth

W hy would anyone ever want to undertake the rather drastic steps
set out in the previous chapter for getting unhooked from growth?
Today most Americans live comfortably and decently and would not
want to endanger their prosperity for trivial reasons. To do what is required to avoid global warming or to limit the spread of human population across the landscape is going to bring costs to the American public
without bringing much in the way of near-term benefits. Substantially
cutting greenhouse gas emissions today will have no perceptible impact
on the climate today or any time soon. Only in the distant future will
such cuts matter. To be willing to do anything about global warming requires, at a minimum, some level of concern for the well-being of future
generations.

Even if concern for future generations is prevalent, a compelling rationale for cutting greenhouse gases may still be absent. By the sheer force
of compound economic growth rates, future generations will be materially better off than present. If the global economy grows by only 2 percent
per year, in a century it will be seven times the size it is today. Surely in
such a massive global economy sufficient resources will be available to
adapt to the problems of a warmer world and still leave everyone materially better off.

In these circumstances a future-generations-based utilitarian-style ethical rationale for containing global warming doesn't seem very convincing. Without our doing anything at all, future generations will inevitably be better off materially than we are today. Other grounds are needed for conserving environmental resources. Global warming, the spreading of human population over the landscape, and the invasion of exotic species will all bring substantial ecological disruption and cause the endangerment of numerous plant and animal species. One cannot say for sure how intensely future generations will value environmental resources. The loss of a diverse natural environment could be so deeply felt that future generations might see themselves as worse off despite their improved material circumstances. Additional economic growth may not be enough to compensate for such a serious loss. If this is the case, then to leave future generations no worse off than present requires preserving a diverse natural environment and serious conservation efforts by the present generation.

Concern for future generations need not be the sole basis for preserving the natural world. As already mentioned in earlier chapters, human beings may see a diverse nature as valuable for its own sake apart from human material concerns. For the sake of nature itself, many in society may want to put environmental protection ahead of economic well-being so long as material standards are not reduced to the point where it is impossible to live a decent life. What kind of ethical thinking would justify such a position? A good place to begin seeking an answer to this question is Aldo Leopold's land ethic.

ALDO LEOPOLD'S LAND ETHIC: AN INTERPRETATION

Anyone interested in the topic of environmental ethics is well advised to begin with Aldo Leopold and his widely acclaimed work, *A Sand County Almanac*. Leopold was a wildlife ecologist who worked for many years in the U.S. Forest Service and later taught at the University of Wisconsin in its wildlife conservation program. Although he was not trained in ethics or philosophy, most environmental philosophers look to Leopold's "land ethic" as the inaugurating work of their discipline.[1]

Leopold begins his discussion of ethics with the famous Greek myth about Odysseus. For Odysseus, who hanged a dozen slave-girls for suspected misbehavior on his return from Troy, slaves were property and treated no differently from any other material instruments. They were a means to an end. Odysseus had no obligation to them as human beings and they had no rights. Since the days of Odysseus, the idea of an obligation not to harm other human beings without good reason has become widely accepted and the view that one person can own and treat another solely as an instrument has been largely rejected.[2] The circle of ethical concern has widened to include all human subjects irrespective of their material role or class position. Slaves in Greek society were not true members of the community and were not accorded the rights of a community member; today slavery is illegal. The concept of community membership has been extended to all human beings. This does not mean that we live in a perfect world. There is still much suffering and human exploitation. It simply means that ethical practices have evolved and the realm of ethical concern has expanded in time.

The essence of ethical behavior is restraint. Behavior is altered or restricted for the purpose of preventing harm to someone or something. Leopold defines ethical behavior as follows:

> An ethic, ecologically, is a limitation on freedom of action in the struggle for existence. An ethic, philosophically, is a differentiation of social from anti-social conduct. These are two definitions of one thing.[3]

Ethical standards emerge from cooperative social practices.[4] Cooperation and community are essential to human survival and prosperity. In order to cooperate we need to get along and to avoid conflict. This is facilitated by ethical standards. Ethical standards are different from rules. Rules are obeyed under the fear of punishment. Ethics are norms of behavior accepted voluntarily out of a sense of community solidarity. Of course, since human beings are imperfect and suffer from weakness of will, ethical norms are often incorporated into rules and laws.

According to Leopold, no ethic yet exists for dealing with the relationship of human beings to the "land." By the "land," Leopold means plants, animals, and their ecological relationships, or, more generally, ecological systems. Thus far, human beings with few exceptions have treated the land just as Odysseus dealt with his slave-girls—strictly as a means to serve human ends. As the scale of social interaction has increased—we now live in a global society—so has the scope of ethical concern. Leopold suggests that the next logical, evolutionary step is to extend ethical concern to the land. Why? Ethics originate in community interaction and interdependence. We are all part of the land community.[5] "The land ethic simply enlarges the boundaries of the community to include soils, waters, plants, and animals, or collectively: the land."[6] The essential point that Leopold makes is that ethical practices evolve as the conception of community membership changes. Recognition of membership in the "land community" calls for still another change in ethical practice.

This is a big step to take, to think of ourselves as more than just members of human groupings. Although we have little choice in the matter of community membership—we are born into particular political jurisdictions and networks of social organizations—we do benefit from being a part of a larger human community both materially and emotionally. Social interaction is important to us for its intrinsic enjoyment as well as for the attainment of common ends. No doubt if we had a choice we would seek the company of others.

To take this idea of belonging to a community beyond its usual human associations involves seeing elements of nature as more than just instruments for our own benefit. Just as we use other human beings to achieve material ends, so would we continue to use plants and animals and the ecological settings in which they reside. Just as we hire plumbers to unplug our pipes or policemen to protect us from criminals, we will still cut down trees for lumber to build our houses or catch fish to feed ourselves. But our attitude would now differ. We would see elements of the natural world as having value in their own right, just as we do with human beings. This doesn't mean that obligations to the natural world would be greater than our human obligations. It means simply that we extend moral concern beyond the strictly human. Leopold puts it as follows:

> a land ethic changes the role of *Homo sapiens* from conqueror of the land-community to plain member and citizen of it. It implies respect for his fellow-members, and also respect for the community as such.[7]

How can such an ethical extension occur? The first step, according to Leopold, is the development of an ecological conscience. We need to understand that the land is a complex living system of interdependent pieces. We also need to understand that human practices historically have been very damaging to the land and to the organisms it supports. "No important change in ethics was ever accomplished without an internal change in our intellectual emphasis, affections, and convictions."[8] Only by gaining knowledge of the land and its complexities can we develop respect and affection for it. Essentially, to internalize a land ethic, we need to recognize that we are a part of the land community and that we have an emotional tie to it. "It is inconceivable to me that an ethical relation to land can exist without love, respect, and admiration for land, and a high regard for its value."[9] Respect is the critical element. But before respect comes consciousness and understanding.

In liberal societies the idea of respect for the human individual is manifested as human rights, which are explicitly or implicitly codified in the constitutional arrangements for political and legal institutions. Rights are usually thought of in connection with duties. A right to freedom of speech carries with it an obligation to respect the same right for others. Respect for the natural world can also be expressed in the form of rights, although the domain of possible rights is more limited than in the human case. Normal predator-prey relationships render infeasible the protection of an individual animal living in a natural community. Since the human species is a part of the food chain, survival requires the consumption of individual plants or animals. We need trees and fish to live. Respectful treatment of plants and animals can nonetheless be demonstrated by conferring rights for the continued existence of particular kinds of organisms or even particular types of ecosystems. In such cases human exploitation of a particular species would be limited in order to avoid its extinction. Similarly, exploitation of particular kinds of ecosystems would be limited to ensure their continued presence and healthful functioning. Conscious reciprocity in the form of duties from species or ecosystems, of course, cannot be expected. Conferring a right to exist on kinds of organisms or ecosystems is simply a demonstration of respect and an expression of the idea that certain pieces of nature ought to have a right to exist. Leopold articulates something like this when he suggests that a "land ethic of course cannot prevent the alteration, management and use of these 'resources,' but it does affirm their right to continued existence." Leopold offers further support for this notion when he claims that "birds should continue as a matter of biotic right, regardless of the presence or absence of economic advantage to us."[10]

Ethics involves specific standards, and the fundamental standard suggested by Leopold for the "land ethic" is as follows: "A thing is right when it tends to preserve the integrity, stability, and beauty of the biotic community. It is wrong when it tends otherwise."[11] This is a very broad and general standard and requires interpretation for specific cases. The focus on stability is perhaps misplaced, given the modern view that many ecosystems experience fluctuations in species populations and undergo change over time as various disturbances occur such as fire, wind storms, pest outbreaks, or shifts in climate. Still, the basic idea is to preserve ecological systems and protect their health and the species they contain to the extent possible within the framework of natural disturbance patterns.

Although he is not very optimistic about the land-use practices of his day, Leopold advocates the approach of adjusting the economy to the environment and reducing reliance on economic standards for deciding how to make use of the landscape. Leopold notes that "Land-use ethics are still governed wholly by economic self-interest, just as social ethics were a century ago."[12] Wisconsin farmers in the 1930s, for instance, engaged in conservation practices only to the extent that an immediate economic return was forthcoming, according to Leopold.[13] Most members of the land community are lacking in economic value, including in some cases entire biotic communities such as bogs and deserts. For this reason much of the land community receives little attention from economically oriented conservationists. According to Leopold, a system of conservation based solely on economic self-interest is hopelessly lopsided. It tends to ignore, and thus eventually to eliminate, many elements in the land community that lack commercial value, but that are (so far as we know) essential to its healthy functioning. It assumes, falsely, I think, that the economic parts of the biotic clock will function without the uneconomic parts.[14]

Leopold's response is to advocate a land ethic that goes beyond strictly economic criteria for making judgments about land-use practices. Such an ethic can only come into practice as a consequence of an understanding of ecological relationships and the development of an ecological conscience.[15] In the end an emotional connection to the land is an essential underpinning of an ethical relationship to the world of nature. The human species is necessarily a part of the land system in an economic sense, but this doesn't mean that economic standards are to be the only basis for deciding how land is to be used.

PHILOSOPHICAL ISSUES AND THE LAND ETHIC

Leopold's land ethic raises a host of interesting conceptual and philosophical questions about the meaning of such a moral commitment. What are the possible underlying human motivations for such an ethic? Why would anyone ever adopt it? Does the natural world truly have intrinsic value apart from human material interests? What exactly do land-ethic advocates value in the natural world? Is it individual organisms, species, or ecosystems? Where does a land ethic stand in comparison to other ethical commitments? These are challenging questions that have generated intense controversy among environmental philosophers.

A critical divide on the question of a justification for a land ethic is between "anthropocentrism" and "biocentrism." An anthropocentric approach to environmental ethics takes human beings as the object of moral concern and focuses on how the environment affects human welfare. A biocentric approach takes beings in the natural world to be objects of moral concern in and of themselves, apart from any benefit they provide to humans. The anthropocentric approach has the virtue of familiarity. The notion that human individuals are of value for their own sake is a common one that is widely supported. The idea that everyone should live decently, be treated justly, and be free to express opinions, practice religion, choose occupations, associate with others, and participate in the political process is hard to argue against. The right to life, liberty, and the pursuit of happiness is something most individuals are willing to defend not only for themselves but for the sake of others as well. Under the anthropocentric approach, the environment is treated as an instrument for human benefit. Environmental resources are to be defended, since they contribute to the well-being of present and future generations. Because of the importance of ecosystem services in supporting life in general and human well-being in particular, some argue that we need go no further than an anthropocentric environmental ethic to justify a serious commitment to environmental conservation.[16]

The trouble is, to satisfy material needs for a decent life, many people may want only the bare minimum in ecosystem services and a maximum possible stock of human artifacts. If this is the case, then attention to such problems as global warming or habitat loss is not so compelling. Many may be perfectly happy living in a material world dominated by human artifacts and may be content with human-constructed adaptations to environmental change. A strictly anthropocentric environmental ethic may not call for very much in the way of protection for the world of nature.

Fortunately for environmentalists, a significant proportion of the public in practice seems to have a more positive attitude toward the natural world than this. Many people seek and experience contact with natural environments and respond empathetically to what they find. They seem to accept that idea that nature is more than just an instrument and has value for more than strictly material ends. This kind of value offers a different kind of justification for a land ethic. In the terminology of Leopold, an "ecological conscience" rooted in the experience of nature engenders a desire to consider more than just human interests in decisions about human uses of the natural environment. Simply put, some may bring to the table of environmental decision making more than just an anthropocentric outlook. Ethics for them are not just anthropocentric but are biocentric as well. While human material interest in the environment is important, the world of nature deserves protection for its own sake apart from material concerns, according to biocentric environmental values. Although commitments to human individuals remain in place, an additional layer of ethical concern is added by those with a biocentric outlook.

A second critical divide in environmental philosophy is between those who see elements of the natural world as intrinsically valuable apart from the human valuer and those who see elements of the natural world as valuable only as a consequence of human valuations. The former argue that environmental values exist "objectively" in nature while the latter argue for environmental values on "subjective" grounds and claim that value without a human valuer cannot exist. According to the "subjectivists," valuing a natural being for its own sake is a human projection of value into nature. According to the principal proponent of the idea of "objective value," Holmes Rolston, III, *"intrinsic natural* value recognizes value inherent in some natural occasions, without contributory human reference."[17]

Whether something is a matter of ethical concern on "objectivist" grounds depends strictly on its characteristics. Under such an environmental ethic, anything organic that pursues its own good would be included. A population of a particular species, for instance, pursues its own continuation through reproduction and genetic adaptation to environmental conditions. Ironically, this is perhaps illustrated most succinctly in the world today by the successful adaptation of pest species populations to new kinds of agricultural pesticides. Individual organisms also count as intrinsically valuable since they pursue their own good through growth and reproduction. Elk defend the young of their kind against predation by wolves, while wolves prey on newborn elk to feed their own young. A young Douglas-fir tree races to the canopy to gain light energy that would otherwise go to its neighbors. Flowers produce sweet nectar to attract the pollinators they need for reproduction. For the objectivists, anything that is an end in itself and has a good of its own is intrinsically valuable and ought to be an object of moral concern.[18] It is the nature of the being that determines whether it is morally considerable, not the particular views of a valuing agent.[19] Objective environmental values are out there in nature only to be found by the perceptive observer.

Critics object to the notion of intrinsic value as something internally determined by the nature of beings in themselves. We cannot fully know the natural world outside of our own perceptions; we cannot look at the world through eyes other than our own. Insofar as we know, only conscious subjects can confer value on other beings. Value doesn't exist in nature; rather it is granted by the human valuer. This calls for a more subjective approach to environmental ethics.

A "subjectivist" and pragmatic environmental ethic results from the interplay of human psychology (capacity for empathy), historical experience, and social practice.[20] Value cannot be discussed independently of a valuing agent. Values from this point of view are a human creation and involve human perceptions and interactions with the world. The recognition of a larger biotic community and a feeling of identification with it can lead to an ethic that takes us beyond strictly instrumental valuations. We may come to feel as a consequence of our experiences in the world that it is simply the right thing to preserve ecosystems and species irrespective of positive human benefits. A scientist studying ecosystems may, for example, start by seeing the world in strictly instrumental terms but experience a change of attitudes towards ecosystems and species and come to feel that they have a right to exist apart from any benefit they provide. Learning to value the natural world for its own sake is the result of gaining an "ecological conscience." Such a conscience may also be a response to publicity about environmental threats (the Rachel Carson effect), increased exposure to environmental education, or perhaps increased outdoor recreation in natural habitats. Ethics don't come out of thin air. Historical, social, and cultural practices are the driving force in their emergence. Natural beings are not automatically objects of moral concern even if they pursue valued ends much as human beings do. It's not so much a discovery of values out there in nature as it is a change in our perceptions, in the way we see things. We see that we, too, are a part of the world of nature along with all other species. As the human genome project has shown, we don't differ genetically from other organisms by very much. We along with all other species are a product of the evolutionary process. We as a species possess the capacity for empathy, and seeing things in a new way can generate empathic feelings for other species and the ecological and evolutionary processes that bring forth the diversity of life present in the world today. As a result, we have the capacity to expand our circle of moral concern beyond the strictly human.

The qualities perceived in nature do matter for a subjectivist. We care that natural beings appear to have interests, organisms appear to perpetuate their species, and ecosystems appear to serve as incubators for new species. As a consequence of our human capacity for empathy and the scientific recognition that human beings, along with all other species, are the product of evolutionary processes, we may see the creative forces of evolution, ecosystems, species, and individual organisms as valuable for their own sake. Interestingly, such a response can be easily interpreted along "objectivist" lines as finding preexisting values in nature.

As a practical matter, objective and subjective approaches to valuing nature needn't be viewed as conflicting. Through our perceptual apparatus, something apart from us in nature is observed that stimulates our moral sensibilities, something that can never be fully experienced in all its details but something that is nonetheless real.[21] Our interpretation of what we see is necessarily influenced by our own experience and for this reason has a subjective quality. After reading a description of old-growth forest ecology, I go for a hike in a remnant old-growth forest somewhere in the Pacific Northwest. I observe the huge old trees that functionally dominate the ecological system through their massive ability to capture the energy of the sun. I also observe a pileated woodpecker, a trout jumping in a local stream, and flying squirrel leaping through the canopy, all of which are dependent ultimately on the big, old trees. These are things that concretely enter my perception. Combining my perceptions and my newfound knowledge of old-growth forests, I feel a new respect for the life I find on my hike and a greater commitment to defend old-growth remnant forests wherever they occur. "Objective" perceptions and "subjective" experience combine to bring forth altered values and commitments. The idea of "intrinsic value" in this more limited sense seems to address some of the key concerns expressed by its critics.

The critics of biocentric environmental ethics also frequently express concerns about how the objects of moral concern are defined or selected.[22] Paul Taylor, for example, focuses on individual organisms as teleological centers of life.[23] Does this mean that every mosquito and every baby salmon smolt deserves our moral attention and our equal concern? Why stop at individual organisms? Why not rocks, whose pattern of existence is defined by geological forces? In actual fact, the choice of objects of moral concern is a matter of personal judgment. Each of us must decide for ourselves when we have reached our threshold of moral concern. This doesn't necessarily mean that such choices are strictly arbitrary and relative. If Baird Callicott is right, human moral sentiments and their limits feature some level of behavioral uniformity and can in theory be discovered through historical, psychological, and sociological investigation.[24]

Given the way ecosystems work, nature itself places important limitations on what we as human beings can do to protect particular organisms. Millions of salmon smolt emerge from eggs laid in clear, flowing, gravel-bottomed mountain streams, but very few will survive the migration back down stream and mature to adulthood in ocean waters. There isn't much anyone can do about this. Nor is there much anyone can do about newborn elk that fall prey to wolves in Yellowstone National Park. To protect particular individual organisms in most cases is impractical and, ultimately, ecologically undesirable. After all, fish-feeding birds need juvenile salmon to survive, just as wolves need newborn elk. Our own participation in the global ecological system necessitates the killing and consuming of particular organisms. About all that can be done is to protect populations of particular species and the habitat they require from human-caused damage.[25] If it is individual organisms in nature that are objects of moral concern, in the end human action to protect them must necessarily be holistic in its emphasis. The actual focus of moral concern ultimately must be species populations and ecosystems. Nature draws the line for us in defining the feasible domain of our ethical attention. Whether it is individual organisms that are the fundamental objects of moral concern, or whether it is species populations or ecosystems in the end really doesn't matter. The protection of the individual requires the protection of the whole.[26] Aldo Leopold recognized this in his emphasis on the "land community" and ecological processes. To repeat, "A thing is right when it tends to preserve the integrity, stability, and beauty of the biotic community. It is wrong when it tends otherwise."[27]

A really fascinating book called *The Orchid Thief* about a horticulturist in Florida who steals wild orchids from natural areas inadvertently raises many of the issues covered by environmental ethics. The greatest prize of all for orchid lovers (and thieves) is the "ghost orchid," a truly beautiful flower only rarely encountered in the Florida swamps. A likely first reaction by readers of the book is that orchids are of exceptional beauty and, because they offer their viewer such sensual pleasure, are of significant human benefit. Many wild orchids no doubt exist unseen in the swamps of Florida. Shouldn't they be allowed to persist even if unseen and to be protected from orchid thieves and other human depredations? If the answer is yes, then what is the reasoning behind protection? Is the final goal to protect the individual orchid? After all, it does have a life of its own. It emerges from a seedling, grows, and flowers. Still, a deer or some other animal may come along and eat it. Individual orchids in the natural scheme of thing are hard to protect. Orchid thieves might be kept out of the swamp, but to do the same for deer and other animals is probably infeasible. A species population as a whole in a given habitat can nonetheless be defended. The swamps of Florida can be protected against damaging human incursions to give orchids a fighting chance for survival. But why would we want to protect a rarely observed species? Orchids are indeed exquisitely adapted to their environment. They are known for their intricate schemes of pollination, carefully designed to suit the needs of specific pollinators. In this way, orchids pursue the end of reproduction and survival through the medium of genetic adaptation. As a species they have what we would call intrinsic value. Those who know about orchids understand such behavior patterns. This understanding and the love of such beauty and life combine to form the desire to protect orchids. The recognition of intrinsic value in orchid species is an interactive process. Something in nature is discovered and that discovery stimulates certain human sentiments. The conferring of value on orchids is a subjective human act, but it can only be motivated by certain kinds of objective stimuli and knowledge. Even orchid thieves contribute through their discoveries, although they too must be restrained for the species' sake. A certain amount of thievery may be a good thing, but not too much.

ENVIRONMENTAL ETHICS AND SUSTAINABILITY

The notion of sustainability, as noted in the last chapter, carries with it a burden of ambiguity. To meet this concern, economists have defined the more specific notion of "weak sustainability." Under weak sustainability, the goal is to preserve the total stock of capital in a society, adding together the value of both human-produced and natural capital under the assumption that one can be substituted for the other. The capital value of the stock of swordfish in the ocean or old-growth forests in the Pacific Northwest can be withdrawn through harvesting and reinvested in business plant and equipment—factories for SUVs, for instance—that yield a greater return on investment. The act of drawing down the stock of natural capital goods and replacing it with human-produced goods presumes that both kinds of goods are commensurable and directly substitutable, one for the other. If everyone in society were a utilitarian where all goods are judged according to the same standard of measure, then weak sustainability would be the appropriate criterion for protecting the ability for successive generations to obtain at least as much utility in their daily lives as previous generations.

If viable populations of swordfish and old-growth forest ecosystems are considered different from typical consumer goods, then the notion of substitutability becomes more constrained. The value of continuously reproducing swordfish populations or healthy old-growth ecosystems may well trump the value of ordinary consumer goods. If so, the notion of "strong sustainability" replaces weak, and human-made capital goods cannot substitute for natural capital. Ethical valuations under such a scheme take precedence over ordinary economic valuations. Technically speaking, this amounts to lexicographical orderings of states of the world. This is a big word that refers to simple orderings of the kind exhibited by the alphabet. All A-words come before B-words, and all B-words come before C-words or D-words. The protection of swordfish populations and old-growth forests under such a scheme could well come before the acquisition of consumer goods to demonstrate status or avoid boredom. On the other hand, the material requirements of a decent life for individuals employed in the forest products industry would no doubt enter into an ethical evaluation of the old-growth forest conservation issue for most people and could well trump the protection of old-growth forests.

Both Baird Callicott and Peter Wenz have used the metaphor of widening concentric circles to describe patterns of ethical evaluations.[28] Occupants of the inner circles, such as family and friends, would take precedence in most ethical decisions over occupants on the outer circles, such as the local neighborhood community, the nation as a whole, and nonhuman species or particular ecological systems. The preservation of old-growth forest ecosystems on an outer ring, for example, may be favored only if displaced forest-products workers on an inner circle can find alternative means of employment that offer a reasonable standard of living. The acceptability of the idea of "strong sustainability" and the trumping of economic by environmental values will be conditional in practice and dependent on specific circumstances. The notion of concentric circles of ethical concern embodies nicely the idea that not all ethical commitments are created equal. For most of us, a standard of living essential for a decent life occupies an inner circle and comes before environmental concerns on an outer circle. For those among us having biocentric environmental values, however, occupants of an outer concentric ring, such as particular species or ecosystems, will trump economic activity needed exclusively for fueling the status-consumption arms race or the inessential acquisition of consumer novelties.

The notions of intrinsic value (as qualified by the above discussion), value-trumping, and strong sustainability are logically connected in the ethical evaluation of specific environmental issues. This can be seen in the discussion of global warming in the previous chapter. The most stringent feasible limits on global warming prevent CO_2 from rising above 450 ppm of ambient concentration. The cost of this limit in terms of global GDP given up could be as much as 4 percent annually. Since the relatively affluent countries of the world emit most of the greenhouse gases, they are the ones who will bear most of the cost, particularly if emission-allowance trading arrangements are established, with a distribution of allowances based heavily on population. Under such a scheme, a country like China, with its very low greenhouse gas emissions per capita, will have more emission allowances than it needs and will be able to sell those allowances to affluent countries and to use the proceeds to fund its own long-term emission control requirements. Such a trading scheme could increase the cost for the United States somewhat, perhaps to 5 or 6 percent of GDP, during the transition to an energy system based on renewable sources.

The point of such a stringent limit on greenhouse gases is mostly for the protection of species and ecosystems. Human societies can probably adapt to global warming while species and ecosystems are less able to, as noted in the last chapter. In fact, the economic burden of global warming is likely to be quite affordable, simply because of the normal pace of economic expansion. A $10 trillion U.S. economy today will expand to $72 trillion economy in a century at a 2 percent annual growth rate. Even if the human adjustment to global warming cost as much as half of what our total economy can produce today, it would still only be around 7 percent of GDP in a hundred years. That human adjustment to global warming is probably quite affordable takes away the justification for sacrificing very much today to limit global warming.

But what about our fellow travelers on the planet? The evidence of the effects of global warming on species and ecosystems presented in chapter 5 suggests that natural ecosystems will be significantly damaged and numerous species are likely to go extinct. If species and ecosystems have intrinsic value, then their protection trumps economic goods not essential for living decently. Intrinsic value trumps economic values. If, however, the cost of limiting global warming results in a substantial increase in the incidence of poverty, then economic values may well trump the intrinsic value of species and ecosystems harmed by global warming. In the concentric circles scheme, basic human well-being for the poorest among us occupies a more central position and trumps ecosystems and species occupying positions farther from the center.[29]

As suggested in the last chapter, strategies to limit global warming will likely result in a less consumption-oriented society, but need not substantially reduce the quality of life. First and foremost, existing air pollution problems will virtually disappear under a regime of strict limits on greenhouse emissions. Indeed, to the degree that more pedestrian-friendly forms of urban design are implemented to improve energy efficiency and reduce greenhouse emissions, in at least some dimensions the quality of life could actually improve, as noted in the last chapter. Also, the shift to an environmentally friendly economy featuring lower rates of economic expansion need not result in rising unemployment and can lead to increased leisure, as also argued in the last chapter. This leaves the question of where the relative economic burden of limitations on greenhouse gases will fall. If it is unduly on the poor, then economic values in the eyes of many will trump environmental values.

In theory, the tax system and social welfare programs could be used to offset any special burdens from controlling global warming for society's poorest. Social welfare benefits could be increased and low-income tax burdens reduced for the lowest 20 percent of the population and paid for with increased taxes on the wealthiest 20 percent, at least in theory. The top fifth of households received 49.1 percent of aggregate income in the United States in 1994. This figure is up from 43 percent in 1969. Imposing the full 6 percent cost of greenhouse gas restrictions on the top fifth would amount to returning the top fifth of households to the share of aggregate income they received in 1969. Since the 1960s was a period of record growth in productivity, there isn't much evidence that a more equitable distribution of income distorts economic incentives for efficient production, as some economists might argue.[30] The politics of income redistribution will no doubt continue to be challenging, but probably not much more challenging than the politics of limiting global warming. If limiting global warming is ever politically feasible, redistributing the cost burden of doing so from poor to rich will probably be politically feasible as well. One strategy for income redistribution that blends nicely with reductions in greenhouse gases is the issuing of carbon emissions allowances on a per capita basis. Since energy consumption tends to rise with income, low-income families will have surplus allowances that can be sold to high-income families.

With measures to offset any special burdens on the poor, the costs of limiting global warming would no longer trump the intrinsic value of species and ecosystems dependent on climate stability. With the cost being borne by the wealthy, the burden will fall on the consumption of goods acquired for demonstrating status or experiencing the psychological stimuli of the new and the novel. Given that the economic cost of controlling greenhouse gases needn't cause anyone to forgo a decent standard of living, land ethic advocates can legitimately argue that the intrinsic value of species and ecosystems trumps economic value and that the final result of environmental policy ought to be "strong sustainability" and a stable climate. Otherwise, we in human society would bear the moral burden of putting a nontrivial dent in the diversity of life created by the very same evolutionary process responsible for our own existence.

ENVIRONMENTAL ETHICS IN PRACTICE

In the end, this debate over the ethical foundations of environmental values is important in a democratic society only to the extent that the public participates in it. If environmental ethics is not a part of the larger public discourse, then debates among academics will have little effect in the world of social and political decision making. Does the public in fact express values anything like those discussed by environmental philosophers?

In the real world of values, pluralism reigns. While each of us ultimately must have an internally consistent scheme of values for resolving the multitude of choices and moral dilemmas we face on a daily basis, values across human populations can be vastly different.[31] Attitudes toward specific issues, such as the problem of global warming, can be fueled by a wide array of underlying value commitments. Republicans, Democrats, Libertarians, Christians, Deep Ecologists, Pantheists, Buddhists, Muslims, Free Market Economists, College Graduates, the Rich, and the Poor will all look at environmental problems somewhat differently.[32] The process by which such values are reconciled and environmental policy emerges is a central concern of the "environmental pragmatists," a group of environmental philosophers who draw on the intellectual traditions of American pragmatists such as William James and John Dewey. Members of this group argue that in reality individuals have diverse values and interests, that the focus of attention should be the seeking out of common ground on solutions to environmental problems, and that the debate over ethical valuation of the natural world is largely a distraction.[33] They argue in favor of elevating democratic processes in the resolution of environmental problems and believe that through political participation and discourse, diverse value commitments can be reconciled and pragmatic solutions can be found. Pragmatists suggest that a monistic commitment to biocentrism and intrinsic value will lead to exclusion and division in environmental debates and be counterproductive.[34]

The pragmatists indeed make an important point about the importance of democracy to environmental decision making. After all, the only reason we have the Clean Air Act, the Clean Water Act, the Endangered Species Act, and a variety of other legislation is the growth of public concern over a deteriorating environment and the rising up of new political interest groups in the 1960s and 1970s in a period of "alarmed discovery and euphoric enthusiasm" for environmental issues, as Anthony Downs would put it.[35]

The pragmatists unfortunately fail to recognize that the notion of intrinsic value in nature can be looked at in another way, one that is actually favorable to the reconciliation of differing views. Underlying the diversity of beliefs and values observed in the world there may well exist common threads and themes. One of these could very well be the idea that the world of nature has value in itself apart from any instrumental benefits to human beings. The literature on environmental values clearly suggests a diversity of beliefs about the natural world. A widely used vehicle for measuring environmental attitudes in survey research is the New Environmental Paradigm (NEP) scale. Large majorities in many studies respond positively to such NEP statements as the following: (1) humans should adapt to nature rather than modify it to suit us; (2) a change in basic attitudes and values is necessary in order to solve environmental problems; (3) humans are presently interfering too much with the natural environment.[36] Other studies find respondent agreement with the notions that nature is "God's creation" and shouldn't be abused, nature should be "preserved for future generations," and "species have a right to evolve" without human interference.[37]

One of the studies is of special interest because it uses question statements formulated in focus groups without the prompting of survey researchers, and it surveys not only the public at large, but specific special-interest groups including Earth First! (a relatively radical environmental group) and the Sierra Club (a relatively moderate environmental group), as well as groups hurt by environmental regulations, such as laid-off sawmill workers in Oregon. Even though Earth First! members and sawmill workers likely have quite different outlooks on life, 76 percent and 78 percent of the two groups, respectively, agree that "because God created the natural world, it is wrong to abuse it." Also, for Earth First! members, sawmill workers, and the public, 100, 82, and 93 percent, respectively, agree that "we aren't justified in using resources to benefit only the current generation if that creates problems for future generations." Finally, the respective proportions in agreement with the following statement for the three groups are 100 percent, 59 percent, and 87 percent: "All species have a right to evolve without human interference. If extinctions are going to happen, it should happen naturally, not through human actions." Given that sawmill workers suffer unemployment partly because of efforts to protect endangered species, it is surprising that their positive response to this question is as high as it is. The critical point of this research is that a high level of agreement on environmental attitudes exists across groups likely to have vastly different values. Despite social differences, there indeed appears to be a common ground for agreement on environmental issues in the form of a belief in rights for species.

Support for environmental issues, however, ends when more personal value commitments are threatened. Agreement with the following statement by Earth First! members, sawmill workers, and the public was respectively 13, 70, and 70 percent: "My first duty is to feed my family. The environment and anything else has to come after this." Sierra Club members were close to the public on this issue, with 73 percent of members agreeing with the statement.[38] Even mainstream environmentalists agree that commitments nearer to the core (inner concentric circles) of most peoples' ethical concerns take precedence over environmental issues. Only radical environmentalists disagree.

The closest most survey research studies of environmental attitudes come to the notion of intrinsic value is in questions addressing the rights of species or individual plants and animals to exist. As already noted, agreement with such rights is fairly high for the public at large as well as particular interest groups. Human rights are normally justified on the grounds that human beings are "ends-in-themselves."[39] Extending this logic, the rights of species to exist implies that they are "ends-in-themselves" and have a good of their own. This is essentially the meaning of intrinsic value. Wide agreement on species rights suggests that diverse interests accept the notion of species having value for their own sake. Of course, different people may justify this view for quite different reasons. Christians, for example, may justify the intrinsic value of species on stewardship grounds. Species as creations of God have value in their own right and humans as stewards of God's creation need to protect those rights. Sierra Club members who are not Christians may come to their support for the intrinsic value of species as a result of their own personal experience in the natural world and acquisition of an "ecological conscience" as discussed by Leopold in the *Sand County Almanac*. This suggests that there is no real inconsistency between moral pluralism and the notion of intrinsic value in the natural world. The pragmatists are right about the presence and importance of moral pluralism, but there isn't any real inconsistency between pluralism and the notion of nature having value for its own sake. Intrinsic value may well be the source of agreement on environmental issues over a broad cross-section of the public.

A recent extension of the NEP scale for measuring environmental attitudes for the first time explicitly confirms that the intrinsic value of the natural environment is a widely held belief. A study of environmental values for a diverse population sample and members of environmental groups in England finds that 97 percent of environmental group members and 96 percent of the public agree with the following statement: "The natural environment has value within itself regardless of any value humans may place on it." Similar results are also found in the same study for statements about humans having moral duties to elements of the natural environment. In my own research on an urban river in Milwaukee, Wisconsin, 78 percent of respondents to a survey agree with the following statement: "The health of urban rivers should be improved for the sake of nature itself."[40] Both of these studies suggest that a relatively large portion of the public accepts the notion that intrinsic values are present in the natural world.

CONCLUSION

What exactly is significant about the acceptance of the idea that species or ecosystems have intrinsic value and rights to exist? What is important about the values of the kind professed in Aldo Leopold's Land Ethic? Such values offer support for the approach of ecological economics in deciding on what should be done about critical environmental issues of the day. The belief that something has intrinsic value implies a commitment to defend its continued existence, or, essentially, that it has a right to exist. Rights are never absolute. Species threatened by global warming, habitat loss, and invasive exotic organisms don't have an absolute right to exist if their defense causes a larger moral harm to something of greater ethical importance. If halting global warming or the spreading of human population into natural habitats is so costly that it results in rising poverty and substantial human misery, then most of us would no doubt agree that the pursuit of such environmental improvements should be given up. Commitments to the opportunity for our fellow human beings to live decently are at the center of moral concern for most of us, while commitments to species and ecosystems occur farther out on our concentric circles of ethical importance. On the other hand, a commitment to the rights of nature implies a willingness to forgo material goods not essential to living a decent life and to avoid trading off such goods against the survival of species and ecosystems. This is exactly the approach of ecological economics—select key environmental commitments and adjust the economy to fulfill those commitments.[41] Don't trade off natural capital in favor of human-made capital.

In the last chapter, strategies were presented for dealing with the critical environmental problems of global warming, the spreading of human population into important natural habitats, and the global movement of exotic species to new environments. The price to pay for dealing with these problems is getting unhooked from perpetual growth in consumption that is really only necessary to fuel the arms race in conspicuous consumption and the psychic stimulus of consumer novelties. Conspicuous consumption, like any arms race, doesn't result in greater well-being, and the pleasure of novelty in consumption is replaceable by the more intangible but fundamental joys of life. The sacrifices required to meet public moral commitments to ecological conservation are not so burdensome as to create a larger moral harm. If this is the case, why isn't more being done about the big environmental problems of the day? This is the central question to be addressed in the final chapter.

NOTES

1. Aldo Leopold, *A Sand County Almanac: With Essays on Conservation from Round River* (New York: Ballantine Books, 1970).
2. Leopold, *A Sand County Almanac*, 237–38.
3. Leopold, *A Sand County Almanac*, 238.
4. Leopold, *A Sand County Almanac*, 238–39.
5. Leopold, *A Sand County Almanac*, 237–39.
6. Leopold, *A Sand County Almanac*, 239.
7. Leopold, *A Sand County Almanac*, 240.
8. Leopold, *A Sand County Almanac*, 246.
9. Leopold, *A Sand County Almanac*, 261.
10. Leopold, *A Sand County Almanac*, 240, 247.
11. Leopold, *A Sand County Almanac*, 262.
12. Leopold, *A Sand County Almanac*, 245.
13. Leopold, *A Sand County Almanac*, 244.
14. Leopold, *A Sand County Almanac*, 251.
15. Leopold, *A Sand County Almanac*, 258–64.
16. Bryan G. Norton, "Why I Am Not a Nonanthropocentrist: Callicott and the Failure of Monistic Inherentism," *Environmental Ethics* 17 (1995): 341–58.
17. Homes Rolston III, "Are Values in Nature Subjective or Objective," *Environmental Ethics* 4 (1982): 125–51.
18. Paul W. Taylor refers to such organisms as having a teleological center of life in his "The Ethics of Respect for Nature," *Environmental Ethics* 3 (1981): 197–218.
19. However, Taylor argues that an attitude of respect for nature is necessary to recognize that intrinsically valuable beings in nature are objects of moral concern. See Taylor, "The Ethics of Respect for Nature," 204. Taylor distinguishes between intrinsic value, the realization of the good of an organism, and inherent worth, a good that is worthy of the concern of moral agents.
20. J. Baird Callicott, a major proponent of a subjectivist approach, argues that the moral sentiments originate in human evolution and are extendable to the natural world. See his "Hume's *Is/Ought* Dichotomy and the Relation of Ecology to Leopold's Land Ethic," *Environmental Ethics* 4, (1982): 163–74. See also Callicott's "Intrinsic Value, Quantum Theory, and Environmental Ethics," *Environmental Ethics* 7 (1985): 257–75.

21. This is, I think, the essential point of Christopher J. Preston's conclusions about the notion of intrinsic value in his "Epistemology and Intrinsic Values: Norton and Callicott's Critiques of Rolston," *Environmental Ethics* 20 (1998): 409–28. Even though intrinsic value in practice can never be free of subjective qualities, to argue for nonsubjective qualities in nature is a reasonable thing to do so long as it is recognized that those qualities are filtered through a subjective perceptual apparatus and that any such knowledge claims are subject to perceptual modification and are thus revisable. It is still possible to observe that organisms out there in the world have a good of their own. This can in turn stimulate our human moral sensibilities.

22. For example, see Jana Thompson, "A Refutation of Environmental Ethics," *Environmental Ethics* 12 (1990): 147–60, and also Norton, "Why I Am Not a Nonanthropocentrist," 347–48.

23. Taylor, "The Ethics of Respect for Nature," 210–11.

24. Callicott, "Intrinsic Value, Quantum Theory, and Environmental Ethics," 265.

25. There is an interesting and challenging question of defining particular species. Drawing boundaries around anything in nature is somewhat arbitrary. Nonetheless, we can talk about species in terms of groupings of organisms that have a common genetic lineage and are subject to genetic selection over time at the level of the genotype. A genotype is a collection of compatible genes within and across species. See Lawrence E. Johnson, "Toward the Moral Considerability of Species and Ecosystems," *Environmental Ethics* 14 (1992): 145–57.

26. This doesn't preclude respectful treatment of individual organisms and the limiting of their use or consumption to no more than that necessary for decent and worthwhile human lives.

27. Leopold, *A Sand County Almanac*, 262.

28. J. Baird Callicott, "The Case against Moral Pluralism," *Environmental Ethics* 12, (1990): 99–124; Peter S. Wenz, *Environmental Justice* (Albany: State University of New York, 1988), 310–35.

29. For a similar discussion of conflicting values and moral dilemmas, see Clive L. Spash, *Greenhouse Economics: Values and Ethics* (London: Routledge, 2002), 237–42.

30. U.S. Bureau of the Census, "Income Inequality—Table 2, "http://www.census.gov/hhes/income/incineq/p60tb2.html.

31. For more on this point, see Peter S. Wenz, "Minimal, Moderate, and Extreme Moral Pluralism," *Environmental Ethics* 15 (1993): 61–74. Wenz argues that no moral theory provides well-defined solutions to all moral dilemmas. In this limited sense, all our schemes of moral values are pluralist. Conflicts between human commitments and the environment will arise and the resolution will not be easy. But extreme moral pluralism precludes a "coherent moral life." In the end moral dilemmas must be resolved.

32. For an interesting treatment of religious and cultural influences on environmental values and ethics, see J. Baird Callicott, *Earth's Insights: A Survey of Ecological Ethics from the Mediterranean Basin to the Australian Outback* (Berkeley: University of California Press, 1994).

33. For example, see Bryan G. Norton, *Toward Unity among Environmentalists* (New York: Oxford University Press, 1991) and his "Why I Am Not a Nonanthropocentrist."

34. Ben A. Minter and Robert E. Manning, "Pragmatism in Environmental Ethics: Democracy, Pluralism, and the Management of Nature," *Environmental Ethics* 21 (1999): 191–207.

35. Anthony Downs, "Up and Down with Ecology—The 'Issue-Attention Cycle.'" *The Public Interest* 28 (1972): 38–50.

36. Riley E. Dunlap and Kent D. Van Liere, "The 'New Environmental Paradigm' A Proposed Measuring Instrument and Results," *Journal of Environmental Education* 9 (1978): 10–19; Helen L. La Trobe and Tim G. Acott, "A Modified NEP/DSP Environmental Attitudes Scale," *Journal of Environmental Education* 32 (2000): 12–20.

37. Minter and Manning, "Pragmatism in Environmental Ethics," 198–201; Willett Kempton, James S. Boster, and Jennifer A. Hartley, *Environmental Values in American Culture* (Cambridge, Mass.: MIT Press, 1995), 87–115.

38. Kempton et al., *Environmental Values in American Culture*, 87–115.

39. See Wenz, *Environment Justice*, 102–54, for a good summary of the justification of human and animal rights.

40. Douglas E. Booth, "Biocentric Environmental Values and Support for the Ecological Restoration of an Urban Watershed," Technical Report 8, Institute for Urban Environmental Risk Management, Marquette University, Milwaukee, Wis., 2000.

41. This means that human preferences for the protection of certain natural beings are lexicographic. Protection is not to be given up in exchange for consumer goods that are not essential for living decently. Protection is always preferred to more inessential consumer goods. While the literature is in its infancy, there is some preliminary evidence for the existence of such preferences. See Clive L. Spash and Nick Hanley, "Preferences, Information and Biodiversity Preservation," *Ecological Economics* 12 (1995): 191–208; Clive L. Spash, "Ethics and Environmental Attitudes with Implications for Economic Valuation," *Journal of Environmental Management* 50 (1997): 191–208; Clive L. Spash, "Ecosystems, Contingent Valuation and Ethics: The Case of Wetland Re-creation," *Ecological Economics* 34 (2000): 195–215.

8

The Politics of Getting Unhooked from Growth

While public acceptance of environmental values will play an essential role in moving society to unhook itself from excessive economic growth and protect the natural world for its own sake, the acceptance of such values will not be enough. Even if most people favor environmental protection, whether it actually occurs depends on the political decision-making process. The natural environment is truly a public good; it affects everyone and everyone's actions affect it. Public goods must necessarily be decided on politically. Under political democracy in this country, powerful economic interests exercise significant influence over economic and political decisions, and these same interests benefit substantially from continuing, unfettered economic expansion. Even if the public favors significant environmental protection that imposes an environmental speed limit on the economy, public desires may not be strong enough to overcome the power of vested economic interests.

The only real countervailing power to interests of this kind consists of voluntary advocacy groups such as the Sierra Club or the National Audubon Society. The efforts of such voluntary organizations benefit individuals whether they contribute funds or not, dampening incentives to join and share in the costs of political action. By their nature, voluntary groups have a tough time attracting supporters. Despite such difficulties, a fairly vibrant environmental movement based on voluntary organizations has managed to carve out a role for itself in the world of interest-group politics. Explaining the forces behind the growth of the environmental movement despite the obstacles facing it offers insight into whether getting unhooked from growth is a reasonable possibility. In order for political interest groups to experience significant success, they must ultimately have widespread public backing. Unquestionably, the environment is an issue that affects one and all regardless of who they are or what they do. If in a pluralistic world the environmental problem is an issue that affects everyone in all walks of life, then the environmental movement at least has a chance of overcoming the economic interests arrayed against it.

To establish the significance of the environmental problem and the likelihood that it will be adequately addressed in a democratic political system is the task of this final chapter. Business interests opposed to environmental regulation are effective not so much because they exercise direct control over public decisions, but because of their ability to dominate the vehicles of public debate and discourse. The real challenge facing the environmental movement is the gaining of permanent access to the avenues of public discussion over the issues of the day.

ENVIRONMENTALISM AND
ENVIRONMENTAL POLITICS

Concepts and Ideas

Some of the ideas about interest-group politics addressed in previous chapters are worth repeating. In the political arena, large corporations opposed to environmental regulation have the natural advantage of small numbers and abundant resources. Voluntary participation in industry trade groups lobbying against environmental regulation pays because each member brings a relatively large share of the total interest group funding pie to the table, the withholding of which could make a big difference in political outcomes. Unlike their corporate opposition, environmental interest groups suffer the disadvantages of large numbers and the free-rider problem. If one of the 777,000 Sierra Club members[1] doesn't renew, the club's political effectiveness will be virtually unchanged. The former member will still benefit from whatever the club accomplishes. This is the essence of the free-rider problem and discourages self-interested beneficiaries of environmental improvement from signing up and sharing the costs of political action. The Sierra Club nonetheless attracts members, many of whom probably see belonging as an act of ethical commitment. Voluntary groups are able to exist by virtue of collective as opposed to private intentionality. Collective intentionality occurs in those instances where members of a group see their group and individual interests as perfectly coincident. Only those in society with strongly held environmental values are likely to behave in this way in their group affiliations.

According to survey research, environmental values are widely held by the American public but are not always given the highest priority. Public interest in environmental problems indeed seems to follow the "issue-attention cycle" pattern described by Anthony Downs. The intensity of commitment to environmental values seems to rise and fall in response to the public awareness of key environmental issues. This awareness in turn seems to respond to the visibility of problems and the degree to which such problems enter the public dialogue in the news of the day, popular culture, and other forms of public communication. Environmental crises such as the London smog, Times Beach, Chernobyl, and Bhopal, unfortunate as they are, increase public interest in environmental problems. Once the news of such events fades away, public interest fades as well. In periods of declining public interest, political lobbies opposed to environmental regulation are often able to reassert their influence and slow the progress begun on environmental issues at the high point of the issue-attention cycle. The central challenge of the environmental movement is to figure out how to sustain public interest in environmental issues and present convincing, more environmentally friendly alternative visions of how life can be lived. This is especially difficult in a world where business corporations exercise significant control over the key vehicles of public communication and where these same corporations focus on consumption-oriented visions of the good life and the need to keep the consumer economy advancing in order to avoid economic decline and unemployment.

To take a brief look at the history of environmental politics is essential for gaining a better understanding of whether the environmental movement can ever overcome its inherent internal weaknesses and the external economic interests arrayed against it. The critical question to be answered is whether the collective intentionality motivating environmental groups can ever be strong enough to offset the free-rider problem and overcome the advantage of small numbers, high stakes, and abundant lobbying resources possessed by the opponents of environmental regulation. Can the kind of attention to environmental issues generated at the peak of the issue-attention cycle ever be sustained on a permanent basis in order to overcome the power of business-controlled communications media promoting a strictly material vision of the good life? Public acceptance of serious environmental protection is likely to come only with a real understanding of alternative, environmentally friendly options for living decently. This understanding is possible only if there is a real public dialogue on environmental issues and a full airing of competing visions, not just the one-sided, growth-oriented view common to virtually all of advertising and much of popular culture.

Historically, this kind of public dialogue has made only brief appearances at the high points of public concern for environmental issues. Only then does attention to environmental issues in the news rise enough to counterbalance the normal pro-growth, pro-materialism message of the business-oriented media outlets.

Historical Background: Media, Public Opinion, and Legislation

Various measures of public concern for environmental issues support the idea of a cyclical pattern as described by the issue-attention cycle. As we will now see, these include space devoted to the environment in the news media, public opinion about environmental issues as measured by pollsters, and environmental legislation passed by Congress.

Prior to World War II, the number of column inches in the *New York Times* devoted to environmental issues was small in comparison to the burst in coverage in the postwar period. Environmentalism didn't truly come of age until the 1960s. Between 1969 and 1977, column inches in the *Times* on environmental issues soared. From 1977 to 1979, column inches devoted to the environment plunged, remained in a slump through 1981 and did not recover significantly until the mid-1980s. While coverage of environmental issues in the latter half of the 1980s and early 1990s by the *Times* was fairly substantial, it didn't come close to the peak in the early 1970s.[2] The emergence of substantial public concern with environmental issues in the late 1960s and early 1970s brought with it a quantum jump in media attention, but it didn't last. Other problems, such as economic decline and the energy crisis, forced environmental issues off the front page. Nonetheless, attention to environmental issues remained high in the news media by historical standards and increased again in the 1980s, partly in reaction to the open hostility of the Reagan administration to environmentalism and partly in response to a series of horrific environmental disasters.[3] Although the data are limited, with the passage of the Clean Air Act Amendments in 1990, increasing economic troubles, and the Gulf War, media attention to the environment in the 1990s appeared to wane.

In addition to media attention, public opinion as sampled in surveys is another measure of interest in environmental issues. Since public opinion researchers in the early 1960s didn't even include questions about the environment in their survey instruments, environmental issues were presumably not yet a matter of much concern.[4] In the latter half of the 1960s this situation changed rather dramatically. With increased media and political attention to environmental issues, public concern as expressed in opinion surveys surged upward. The proportion of respondents to an Opinion Research Corporation survey who viewed air pollution as very or somewhat serious increased from 28 percent in 1965 to 69 percent in

1970. The comparable figures for water pollution are 35 percent in 1965 and 74 percent in 1970. Responses to questions about the environment in other surveys exhibit similar trends during this period of time. Public concern for the environment as expressed in opinion surveys clearly increased in the late 1960s.[5] The symbolic culmination of this upsurge in environmental concern was the first Earth Day celebration in 1970.

Public opinion favorable to environmental issues reached its peak in the early 1970s and began a slow downward slide that continued through the decade. Unfortunately, opinion pollsters modified the language of the questions they asked concerning environmental issues in the late 1970s, precluding comparisons to the 1960s. The downward slide in the 1970s can nonetheless be observed in responses to new kinds of questions asked by pollsters. The proportion of respondents concerned a great deal about air pollution declined, for example, from 61 percent in 1972 to 39 percent in 1980. The comparable figures for water pollution are 60 percent in 1972 and 36 percent in 1980. While decline occurred relative to the peak, the level of concern at the end of the 1970s appeared to remain above what it had been in the mid-1960s. Environmental concern rose dramatically in the period of "euphoric enthusiasm" and then dropped back, but still remained at a significant level. Concern lessened but didn't go away.[6]

The big change in the 1980s was the election of a president predisposed against big government in general and the regulation of private sector activities in particular. The Reagan administration quickly reversed course on efforts to expand environmental regulation, dismantling the Council on Environmental Quality and cutting the Environmental Protection Agency's budget. The public did not take kindly to this attack on environmental regulation and expressed growing concern for the environment throughout the 1980s and into the early 1990s. In a 1980 Roper survey, 33 percent of respondents felt that "environmental protection laws and regulations have not gone far enough," and by 1992 this figure had jumped to 52 percent. This trend is comparable for other environmental questions asked in various surveys over this period of time.[7] For those survey items asked both in 1990 and the early 1970s, public support for environmental improvement was actually higher in 1990.[8] This suggests that the issue-attention cycle has the potential for repetition, as Downs himself argued, at least in terms of public opinion.[9]

In the early 1990s, the Persian Gulf War and problems with the economy crowded environmental issues out of news headlines, and public concern with environmental issues weakened. By 1998 only 2 percent of respondents voluntarily listed the environment among the most important issues facing the country in a Gallup Poll.[10] In a similar question asked in 1990, 17 percent of respondents had volunteered that the environment was among the two most important problems facing the nation.[11]

The term pollsters use to describe the intensity of public interest in an issue is "salience." An issue has a high degree of salience if it is something that is on the minds of many individuals. A decline in salience does not mean that concern about an issue has dropped, only that the prominence of the issue in the public attention span has declined. When asked specific questions about environmental problems, large proportions of respondents in surveys in the late 1990s still expressed the belief that more needs to be done to protect the environment. As the 1990s progressed, the environment nonetheless received less media attention and became less prominent in the public dialogue over issues of the day. In short, the salience of environmental issues declined.

The volume of significant environmental legislation also follows a pattern that parallels public attention to environmental issues. In the first half of the 1970s an amazingly wide range of significant environmental legislation was passed by Congress, including the Clean Air Act, the Clean Water Act, the Federal Insecticide, Fungicide, and Rodenticide Act (FIFRA), and the Endangered Species Act. Legislation passed in the second half of the 1970s was of a lesser order of importance. With the exception of the Superfund Act passed in 1980, not much else of significance made it through the legislative process during the Reagan administration. The next real surge in legislation came in the first Bush administration, led by the passage of the Clean Air Act Amendments in 1990, although the administration's support for environmental issues quickly subsided after that.[12] Despite the Clinton administration's backing for a variety of environmental measures, including Clean Water Act revisions with standards for nonpoint pollution and stricter corporate average fuel economy (CAFE) standards for new motor vehicles, little was accomplished in terms of new legislation. This lack of legislative action no doubt occurred partly because of the Republican victory in the 1994 House and Senate elections, leading to political gridlock on environmental legislation.[13] Through administrative measures, the Clinton presidency was nonetheless able to make significant progress in the enforcement of measures already on the books and in the writing of stricter regulatory rules, including tighter ambient air quality standards for ozone and small particulate matter. Toward the end of his administration, Clinton used executive powers under the Antiquities Act of 1906 to protect large amounts of public lands from the forces of development, most notably the Grand Staircase–Escalante red rock canyon area in Utah.[14]

Growth of Environmental Groups

Three phenomena seem to move together over time: media attention to environmental issues, public concern with environmental problems, and environmental legislation. Given the nature of politics in a democracy, media and public concern with environmental issues logically precede legislative action. Environmental groups, such as the Sierra Club and the Audubon Society, have seen growth in their membership ebb and flow in parallel with the cycle of media attention and public concern. These groups transformed themselves into a significant lobbying force in the 1960s and expanded their concerns to include increasingly visible air and water pollution problems. In the 1950s and 1960s, the Sierra Club gained a reputation as a potent political force in fights to prevent dam construction on the Colorado River and to pass the Wilderness Act of 1964.[15] Environmental groups undoubtedly gained a foothold in the 1960s in large part because environmental problems were becoming much more visible and more serious. Although the California congressional delegation had long pushed for federal government attention to air pollution regulation because of the horrendous air-pollution problem in the Los Angeles basin,[16] national concern with the air-pollution issues awaited the appearance in the 1960s, in other large cities, of photochemical smog of the type experienced in Los Angeles.[17] As already noted, the publication of Rachel Carson's *Silent Spring* in 1962 aroused public concern with the growing threat to the environment from DDT and other toxic chemicals.[18] A virulent attack on Carson and *Silent Spring* by the chemical industry backfired and brought unprecedented public attention to the book.[19] Catastrophes such as the Santa Barbara oil spill in 1969 and the famous burning of Cleveland's Cuyahoga River offered further evidence of the growing importance of environmental issues.[20] By 1970 the public clamor for clean air was so intense that industry interests could no longer forestall national clean-air standards, and the landmark 1970 Clean Air Act was passed.[21]

With environmental issues raised to such a high level of public prominence, the free-rider problem that normally limits membership in voluntary organizations was overcome and environmental groups gained the resources needed to expand their lobbying activities. The initial surge in Sierra Club membership from 35,000 to 181,000 occurred during the "euphoric enthusiasm" phase of the issue-attention cycle in the late 1960s and early 1970s. While membership was fairly stable through the retrenchment phase of the cycle over the rest of the 1970s, the membership growth was explosive in the 1980s in response to the Reagan reaction to environmentalism, attaining 630,000 by 1990. With the Reagan attack on environmental progress, the Sierra Club and other groups experienced a surge in membership in the 1980s, but with declining public attention to environmental issues in the 1990s, membership for many of the old-line groups leveled off or, as with the Sierra Club, actually dropped.[22] By the early 1990s, a second upswing in the issue-attention cycle for environmental issues had run its course and the environment for much of the rest of the decade took a back seat to other concerns.

Just because environmental issues were able to elbow their way onto the stage of public concern does not mean that the opposition was completely neutralized. Legislative measures of unprecedented regulatory strength were included in environmental legislation passed in the early 1970s. The Clean Air Act called for ambient air quality standards to be set for the purpose of protecting human health without regard to cost.[23] The Clean Water Act called for elimination of pollution discharges into navigable waters by 1985.[24] However, lobbyists from the major automobile companies and the American Petroleum Institute warned that a 90 percent reduction in pollution emissions required by 1975 in the Clean Air Act would shut the motor vehicle industry down, although they could do nothing to influence the legislation.[25] Despite that substantial defeat at the legislative level, the environmental opposition was able to make a significant comeback at the implementation stage.

The Environmental Opposition and the Issue-Attention Cycle

The first victory for the automobile industry in the regulatory process was the postponement of the automobile emissions reduction deadline from 1975 to 1976. After testimony by General Motors Corporation that "business catastrophe" would result if the 1975 deadline had to be met, William Ruchelshaus, EPA administrator, ordered a one-year delay and weaker interim emission standards, with tougher requirements for California than elsewhere. GM met the interim standards for California by installing catalytic converters across the board on all models—the technology ultimately used to meet the 90 percent emissions reduction requirement—without experiencing any disruptions. Apparently GM's prediction of catastrophe was unfounded.[26] In the 1977 Clean Air Amendments, the automobile industry won further delays and a weakening of the emissions standards in comparison to the 1970 provisions. With the 1973–1974 Arab oil embargo against the United States and subsequent increases in energy prices, concerns about dependence on foreign energy rose to rival environmental issues for public attention. Despite evidence to the contrary, auto industry executives claimed that the 1970 standards and timetable would cause significant increases in fuel consumption, rising automobile prices, and even industry shutdowns and employment losses.[27] With the election of Ronald Reagan to the presidency in 1980, the automobile industry saw an opportunity to roll back emission requirements. The Reagan administration's comprehensive attack on environmental regulation reinvigorated public support for environmental regulation, and the automobile industry was defeated in its efforts to weaken motor vehicle emissions standards. The industry was able to fend off legislation that would require the installation of catalytic converters on heavy trucks.[28] Congress remained in gridlock for most of the 1980s on the question of reauthorizing the Clean Air Act, but in the 1988 presidential election environmental issues rose to prominence with George Bush declaring himself to be an environmentalist.[29]

With the end of the Reagan Administration and a decade of rising public concern for environmental issues, the stage was set by 1990 for passage of the Clean Air Act Amendments. Environmentalism was making a comeback, and industrial interests were put on the defensive. The result was more stringent emissions standards for nitrogen oxides and hydrocarbons, the installation of canisters to trap volatile organic compounds during refueling on all new cars by 1999, increased durability requirements for pollution-control equipment, and increased use of less polluting reformulated gasoline.[30] A groundbreaking program for controlling sulfur emissions from electric generating facilities causing acid rain was also included in the 1990 Clean Air Amendments. The program placed a cap on emissions and allowed for emission allowance trading within the cap as a measure to reduce compliance costs for electric utilities. The National Clean Air Coalition, which included such groups as the Sierra Club, the Audubon Society, the Natural Resources Defense Council, and the American Lung Society, was the primary force lobbying in favor of a strong clean air bill. The industrial opposition included industry trade associations from the affected industries (electric utilities, coal, steel, chemicals, and automobiles), the National Association of Manufacturers, and the Business Roundtable. In 1989 political action committee money was distributed freely to key House members to solidify opposition to stiff regulatory measures in the new Clean Air Act. The powerful Senator Byrd from West Virginia fought for an expensive measure to compensate coal miners in his state who would lose their jobs because of utilities' switching to western low-sulfur coal, but he had to settle for a scaled-down displaced-worker assistance package. With President Bush pushing for new air-pollution regulations and high levels of public concern with pollution problems, industry lobbying pressures were overcome and the Clean Air Act Amendments of 1990 became law.[31]

For the rest of the decade, little of significance was accomplished in improving air pollution regulation. This was the case even though global warming driven by carbon dioxide emissions and other greenhouse gases gained substantial traction as an environmental issue. Industrial interests whittled away at air-quality regulations, getting provisions for zero emissions vehicles in California and requirements for car pools in highly polluted urban areas scrapped.[32] Business groups also successfully resisted EPA toughening of the ambient ozone standard from 120 to 80 parts per billion.[33]

A crying need for dealing with the global warming problem was increased fuel efficiency for both automobiles and trucks. The growing popularity of truck-based sport utility vehicles served to drag down the overall efficiency of the country's motor vehicle fleet and made meeting carbon emission limits suggested in the Kyoto accord on global warming even harder. Light trucks, sport utility vehicles, and minivans were subject to a more lenient "corporate average fuel efficiency" (CAFE) standard and less stringent emission control requirements than passenger cars.[34] The Clinton administration proposed tougher emission standards for all motor vehicles and a closing of the "light truck loophole," but these measures have yet to be adopted.[35] The 1990 Clean Air Act marked a second peak in the saliency of environmental issues and the winning of significant regulatory reforms, but with declining public attention to environmental issues, business interests opposed to regulation appear to have again increased their influence over their regulatory process.

The struggle over environmental regulation took place not only in the halls of Congress, but in the courtroom as well. In 1972 the Sierra Club won a major victory in a court ruling requiring the EPA to not only enforce ambient air quality standards but to prevent significant deterioration of air quality even if it is well above Clean Air Act standards. This requirement was formally incorporated into the 1977 Clean Air Act Amendments, by which the country was divided up into regions with different allowable reductions in air quality. Class I regions included national parks and wilderness areas and are assigned the smallest allowable increments of air quality reduction. Most areas are designated as Class II, in which a somewhat larger increment is allowed. New sources in such areas are required to install the best available control technology, and once the allowed increments to air quality decline is used up no more new sources can get a permit to locate in the area. New sources are still not totally precluded from locating in such areas, since the EPA does allow for offsets where new sources get older sources to reduce emissions by a greater amount than the increase from the new source.[36]

While environmentalists have made significant gains in the courts, businesses have also used the courts to successfully delay or fend off costly environmental regulations. This occurs most frequently at the rule-making stage of the regulatory process and has been especially significant in delaying the implementation of the landmark 1972 Clean Water Act. The act established the ambitious goals of eliminating the discharge of pollutants into navigable waters by 1985 and water quality that "provides for the protection and propagation of fish, shellfish, and wildlife" by 1983 where attainable.[37] Unlike the Clean Air Act, the focus in the Clean Water Act is on pollution discharges, with little attention being paid to the ambient quality of receiving waters. The critical task for the EPA has been to establish discharge limits that are technologically feasible and impose costs that are reasonable in light of water quality improvements attained.[38] This standards-setting procedure as a consequence was inherently complex, opening it up to challenge by polluters in court at every step of the way. The inevitable result was delays in the standards-writing and implementation process.[39] A decline in funding for EPA administration and research in the 1980s rendered the agency even more vulnerable to challenges in the courts on both the cost and technological feasibility of water pollution control.[40] Enforcement is at least half the battle in environmental regulation, and enforcement suffered significantly in the anti-environmental Reagan years.

Successes and Failures

The rise of an environmental movement clearly transformed the politics of environmental issues. Progress on reducing environmental problems is perhaps most significantly manifested in the successes of the Clean Air Act. With the exceptions of nitrogen oxides and small particulates, all of the conventional pollutants covered by the Clean Air Act have experienced dramatic reductions and ambient measures of air pollution have significantly improved since the inception of the Clean Air Act. Between 1970 and 2001, declines in emissions of conventional pollutants were 44 percent for sulfur dioxide, 19 percent for carbon monoxide, 38 percent for volatile organics, 76 percent for large particulates, and 98 percent for lead. Ambient ozone levels, resulting from the interaction of nitrogen oxides and volatile organics with sunshine, have declined by about 11 percent since 1982. Despite such improvements, the problem of air pollution remains with us. Ozone levels have remained stable in the 1990s, partly because nitrogen oxide emissions have not been significantly reduced.[41] In 2002, ozone standards were still violated 700 times, up from 532 in 2001 and 516 in 2000.[42] Small particulate emissions, a serious health threat, remain at damaging levels.[43] When public attention to environmental problems is at its height, progress is made. The opposition to environmental improvement is nonetheless resilient and well funded. Once public attention fades away, business interests are able to limit regulation through lobbying efforts in the halls of Congress and legal actions in the court system. More often than not, the result is either overly modest incremental progress or regulatory stalemate.[44]

The key lesson offered by the political history of environmentalism is that the most progress is made on environmental issues when public awareness is at its peak. Only then does public discourse in the media explicitly address the desirability and feasibility of reforms in economic arrangements that will bring about a more environmentally friendly world. At other times, media attention focuses more intently on the threats of environmental reform to employment and consumption opportunities and ignores the feasibility of living differently and organizing economic production in a different way. The periods of euphoric enthusiasm at the peak of the issue-attention cycle cannot be completely relied on to bring about an environmentally sustainable world. Doing that requires a more persistent balance of participation in public dialogue and a reduction in the dominance of business interests over public communications media. Only if the public has a full understanding of how a good life is possible while protecting the natural environment will they ever support the economic reforms needed to bring about environmental sustainability. Such an understanding comes only with a full public airing of the issue. Given the high level of public support for environmental improvement, the lack of more extensive public discourse on sustainability in a democracy is a little surprising and requires explaining. To understand how a significant public discourse on environmental issues would ever be possible requires us to have some insight into why public dialogue is normally dominated by the interests of business institutions.

ECONOMIC INTERESTS, PUBLIC DISCOURSE, AND THE ENVIRONMENT

Discourse Ethics

The ethics and practice of public discourse in a democracy is a central theme in the works of the German philosopher, Jürgen Habermas. Habermas sees balanced and equitable public discourse as the essence of democracy and as the fundamental means for resolving disagreements on social practices and moral norms in a pluralistic world. Numerous visions of how to lead a good life stand side by side in modern reality, each with its own complex of values and attitudes. There is no single view of how one ought to live. Yet in an interconnected world moral norms that affect everyone must be agreed upon. For Habermas, moral norms are ideally decided on through application of the principles of communication revealed in the practices of everyday life.[45]

A key purpose of discussion with others in the normal course of daily events is to come to an agreement about some course of action. This could be as simple as two friends deciding how to spend an afternoon together. Each presents different possibilities and talks about their relative advantages and makes evaluative comments on the options presented by the other. Ideally both consider in their deliberations not only their own interests and desires, but those of their friend as well. Through discussion and debate, a jointly agreed-upon plan of action is arrived at, one that is satisfactory to the interests and desires of both.

Such a discussion or discourse has certain essential features. Among them are these: freedom to participate by all who are affected and are competent to do so; absence of the use of coercion by any party; honesty in expression of views and the avoidance of deception or strategic behavior; the freedom to express views fully and to question any assertion made; consideration by everyone of the effects of the group's decision on the interests of all; and unanimous agreement with the group's final decision. These are the key ideal features of Habermas's discourse ethics.[46] Participants in such discussions are concerned with discovering and clarifying a common interest or a common activity in the normal course of daily life.

In practice this ideal form of discourse is not always attainable. Where differing interests are irreconcilable, compromise is called for. The best that can be done is striking a balance between competing particular interests. Discourse ethics differs distinctly from the notion of a compromise.[47] In the case of a compromise, the goal of each participant is to get the biggest share of the pie possible in a zero sum game, and the final result depends on the relative bargaining strength of the participants. In discourse ethics, the goal is to act not as an individual but as a citizen and to make a judgment about the best course of action to pursue, taking into account the interests of all concerned.

In the real world of politics, discourse ethics is only an ideal or benchmark against which actual public decision making can be judged. In practice, compromise and the exercise of raw power tend to dominate the reality of public decision making. As Habermas puts it, "practical discourses resemble islands threatened with inundation in a sea of practice where the pattern of consensual conflict resolution is by no means the dominant one."[48]

Discourse ethics suffers from its own "large numbers" problem. In reality not everyone can participate fully in public discourse on the big issues of the day, simply because there are too many of us for the discussion that obeys the premises of discourse ethics. As a mode of decision making, discourse ethics works best at the smaller scale of families and other small groupings. Still, approximations to discourse ethics in the larger public realm are a possibility, given proportionate representation of different views and interests. In theory, the institutions of representative democracy can ideally serve as a forum for a public discourse that roughly follows the practice of discourse ethics. Representatives carry out the actual discourse, but the result is roughly the same as if all participated so long as a reasonable breadth of public opinion is reflected in the decision-making body. As Habermas argues, "Only those norms can claim to be valid that meet (or could meet) with the approval of all affected in their capacity *as participants in a practical discourse.*"[49] The important term to consider in this assertion is "or could meet." This opens up the possibility of an acceptable form of real dialogue over public issues in a world of large numbers through representative democracy. The outcome of a dialogue under ideal democratic representation would not in theory change as the particular individuals serving as representatives change, so long as the spectrum of opinion occurring in the larger society continues to be accurately approximated in the legislative body. "Advocatory discourse," or advocating for the views of others, according to Habermas is an acceptable substitute for actual participation by all in discussions and decisions dealing with social norms.[50]

The real trouble with democracy is that standards established by discourse ethics are seldom realized in practice. The goals of a political representative are strategic in most circumstances, not to serve the ideals of discourse ethics. The critical practical task of an elected representative is to get reelected. This need makes representatives vulnerable to lobbyists who can provide campaign funds and interest groups that can deliver votes. Political representatives are also typically in need of information on complex issues under legislative consideration, and such information is often costly to generate. This is certainly the case for environmental problems, whose effects can be complex and challenging to understand. Supplying such information to representatives provides still another avenue of influence for lobbyists and political interest groups. As a consequence, elected representatives won't necessarily fully and accurately reflect the values and attitudes of their constituents. They will at least partly reflect the goals of organized political interests.[51]

Even if elected politicians did fully represent the views of their constituents, interest groups have the capacity to influence public opinion through the media. This can be done through various forms of paid advertising, through public relations efforts to influence the news media, or through direct and indirect influences on the content of popular culture. Under ideal conditions, in a public discourse on a particular issue, all views and ideas would be fully represented. In practice, economic and political interests with the resources to do so can strategically supply information through mass media with the intention of shaping public opinion in certain ways. In getting their message out to the public, large corporations rich in financial resources for advertising and public relations have an obvious advantage in comparison to voluntary interest groups dependent on contributed funds.

Much of Habermas's principal work, *The Theory of Communicative Action*, focuses on the relative shrinkage of participatory discourse as a vehicle for social and public decision making and action.[52] Habermas postulates a social world composed of three critical arenas: the market-driven capitalist business economy; governmental bureaucracies dependent on tax revenues from the business economy; and the private "life-world" of norm-guided human interaction. In the life-world of social intercourse, actions taken together with others are often decided on in a process of discussion and debate about what to do. In families, husbands and wives discuss, debate, and decide such things as where to live, how much money to save each week, whom to invite over for dinner, where to go on vacation, what charities to give money to, and a host of other issues. Local voluntary service group members jointly decide what projects to undertake, how to raise money, and how to spend it. Amateur sports teams work out their schedule of play collectively. Local municipal governments hold hearings on capital spending proposals for libraries, public school buildings, roads, and other facilities. These are all examples of discussion and debate between individuals that occur with the goal of arriving at a consensus, or at least something close to it. The "life-world" is also the arena where the socialization of the young occurs and cultural values are transmitted from one generation to another. The hallmarks of the life-world are face-to-face contact and communication and action arrived at through collective decision making.

Discussion and debate of any kind are premised on the use of language. For language to function as a means of communication, the language-using community must agree on the meaning of terms. Language itself is a product of social consensus about the meaning and interpretations of what is true in the observed world. Before the question of what to do in the world can even be raised, questions of meaning and interpretation—the way language is used to describe perceived circumstances—must be settled. Language is rooted in community consensus and particular visions of the good life.[53]

The guiding forces in the economic and government spheres are entirely different from those in the discussion-oriented world of everyday life. Economic decision making is driven by monetary incentives, while public sector decision making proceeds from the exercise of political power. In an earlier era, the connection between the private sphere and the economy was fairly simple. One had to work to live and earnings went for the necessities of life. Incentives were entirely monetary. The connection between the private sphere and government was simple as well. Taxes had to be paid and public authorities obeyed.[54] Apart from these intrusions, the private sphere of the life-world retained its autonomy and reliance on actions taken in response to discussion and debate about what things mean and what to do.

Public Discourse in Practice

In modern reality, things are more complex. To sustain economic growth, consumers must be encouraged to spend, and in a world of interest-group politics, votes must be won. The result is strategic efforts by economic and political institutions to influence the actions of private individuals. In his writings Habermas clearly worries that economic incentives and motivations are increasingly invading the life-world and reducing the scope of decisions arrived at through discussion and debate.[55] Consumers increasingly decide what to buy in reaction to what their neighbors already have, in response to desires for exhibiting economic status and obtaining sensual fulfillment, and in reaction to messages in the public media about the amazing array of goods available and the wonders of their possession. Public discourse about what one ought to do in the world has a diminishing impact on private consumer decisions, while the influence of popular culture and the public media on such decisions is ever expanding.[56] Similarly, political positions on public issues are less a product of debate and discussion than a response to messages offered by the public media.

Instead of offering a balanced presentation of actual alternatives, public relations and advertising are used by business and other interest groups to strategically mold public opinion.[57] This is important because the information in the hands of the public sets the terms of debate over public issues. Big oil companies with their vast financial resources, for example, can easily afford the cost of communicating to the public the virtues of oil drilling in the Arctic National Wildlife Refuge. Public favor for drilling can be won by pointing to everyone's desire to avoid long lines and high prices at the gas pump, and the arguments of environmentalists opposed to drilling can be trumped by explaining how little land is actually required for oil production operations and how wildlife easily adapts to oil operations without harm.

To make sensible choices about a big issue of the day such as global warming, the public should be fully aware of all its ramifications, including the need to change the way many of us live in order to solve the problem. Today in the United States, daily life for most of us includes the automobile as the predominant means for getting around, huge auto-oriented shopping malls, and spacious homes on big lots in the suburbs.[58] These features of modern cultural reality are constantly reinforced in advertising and are seldom questioned publicly. Alternative arrangements that dramatically reduce energy consumption and greenhouse gas emissions are available—arrangements that have the potential to actually improve the quality of life. A simple trip to Europe with its beautiful cities and efficient mass transit provides a glimpse of the possibilities.[59] Yet we don't see much if any public discussion of such alternatives in corporate sponsored ads or the public media. Corporations have a strong vested interest in current modes of life and thus have a stake in providing information to the public that encourages and supports the status quo. Without credible information on alternatives, the public will naturally fear anything that threatens the way it lives currently.

Individuals in the modern world are certainly capable of making judgments on the issues of the day. Such judgments, however, require knowledge that often appears to be quite complex. How an auto-oriented, low-density urban area can be transformed into a mass transit–oriented, pedestrian-friendly, high-density urban environment might not be immediately clear to the general public. The high cost of gathering knowledge on an issue of this sort opens up strategic opportunities for those with resources to gather information and provide it to the decision-making public. The motor vehicle industry, for example, bombards us daily with advertising promoting the virtues of the automobile, the sport utility vehicle, and the light truck as means for getting around. We don't see ads promoting mass transit alternatives.

Information of this sort has the classic features of a public good. Once it is produced, it is hard to exclude anyone from acquiring it and benefiting from it, and the cost of providing information to another person is very low. Since it is a public good, information is subject to the free-rider problem. We all benefit from honest, balanced information about the issues of the day, but each of us is a potential "free rider" on information provided by others. In a world of large numbers, none of us has much incentive to work at the task of generating information on the public issues of the day even though the public benefits could be huge.[60] Concentrated private interests, on the other hand, have ample incentives to provide information that benefits their particular ends. It makes sense for the auto industry to shower us with ads for cars because it enhances industry sales and profits. It doesn't pay anyone to buy ads that promote publicly funded mass transit. We may be skeptical of the information we do get in a world where corporations are the primary suppliers, but we don't have very many alternative sources untainted by economic interests.[61]

The rationale for unbalanced presentations in the world of advertising is clear enough. The immediate goal of advertising is to sell specific products. This is done by convincing the public that particular products satisfy consumer needs and wants, including the demonstration of status and the psychic stimulus of the new and the novel.[62] Advertising communicates a more general message as well. The overriding goal of life is the acquisition, possession, and use of goods and services produced by private sector corporations. A life of material abundance is the ultimate form of satisfaction. One becomes beautiful, handsome, sexually attractive, powerful, intelligent, physically hygienic, and sensually fulfilled through consumption.[63] The essence of the good life is material and economic! There is nothing dishonest or misleading in this. Advertising appeals to real wants and desires and offers opportunities for their satisfaction.[64] Advertising in the end is not especially manipulative or deceptive. The only real problem with advertising is its failure to offer a balanced view of possibilities for living a good life.[65] The subject matter of advertising is confined to the ways in which private goods fulfill human needs and has nothing to say about public goods despite their importance in daily life. Why? The answer is simple. Nothing is to be gained by advertising public goods. The advertising of parks and other public places, public schools, libraries, public transportation systems, locations with beautiful sunsets, clean air, clean water, climate stability, biological diversity, scenic beauty, and other public assets adds nothing to anyone's profits.

Without real alternatives, the public has little choice but to give at least some credence to existing media messages and little reason to resist trying on the form of life offered by advertisements.[66] Doing so is further eased by the knowledge that modern economic life in fact depends on the consumption practices promoted by advertising. Growth in the kind of consumption motivated by advertising is essential for continued economic expansion and the avoidance of unemployment. If the messages of advertising are disobeyed, the economy stops growing and the underpinnings of the good life are threatened. Growth in such a world automatically takes priority over other goals that jeopardize economic expansion, such as the regulation of greenhouse gases and measures to improve the quality of the environment.

Advertising isn't the only vehicle for influencing public values and opinions. Public relations offers another alternative. The business of public relations, or "corporate advocacy," is "a battle for control over the vocabulary, the grammar and the syntax of everyday life . . . to incorporate into the public consciousness myths and story structures amenable to corporate priorities."[67] While advertising is one of the tools available for public relations, the favored approach is to get desirable coverage in the news media. The corporate world has a distinct advantage in accomplishing this for interesting economic reasons. Print and broadcast media are likely to be business-oriented in part because media enterprises are themselves businesses first and foremost. Not everyone can get into the media business. Capital requirements are substantial and growing over time; access to capital requires close attention to income-earning capacity. Those who do manage to solve the capital problem will be naturally predisposed to a business outlook because they have to in order to remain profitable. This predisposition is reinforced by media dependence on advertising. While advertisers are strongly oriented to the amount of public exposure a particular media outlet generates, they will also be sensitive to the "program environment" and will avoid outlets that are strongly antibusiness or call for substantial social changes. The difficulty the Adbusters Media Foundation, an anti-advertising organization, has had in placing its own ads that parody conventional advertising is a case in point. Television networks have persistently rejected Adbusters' attempts to purchase advertising time on the grounds that their ads are too controversial, are contrary to public policy that promotes economic growth, and will hurt TV station business by alienating other advertisers.[68]

Because of their profit orientation, media outlets will be predisposed to cheap, credible sources of information that corporations and established government bureaucracies are able to provide. As a consequence of the complexity of most environmental issues, environmental reporters are heavily dependent on press releases for the information they use in their stories. In one study of press releases on environmental issues, 42 percent came from government agencies, 23 percent from corporations, 17 percent from universities and other institutions, and 17 percent from activist groups.[69] Government sources are referred to most frequently in stories and serve as the basis for much environmental reporting, although corporate, university, and activist sources are referred to as well. While government is no doubt seen as a credible source of basic factual information on environmental issues, government agencies are unlikely to be the author of revolutionary solutions to problems that upset existing economic arrangements. The position of government agencies will reflect the existing complex of interests that bring pressure on political representatives and agency bureaucrats, and the composition of groups who lobby in Washington, D.C., as well as at the state and local government levels is strongly business oriented.[70] Not all press releases are necessarily created equal. Dissident sources that provide a significant alternative can be hard to locate and costly to substantiate.[71] A radical environmental group such as Greenpeace is able to attract media attention using protests staged with a dramatic flare, but the group's credibility among journalists suffers by such actions and the information provided by the group is often not trusted.[72]

The media are most often attracted to those environmental issues that have an immediate emotional appeal. Pictures of dying, oil-soaked birds make for compelling television images that grab the public's attention and sympathy. While such coverage is a plus because it raises public consciousness, important but less noticed environmental problems that are difficult to explain, such as global warming, tend to go underreported.[73] Global warming is no doubt the predominant environmental threat of the present century, but its consequences are not immediately experienced by the public, and to fully explain its causes and effects in a simple and compelling way is a real challenge.[74] For these reasons, media outlets are unlikely to give global warming much attention.

Overcoming the inherent bias in the media against consideration of invisible but important environmental threats is a serious problem for environmental groups. Reporting on the need for radical change to resolve

environmental problems is not in the interests of established media outlets. This does not mean that environmental groups are totally ineffectual
in their efforts to influence the media. Focused campaigns on specific issues have brought results. After a concerted media campaign against Mc-
Donald's, the fast-food giant gave up using the nonbiodegradable poly-
styrene clamshell container for its hamburgers.[75] Through a clever media
campaign involving a famous actress as spokesperson on a popular TV
show, the Natural Resources Defense Council was able to get the EPA to
ban Alar, a chemical growth regulator used on apples.[76] While such campaigns can be successful, they ultimately depend on voluntary organizations' resources, which are limited, especially in comparison to the resources of businesses opposed to environmental regulation.

Environmentalists can and do take advantage of particular events that
bring media attention to specific environmental problems. Crisis circumstances, such as a chemical spill, a sinking oil tanker, or a killer smog,
make for good stories that attract audiences to broadcast news programs
and newspapers.[77] Environmental interest groups, as pinched as they are
for resources, can benefit from dramatic situations by offering and supporting significant reforms that bring forth a more environmentally
friendly world. The public relations game can be played on the cheap by
environmental groups so long as events are provoking media interest.

At those points of "euphoric enthusiasm" when the public is intensely
interested in environmental issues, the opportunity presents itself to create a more balanced discourse and offset the usual dominance of public
dialogue by established interests. At such times the fundamental rules of
the game are open to challenge and reform. This is exactly what happened
in the 1970s. The Clean Air Act of 1970 went so far as to give priority to
health standards over questions of costs. The ambient air quality standards for ozone, sulfur dioxide, nitrogen oxides, carbon monoxide,
volatile organics, and lead are set by the act to provide a margin of safety
for public health regardless of the cost. This amounts to saying that the
public has a right to healthful air quality, a right that trumps economic
concerns. This is surely a fundamental change in the rules of the game.
Under the Clean Air Act of 1970, the right to use business property for income-earning purposes and in the process to emit pollutants into the air
is subordinated to the right of the public to enjoy healthful air quality.[78]

Media enthusiasm for air pollution problems and other environmental
issues wanes as crises go away and other events emerge to dominate the
news. For this reason sustaining rights to environmental quality established at the height of media and public concern becomes a serious challenge for environmental groups. Ambient air quality standards in the
Clean Air Act have yet to be fully implemented, in no small measure because of successful industry challenges to the regulatory process made

easier by an absence of public attention to the matter. Passing strong legislation is only half of the battle. Intense media and public concern for environmental issues are unsustainable in a world where other problems, such as economic decline, crime, and national security, periodically bubble up to the top of the public agenda, displacing everything else. Environmental protection is important to most people, but it is not the issue on the minds of most except when reminded by an environmental crisis. Critics of the environmental movement fault the big organizations, such as the Sierra Club, the Audubon Society, or the National Resources Defense Council, for collectively becoming just another Washington lobby, one that pursues moderate proposals for environmental improvement and is willing to compromise when need be.[79] When public attention is directed elsewhere not much more is possible. If these groups continue to play the same game when public interest in the environment is at its maximum and more is possible, then they are open to legitimate criticism.

Public Discourse and Environmental Rights

What interesting conclusions can be extracted from the political history of the environmental movement? First, as Habermas suggests, under normal conditions public discourse in modern society is largely under the thumb of economic interests. This profoundly limits progress in protecting the natural environment from the damaging impacts of economic activity. Second, at the height of the "issue-attention cycle," normality is suspended and environmental issues enter the public dialogue; opportunities open up for passing legislation that can significantly alter the rules of the environmental game and even establish environmental rights. Environmental rights are especially important because they imply a commitment to "strong sustainability" and the trumping of economic by environmental concerns. Strong sustainability in turn requires getting unhooked from growth.[80] The passage of legislation creating environmental rights sets the stage for an environmentally friendly economic world with more moderate rates of expansion of GDP than currently experienced. The issue-attention cycle proves the point that public dialogue matters.

Environmental rights established so far in legislation are fairly limited in scope. The Clean Air Act presumes a right to breathe reasonably healthful air. The Endangered Species Act presupposes that threatened species have rights to protection regardless of economic consequences. The Endangered Species Act in its original form precluded federal government agencies from undertaking actions that harm endangered species no matter what the economic effects. In 1978, Congress weakened the act somewhat by establishing the Endangered Species Committee and giving it the authority to grant exemptions from species protections in cases where significant economic harm would result. In practice, the committee has set the bar fairly high for exemptions, granting only one so far.[81]

Just because environmental rights are established in law does not mean that they are always successfully defended in practice.[82] Once public interest wanes in environmental protection, economic interests reassert themselves and take advantage of loopholes in legislation, limitations in enforcement resources, and legal challenges to avoid full enforcement of environmental laws. Ambient standards for pollutants in the Clean Air Act, for instance, continue to be violated in many metropolitan areas.[83] Such violations raise two issues. Are environmental rights, such as the right to clean air, fully accepted and truly legitimate in the context of modern constitutional democracy? If so, what reforms are needed to ensure that such rights can be adequately defended? These are important questions that ultimately have to be answered if the notion of environmental rights is to be taken seriously.

DEMOCRACY AND ENVIRONMENTAL RIGHTS

Ideally, the rights that a society defends command wide consensus, and judgments about those rights are made by citizens willing to set aside their private interests and consider what is good for society as a whole, taking into account the interests of all. The work of John Rawls provides a philosophical framework for thinking about society's basic structure in a pluralistic setting where a variety of conceptions of how to live stand side by side.[84]

The affirmation of particular rights in such circumstances takes form as an "overlapping consensus" about the basic structure of political and economic arrangements. As Rawls put it, "the basic structure of society is the way in which the main political and social institutions of society fit together into one system of social cooperation, and the way they assign basic rights and duties and regulate the division of advantages that arises from social cooperation over time."[85] The basic structure of society is to be founded on principles of fairness, and the features of that structure are to be selected from the neutrality of what Rawls refers to as the "original position." In the original position, society's basic terms of fair cooperation are agreed upon by participants as if they were behind a veil of ignorance where they have no knowledge of their actual, "real world" economic and social roles. The original position is a kind of thought experiment allowing each to step into the shoes of others in order to discuss and analyze from a neutral position society's basic structure of cooperation.[86] The crucial shared value in this process is "the end of giving one another justice."[87] The willingness to do so is the essence of having a sense of justice.

A sense of justice implies a commitment to abide by society's agreed-upon basic structure, regardless of how one lives and the other values one holds. A shared sense of justice doesn't mean that everyone sees eye to eye on the details of life. The task in the original position is to work out the best possible arrangements that allow for differences in religious or philosophical beliefs, sexual orientation, choice of occupation, literary interests, political activities, and the other important dimensions of daily living. The result of this process is what Rawls calls an "overlapping consensus."[88] The original position is clearly a fiction, but it offers an intellectual framework for thinking about what, ideally, the basic structure of society should look like.

The first essential question to address from the perspective of the original position is what to include in the basic structure. Do environmental rights count as basic? Rawls argues against this. He claims that environmental questions are to be decided legislatively once the basic structure is in place.[89] The basic structure of society is established for Rawls by the two principles of justice: "(a) Each person has the same indefeasible claim to a fully adequate scheme of equal basic liberties . . . (b) Social and economic inequalities are to satisfy two conditions: first, they are to be attached to offices and positions open to all under conditions of fair equality of opportunity; and second, they are to be to the greatest benefit of the least-advantaged members of society (the difference principle)."[90] Rawls's concerns, one might say, are pre-ecological. Society's basic structure, in his view, "comprises social institutions within which human beings may develop their moral powers and become fully cooperating members of a society of free and equal citizens."[91]

A simple and obvious addition to Rawls's conception of society's basic structure is a human right to a healthful natural environment. Such a right doesn't really go beyond Rawls's conception of basic liberties, given that a healthy natural environment is necessary for human beings to develop their moral powers. To argue for a right to a healthy environment is no different from arguing for a right to health care as a prerequisite to fair equality of opportunity and the enjoyment of basic rights and liberties.[92] Rawls agrees that a right to health care ought to be a part of a society's constitutional structure if fairness is to be achieved.

A more substantial extension of the Rawlsian framework recognizes that human beings are not only members of the human social community, but are also members of the "land community," as Aldo Leopold would put it. Given this wider definition of community, a reasonable next step is to extend society's basic structure of rights beyond the strictly human to encompass nonhuman species and the ecosystems they depend on.[93] Doing so recognizes that human beings, along with other species, are members in common of the global ecological system, have a common evolutionary heritage, and share in common the resources of the global natural environment. Rawls's sense of justice, a moral commitment to a fair and just world for all human beings, would now be expanded to include justice for nonhuman species in the form of rights to exist.

For Rawls, the original position is a point of view from which to make reasonable arguments about the structure of a just and democratic society. His views fit in nicely with the idea of widening concentric circles of moral concern discussed in the last chapter. The innermost circles cover those beings held to be of highest moral concern, while the outmost circles are of a lesser rank in the ethical hierarchy. Presumably, for most people a Rawlsian human-oriented commitment to "justice as fairness" would be located on an inner concentric circle, while a Leopoldian commitment to nonhuman species and the land community would be found on an outer ring.[94] Species would have rights, but the rights of human beings to just and fair social arrangements, as described by Rawls, would take precedence.

The original position is not a historical occurrence as such, but citizens and politicians can, if they so choose, conceptually step into the shoes of others and consider a full spectrum of viewpoints (including those of nonhuman species) in making key political decisions about the basic content of economic and social arrangements. This could occur, for instance, in deciding legislatively that the protection of health from the dangers of air pollution and the protection of species from extinction will take precedence over questions of benefits and costs. This is exactly the process described by Habermas's discourse ethics, where the participants in public discussions take on something like Rawls's original position in arriving at unanimous agreement on elements of society's basic structure. The subject of discourse ethics is a concern that can be generalized across all walks of life and is not unique to a particular set of values. Global warming, air pollution, impaired water quality, the problem of species declines are issues that affect everyone. Since everyone is a natural being and a part of the global complex of natural systems, the relationship of humankind to the rest of nature is a concern of everyone, no matter what their chosen way of life. The purpose of discourse ethics is to step out of one's own shoes in order to unanimously establish through public debate and discussion norms that are good for all.[95] Rawls's original position and the perspective of discourse ethics are essentially the same: to take a neutral stance on questions of society's basic norms.[96] What discourse ethics allows, as opposed to the idea of the original position, is a more dynamic view of public decision making on basic institutional arrangements. Public discourse is an ongoing and continuous process. Discourse ethics can account for a historical widening of moral concern to take into account new kinds of ethical commitments not previously held. This is exactly the procedure Aldo Leopold suggests in justifying an extension of ethics to the land community.[97]

Whether society is actually willing to take the next step and count ecological relationships as a part of its basic structure and establish rights for the natural world is, of course, a historical and empirical question. Assessing this possibility from the standpoint of the original position or discourse ethics amounts to judging whether an overlapping consensus on the rights of nature is feasible. This means evaluating whether those holding differing conceptions of the good life would strongly object to the idea of rights for the natural world. If getting unhooked from growth and fully protecting the environment still allows for a decent standard of consumption and a satisfying way of life, as chapter 6 suggests, then it is hard to see that anyone would find offense in the conferring of rights on species or ecological systems.

Nonetheless, there are holders of well-known philosophical views who would likely be outraged by the governmental enforcement of environmental rights. A libertarian with views of the kind described in Robert Nozick's *Anarchy, State, and Utopia* would not be pleased with sacrificing private property rights for the sake of species conservation.[98] The foundational values articulated by Nozick are the right to noninterference by others (especially the state) in the pursuit of private interests and the right to the holding of property so long as it is justly acquired (entitlement theory of justice). Just acquisition occurs through appropriation of goods unclaimed by others, the production of goods using justly acquired property, and the voluntary transfer of justly acquired goods. Given Nozick's entitlement theory of justice, the role of government is to do no more than protect property and rights to noninterference. The actions of anyone, including government, are constrained by side-obligations not to harm or interfere with the lives of others. Government can't interfere with individuals by involuntarily taxing them to fund social welfare programs that benefit the poor. Libertarians would find the enforcement of Rawls's difference principle through government action to be unacceptable. They would also find unacceptable government interference in the form of land-use restrictions on private property to protect endangered species. The idea of private property is to do what you will with it, short of harm to others, and the definition of "others" does not include nonhuman species. The harvesting of old-growth forests providing habitat for endangered Spotted Owls is perfectly acceptable behavior for a libertarian who ranks the rights of property as having the highest priority in society's basic constitutional structure.

The entitlement theory of justice does not easily account for the needs of the natural world. The creation of private property divides up the landscape into separate and independent units while ecological relationships cause different parcels of land to be interconnected and interdependent.[99] The pursuit of private property interests will not necessarily take into account the needs of ecological systems and the species they support. Parceling up the landscape into private holdings fits the entitlement theory of justice but denies ecological interconnectedness. Creating an open-pit mine or clear-cutting a forest may be the highest and best economic use of a parcel of land, but doing so will likely destroy the ecological values of the land and the species dependent on those values. The entitlement theory is nonetheless a possible viewpoint in the original position, one that would preclude a land ethic of the sort advocated by Aldo Leopold.

Despite Nozick and the libertarians, government does indeed interfere with the rights of private property in order to protect the environment, and they do so with popular public support. As already noted, a right to a healthful environment in terms of air quality is established in the Clean Air Act and a right for the continued existence of species is established in the Endangered Species Act. These two pieces of legislation suggest the possibility of a more general movement in the direction of environmental rights and the incorporation of those rights in society's basic structure. Survey research offers evidence of a strong public commitment to environmental protection and the rights of species to exist, as noted in the last chapter. Leopold's vision of human beings as members and citizens of the land community seems to be on the way to gaining a broader public acceptance.

THE PROBLEM OF RESISTANCE TO STRONG SUSTAINABILITY, GETTING UNHOOKED FROM GROWTH, AND ENVIRONMENTAL RIGHTS

Strong sustainability, getting unhooked from growth, and environmental rights come as a package. Strong sustainability and environmental rights give priority to the environment. Except in extreme circumstances where human prospects for living decently are threatened, environmental concerns take priority over concerns about economic costs in a world of environmental rights and strong sustainability. To realize strong sustainability and to protect environmental rights, environmental productivity will establish a new economic-growth speed limit, and this new speed limit will in all probability fall below historical trends in economic growth. In other words, to achieve strong sustainability and protect environmental rights, getting unhooked from growth will be necessary.

The problem with getting unhooked from growth is political as much as it is economic. Powerful economic interests depend on a high-growth economy and have the political capacity to place roadblocks in the way of a movement toward strong sustainability and the protection of environmental rights. The process of public discussion and debate that could lead society down the path to more extensive environmental rights is unrealizable in a world of powerful corporations capable of dominating public discourse and public-sector decision making. The same problem no doubt stands in the way of attaining other key social goals, such as universal health care, reducing poverty, or decreasing economic inequality. Although most probably agree with Rawlsian principles of justice and many favor a Leopoldian land ethic, interest-group politics and concentrated economic interests create a barrier to full implementation of these ideas.

The root of the problem is the lack of balanced access to the public means of communication and debate. Concentrated economic interests have an incredible abundance of resources to devote to getting their message out—an abundance that advocacy groups, which suffer the serious disadvantage of dependency on large numbers of small contributions, find impossible to match. The only final answer to this dilemma is a transformation of existing economic arrangements that would bring corporations themselves under the influence of democratic decision making. One possibility is to move in the direction of an economy where employees own and control the businesses for which they work. Certainly narrow economic interests will still matter for employee-controlled businesses, but the full spectrum of employee values would have at least a chance of shaping the political pursuits of democratically administered business organizations. Employee democracy is a huge topic in itself that has received much attention elsewhere and cannot be covered here in any real depth.[100] The employee democracy issue is raised here simply to note that the lack of serious progress on the environment and other social issues is a problem that is endemic to corporate, capitalist economic arrangements and that alternatives to such arrangements are feasible. Concentrated economic power singularly devoted to the accumulation of material wealth in a constitutional democracy invariably influences and perverts the public decision-making process. This is a rather depressing conclusion about modern political reality. Transforming basic economic arrangements appears to be an insurmountable task when compared with the pursuit of incremental reforms that will protect the environment or reduce poverty. Still, there is a chance that the realization of the need to fundamentally remake economic arrangements can serve as a unifying theme for disparate groups pursuing diverse social goals. The democratic nature of these groups can serve as a model for the economic institutions of the future.

The simple conclusion of all these pages is that economic institutions ought to be rearranged to unhook modern society from high rates of growth and to bring the process of environmental degradation to a halt.

Chapter 8

Most Americans desire a healthful environment, the conservation of natural landscapes, and the preservation of nonhuman species. Convincing arguments can also be made that modern consumerism is something that most Americans want as well.[101] After all, 350 million American consumers can't be entirely wrong. A mild addiction to the finer material things in life can hardly be seen as a serious problem. What is being called for here is a modest lowering of the stakes in the race for more consumer goods, perhaps 1 or 2 percent less economic growth a year, in order to make room for the rest of nature and to allow everyone a little more time to enjoy all that life has to offer, material and immaterial. The problem is, even to achieve something so modest may require a fairly radical reshaping of our economic institutions.

NOTES

1. Sierra Club, "Sierra Club Yearly Election Results," http://www.susps.org/info/election_results.html.
2. W. Douglas Costain and James P. Lester, "The Evolution of Environmentalism," in *Environmental Politics and Policy: Theories and Evidence*, ed. James P. Lester (Durham, N.C.: Duke University Press, 1995), 15–38. The averages for the 1960s, 1970s, and 1980s were, respectively, 285, 945, and 689 column inches per year. The peak in 1971 was approximately 1,400 column inches.
3. These include the chemical spill in Bhopal, India, in 1984, the nuclear reactor melt-down and radiation release at Chernobyl in 1986, and the oil spill from the *Exxon Valdez* in Alaska in 1989. While two of these disasters occurred outside the United States, they kept environmental issues in the news. Dioxin contamination discovered in the community of Times Beach, Missouri, in 1982 and the efforts by the federal government to deal with it was a continuing news item throughout much of the 1980s as well. For a discussion of public interest in environmental issues in the 1980s, see Riley E. Dunlap, "Public Opinion and Environmental Policy," in *Environmental Politics and Policy: Theories and Evidence*, ed. James P. Lester (Durham, N.C.: Duke University Press, 1995), 87–93.
4. Dunlap, "Public Opinion and Environmental Policy," 70–71.
5. Dunlap, "Public Opinion and Environmental Policy," 70–73.
6. Dunlap, "Public Opinion and Environmental Policy," 81–87.
7. Dunlap, "Public Opinion and Environmental Policy," 87–93.
8. Dunlap, "Public Opinion and Environmental Policy," 93.
9. Anthony Downs, "Up and Down with Ecology—The 'Issue-Attention Cycle.'" *The Public Interest* 28 (1972): 41–42.
10. Christopher J. Bosso, "Environmental Groups and the New Political Landscape," in *Environmental Policy: New Directions for the Twenty-First Century*, ed. Normal J. Vig and Michael E. Kraft (Washington, D.C.: CQ Press, 2000), 55–76.
11. Dunlap, "Public Opinion and Environmental Policy," 93.

12. James P. Lester, "Introduction," in *Environmental Politics and Policy: Theories and Evidence*, ed. James P. Lester (Durham, N.C.: Duke University Press, 1995), 1–14; Dunlap, "Public Opinion and Environmental Policy," 94–95.

13. Michael E. Kraft, "Environmental Policy in Congress: From Consensus to Gridlock," in *Environmental Policy: New Directions for the Twenty-First Century*, ed. Normal J. Vig and Michael E. Kraft (Washington, D.C.: CQ Press, 2000), 128–40.

14. Normal J. Vig, "Presidential Leadership and the Environment: From Reagan to Clinton," in *Environmental Policy: New Directions for the Twenty-First Century*, ed. Normal J. Vig and Michael E. Kraft (Washington, D.C.: CQ Press, 2000), 107–15.

15. Samuel P. Hays, *Beauty, Health, and Permanence: Environmental Politics in the United States, 1955–1985* (Cambridge: Cambridge University Press, 1987), 53, 458–69; Robert Gottlieb, *Forcing the Spring: The Transformation of the American Environmental Movement* (Washington, D.C.: Island Press, 1993), 41–46.

16. Scott Hamilton Dewey, *Don't Breathe the Air: Air Pollution and U.S. Environmental Politics, 1945–1970* (College Station: Texas A&M University Press, 2000), 226–54; Christopher J. Bailey, *Congress and Air Pollution: Environmental Policies in the USA* (Manchester, U.K.: Manchester University Press, 1998), 84–109.

17. Dewey, *Don't Breathe the Air*, 228–29.

18. Hays, *Beauty, Health, and Permanence*, 28; Rachel Carson, *Silent Spring* (Boston: Houghton Mifflin, 1962).

19. Gottlieb, *Forcing the Spring*, 81–86.

20. Bailey, *Congress and Air Pollution*, 140.

21. Dewey, *Don't Breathe the Air*, 226–49; Bailey, *Congress and Air Pollution*, 140–56.

22. Bosso, "Environmental Groups and the New Political Landscape," 64; Helen M. Ingram, David H. Colnic, and Dean E. Mann, "Interest Groups and Environmental Policy," in *Environmental Politics and Policy: Theories and Evidence*, ed. James P. Lester (Durham, N.C.: Duke University Press, 1995), 115–45.

23. Tom Tietenberg, *Environmental and Natural Resource Economics*, 5th ed. (Reading, Pa.: Addison-Wesley Longman, 2000), 364–65.

24. Tietenberg, *Environmental and Natural Resource Economics*, 446.

25. Jack Doyle, *Taken for a Ride: Detroit's Big Three and the Politics of Pollution* (New York: Four Walls Eight Windows, 2000), 66–73.

26. Doyle, *Taken for a Ride*, 86–88.

27. Doyle, *Taken for a Ride*, 125–28.

28. Doyle, *Taken for a Ride*, 173–91.

29. Doyle, *Taken for a Ride*, 211–12.

30. Doyle, *Taken for a Ride*, 217–38.

31. Gary C. Bryner, *Blue Skies, Green Politics: The Clean Air Act of 1990 and Its Implementation*, 2nd ed. (Washington, D.C.: CQ Press, 1995), 96–135.

32. Doyle, *Taken for a Ride*, 299, 344–45.

33. Doyle, *Taken for a Ride*, 345–67.

34. Doyle, *Taken for a Ride*, 395–419.

35. Doyle, *Taken for a Ride*, 431–38.

36. Tietenberg, *Environmental and Natural Resource Economics*, 367; Lettie McSpadden, "The Courts and Environmental Policy," in *Environmental Politics and Policy: Theories and Evidence*, ed. James P. Lester (Durham, N.C.: Duke University Press, 1995), 242–74.

37. Tietenberg, *Environmental and Natural Resource Economics*, 446.

38. Tietenberg, *Environmental and Natural Resource Economics*, 447.

39. Tietenberg, *Environmental and Natural Resource Economics*, 451; McSpadden, "The Courts and Environmental Policy," 248–53.

40. McSpadden, "The Courts and Environmental Policy," 250.

41. U.S. EPA, *Latest Findings on National Air Quality: 2001 Status and Trends* (Research Triangle Park, N.C.: Office of Air Quality and Standards, Environmental Protection Agency, September 2002).

42. Seth Borenstein, "U.S. Smothered in Dangerous Smog 32% More in 2002: Auto Emissions, Power Plants Blamed for the Increase," *Milwaukee Journal*, March 21, 2003, A18.

43. U.S. EPA, *Latest Findings on National Air Quality: 2001*, 12–13.

44. The discussion of environmental politics has focused here on air pollution issues and to a modest degree on water pollution. A similar story can be told with other environmental issues such as the regulation of pesticides, the regulation of toxic waste, and public lands management. See Samuel P. Hays, *Beauty, Health, and Permanence*; Christopher J. Bosso, *Pesticides and Politics: The Life Cycle of a Public Issue* (Pittsburgh: University of Pittsburgh Press, 1987).

45. Jürgen Habermas, *Moral Consciousness and Communicative Action*, trans. Christian Lenhardt and Shierry Weber Nicholsen (Cambridge, Mass.: MIT Press, 1990).

46. Habermas, *Moral Consciousness and Communicative Action*, 43–109.

47. Habermas, *Moral Consciousness and Communicative Action*, 72.

48. Habermas, *Moral Consciousness and Communicative Action*, 106.

49. Habermas, *Moral Consciousness and Communicative Action*, 66.

50. Habermas, *Moral Consciousness and Communicative Action*, 122.

51. Anthony Downs, *An Economic Theory of Democracy* (New York: Harper & Row, 1957), 238–59.

52. Jürgen Habermas, *The Theory of Communicative Action: Volume 1, Reason and Rationalization of Society*, trans. Thomas McCarthy (Boston: Beacon Press, 1984); Jürgen Habermas, *The Theory of Communicative Action: Volume 2, Lifeworld and System: A Critique of Functionalist Reason* (Boston: Beacon Press, 1984).

53. Habermas, *The Theory of Communicative Action: Volume 2*, 119–52.

54. Habermas, *The Theory of Communicative Action: Volume 2*, 153–97.

55. Jürgen Habermas, *The Structural Transformation of the Public Sphere: An Inquiry into a Category of Bourgeois Society*, trans. Thomas Berger (with Frederick Lawrence) (Cambridge, Mass.: MIT Press, 1991), 141–80.

56. For a fuller treatment of consumer behavior, see chapter 2.

57. Habermas suggests that a public sphere of private individuals existed historically in early bourgeois society in which occurred public debate over the issues of the day, the results of which directly influenced political representatives and public sector decision making. See Habermas, *The Structural Transformation of the Public Sphere*, 31–43, 141–205. With the emergence of a large-scale corporate capitalism and the welfare state, a public sphere featuring wide participation in public debate disappeared.

58. See chapters 2 and 5 for a more detailed treatment of the modern consumption-oriented vision of the good life.

59. The option of more pedestrian-friendly, high-density urban areas as a means for reducing energy consumption and improving the quality of life is discussed in more detail in chapter 6.

60. See the discussion of the free-rider problem in chapter 4. Again, the size of the group and the per capita potential for gain matters. Because each firm's contribution is a big part of the total in the automobile industry, each will no doubt contribute to the production and dissemination of information on the high cost of carbon emission reductions through automotive emissions restrictions. Because the typical citizen is an extremely small part of the total, the potential contribution of each to the production of information on transportation alternatives will be a small part of the total and won't in the end have a significant impact on the amount of information produced. Since a voluntary contribution will have no real impact and because an information that does get produced voluntarily is a public good and freely available to all, the pursuit of private interests would result in an absence of information on transportation alternatives to the automobile. See Downs, *Economic Theory of Democracy*, 238–59.

61. Robert Goldman, *Reading Ads Socially* (London: Routledge, 1992), 1.

62. See chapter 2 for a more detailed discussion of consumer behavior.

63. Again, see chapter 2 for a discussion of consumer behavior. For an interesting discussion of the messages communicated through advertising, see Goldman, *Reading Ads Socially*.

64. A conception of the good life rooted in consumerism is certainly a legitimate choice in the world. This point is central in James B. Twitchel, *Lead Us into Temptation: The Triumph of American Materialism* (New York: Columbia University Press, 1999).

65. This is more or less the position of an anti-advertising organization, Adbusters Media Foundation. See Maryilyn Bordwell, "Jamming Culture: Adbusters' Hip Media Campaign against Consumerism," in *Confronting Consumption*, ed. Thomas Princen, Michael Maniates, and Ken Conca (Cambridge, Mass.: MIT Press, 2002), 237–53.

66. Goldman, *Reading Ads Socially*, 3.

67. Barry Alan Morris, "Wall Street to Main Street: A Narrative Approach to Organization Crisis," in *Corporate Advocacy: Rhetoric in the Information Age*, ed. Judith D. Hoover (Westport, Conn.: Quorum Books, 1997), 131–47.

68. Bordwell, "Jamming Culture," 244–46.

69. David B. Sachsman, "The Mass Media 'Discover' the Environment: Influences on Environmental Reporting in the First Twenty Years," in *The Symbolic Earth: Discourse and Our Creation of the Environment*, ed. James G. Cantrill and Christine L. Oravec (Lexington: University Press of Kentucky, 1996), 241–56.

70. Michael E. Kraft and Dana Wuertz, "Environmental Advocacy in the Corridors of Government," in *The Symbolic Earth: Discourse and Our Creation of the Environment*, ed. James G. Cantrill and Christine L. Oravec (Lexington: University Press of Kentucky, 1996), 95–122.

71. Edward S. Herman, *Triumph of the Market: Essays on Economics, Politics, and the Media* (Boston: South End Press, 1995), 168–69.

72. Kraft and Wuertz, "Environmental Advocacy in the Corridors of Government," 113.

73. Kraft and Wuertz, "Environmental Advocacy in the Corridors of Government," 112; Roger Harrabin, "Reporting Sustainable Development: A Broadcast Journalist's View," in *The Daily Globe: Environmental Change, the Public and the Media*, ed. Joe Smith (London: Earthscan, 2000), 49–63.

74. Cherry Farrow, "Communicating about Climate Change: An NGO View," in *The Daily Globe: Environmental Change, the Public and the Media*, ed. Joe Smith (London: Earthscan, 2000), 189–97.

75. Patricia Paystrup, "Plastics as a 'Natural Resource': Perspective by Incongruity for an Industry in Crisis," in *The Symbolic Earth: Discourse and Our Creation of the Environment*, ed. James G. Cantrill and Christine L. Oravec (Lexington: University Press of Kentucky, 1996), 176–97.

76. Kraft and Wuertz, "Environmental Advocacy in the Corridors of Government," 113.

77. Sachsman, "The Mass Media 'Discover' the Environment," 241–44; Mark Neuzil and William Kovarik, *Mass Media & Environmental Conflict: America's Green Crusades* (Thousand Oaks, Calif.: Sage Publications, 1996), 163–93.

78. Tom Tietenberg, *Environmental and Natural Resource*, 364–74.

79. See Mark Dowie, *Losing Ground: American Environmentalism at the Close of the Twentieth Century* (Cambridge, Mass.: MIT Press, 1995), and Gottlieb, *Forcing the Spring*.

80. See chapter 6.

81. Douglas E. Booth, *Valuing Nature: The Decline and Preservation of Old-Growth Forests* (Lanham, Md.: Rowman & Littlefield, 1994), 209–12; Patrick A. Prenteau, "The Exemption Process and the 'God Squad,'" in *Endangered Species Act: Law, Policy, and Perspectives*, ed. Donald C. Baur and Wm. Robert Irvin (Chicago: American Bar Association, 2002), 131–54. The exemption was eventually withdrawn after being turned back to the Endangered Species Committee by the courts.

82. The Endangered Species Act interestingly has not been successfully challenged by landowners on the grounds that a taking of private property results from enforcement of the act. See Glenn P. Sugameli, "The ESA and Takings of Private Property," in *Endangered Species Act: Law, Policy, and Perspectives*, ed. Donald C. Baur and Wm. Robert Irvin (Chicago: American Bar Association, 2002), 441–58.

83. U.S. EPA, *Latest Findings on National Air Quality: 2001*.

84. John Rawls, *A Theory of Justice* (Cambridge: Belknap Press, 1971); John Rawls, *Political Liberalism* (New York: Columbia University Press, 1993); John Rawls, *Justice as Fairness: A Restatement*, ed. Erin Kelly (Cambridge, Mass.: Belknap Press, 2001).

85. Rawls, *Justice as Fairness*, 10.

86. Rawls, *Justice as Fairness*, 14–18.

87. Rawls, *Justice as Fairness*, 19–20.

88. Rawls, *Justice as Fairness*, 32–8.

89. Rawls, *Justice as Fairness*, 91.

90. Rawls, *Justice as Fairness*, 42. It is indeed hard to argue against the idea of basic rights and equality of opportunity. One could quibble with Rawls's difference principle. Some may not need much to live well in the context of their own culture arrangements and religious or philosophical beliefs. This could be the case for cloistered monks or Buddhist priests. The real issue may be to assure a minimum

standard of living sufficient for each to live a decent life. The role of economic inequality in achieving this is by no means clear, although something is doubtlessly wrong with a world where many are starving and some are very rich. If living decently and happiness are strongly dependent on the relative distribution of income, then the degree of inequality matters. Evidence suggests that happiness is largely a noneconomic phenomenon and is only weakly related to one's relative position in the income distribution.

91. Rawls, *Justice as Fairness*, 57.

92. Rawls, *Justice as Fairness*, 174.

93. See chapter 7 for a discussion of Leopold's views.

94. One point of conflict between justice as fairness and a land ethic could occur in the application of the Rawlsian difference principle. The difference principle calls for arranging institutions so as to maximize the economic well-being of the worst-off person in society. This principle could come into conflict with species protections if achieving it required, say, continued global warming or critical habitat loss. The loss of species protections could possibly be avoided if the social goal were weakened to simply achieve a standard of living for the worst-off person that allows for a decent life as opposed to maximizing that standard of living.

95. Habermas, *Moral Consciousness and Communicative Action*, 43–109.

96. Habermas, *Moral Consciousness and Communicative Action*, 116.

97. Aldo Leopold, *A Sand County Almanac: With Essays on Conservation from Round River* (New York: Ballantine Books, 1970), 237–39.

98. Robert Nozick, *Anarchy, State, and Utopia* (New York: Basic Books, 1974).

99. Nozick comes tantalizingly close to the notion of animal rights for sentient creatures. He isn't willing to draw any final conclusions on the question of animal rights and doesn't make it an integral part of his theory. If he did, he would have to account for the incompatibility of private property and ecological interconnectedness. See Nozick, *Anarchy, State, and Utopia*, 35–45.

100. Douglas E. Booth, "Economic Democracy as an Environmental Measure," *Ecological Economics* 12 (1995): 225–36.

101. For a fascinating statement of this position, see Twitchell, *Lead Us into Temptation*. Twitchell's analysis substantiates many of the conclusions voiced in the discussion of consumer behavior in chapter 2.

Bibliography

Abrahamson, Dean E. "Global Warming: The Issue, Impacts, Responses." In *The Challenge of Global Warming*, ed. Dean E. Abrahamson, 3–34. Washington, D.C.: Island Press, 1989.

Ackerman Bruce A., and William T. Hassler. *Clean Coal/Dirty Air: or How the Clean Air Act Became a Multibillion-Dollar Bail-Out for High-Sulfur Coal Producers and What Should Be Done About It.* New Haven, Conn.: Yale University Press, 1981.

Alexander, Susan E., Stephen H. Schneider, and Kalen Lagerquist. "The Interaction of Climate and Life." In *Nature's Services: Societal Dependence on Natural Ecosystems*, ed. Gretchen C. Daily, 71–92. Washington, D.C.: Island Press, 1997.

Allessie, Rob, and Arie Kapteyn. "Habit Formation, Interdependent Preferences and Demographic Effects in the Almost Ideal Demand System." *The Economic Journal* 101 (1991): 404–19.

American Rivers. "Yellowstone River Named One of Nation's Most Endangered Rivers." http://www.amrivers.org/pressrelease/pressmeryellowstone1999 .htm, 1999 (accessed January 12, 2002).

Argyle, Michael. "Causes and Correlates of Happiness." In *Well-Being: The Foundations of Hedonic Psychology,* ed. Daniel Kahneman, Ed Diener, and Norbert Schwartz, 353–73. New York: Russell Sage Foundation, 1999.

Astous, Alain d'. "An Inquiry into the Compulsive Side of 'Normal' Consumers." *Journal of Consumer Policy* 13 (1990): 15–31.

Atkinson, Thomas, Ramsay Liem, and Joan H. Liem. "The Social Costs of Unemployment: Implications for Social Support." *Journal of Health and Social Behavior* 27 (1986): 317–31.

Bailey, Christopher J. *Congress and Air Pollution: Environmental Policies in the USA.* Manchester, U.K.: Manchester University Press, 1998.

Bassmann, Robert L., David J. Molina, and Danile J. Slottje. "A Note on Measuring Veblen's Theory of Conspicuous Consumption." *The Review of Economics and Statistics* 70 (1988): 531–35.

Bearden, William O., and Michael J. Etzel. "Reference Group Influence on Product and Brand Purchase Decisions." *Journal of Consumer Research* 9 (1982): 183–94.

Bearden, William O., Richard G. Netemeyer, and Jesse E. Teel. "Measurement of Consumer Susceptibility to Interpersonal Influence." *Journal of Consumer Research* 15 (1989): 473–81.

Beier, Paul. "Dispersal of Juvenile Cougars in Fragmented Habitat." *Journal of Wildlife Management* 59 (1995): 228–37.

Belk, Russell W. "Possessions and the Extended Self." *Journal of Consumer Research* 15 (1988): 139–68.

——. "Materialism: Trait Aspects of Living in the Material World." *Journal of Consumer Research* 12 (1985): 265–80.

Blair, Robert B. "Land Use and Avian Species Diversity Along an Urban Gradient." *Ecological Applications* 6 (1996): 506–19.

Bluestone, Barry, and Stephen Rose. "The Enigma of Working Time." In *Working Time: International Trends, Theory and Policy Perspectives*, ed. Lonnie Golden and Deborah M. Figart, 21–37. London: Routledge, 2000.

Bockerman, Petri, and Jaakko Kiander. "Has Work-Sharing Worked in Finland?" *Applied Economic Letters* 9 (2002): 39–41.

Bogue, Allan G. *From Prairie to Corn Belt: Farming on the Illinois and Iowa Prairies in the Nineteenth Century.* Chicago: University of Chicago Press, 1963.

Bolger, Douglas T., Thomas A. Scott, and John T. Rotenberry, "Breeding Bird Abundance in an Urbanizing Landscape in Coastal Southern California." *Conservation Biology* 11 (1997): 406–21.

Booth, Douglas E. *Searching for Paradise: Economic Development and Environmental Change in the Mountain West.* Lanham, Md.: Rowman & Littlefield, 2002.

——. "Biocentric Environmental Values and Support for the Ecological Restoration of an Urban Watershed." Technical Report 8, Institute for Urban Environmental Risk Management, Marquette University, Milwaukee, Wisc., 2000.

——. "Spatial Patterns in the Economic Development of the Mountain West." *Growth and Change* 30 (1999): 384–405.

——. *The Environmental Consequences of Growth: Steady-State Economics as an Alternative to Ecological Decline.* London: Routledge, 1998.

——. "Economic Democracy as an Environmental Measure." *Ecological Economics* 12 (1995): 225–36.

——. *Valuing Nature: The Decline and Preservation of Old-Growth Forests.* Lanham, Md.: Rowman & Littlefield, 1994.

——. "Hydroelectric Dams and the Decline of Chinook Salmon in the Columbia River." *Marine Resource Economics* 6 (1989): 195–211.

Bordwell, Maryilyn. "Jamming Culture: Adbusters' Hip Media Campaign against Consumerism." In *Confronting Consumption*, ed. Thomas Princen, Michael Maniates, and Ken Conca, 237–53. Cambridge, Mass.: MIT Press, 2002.

Boren, Jon C., David M. Engle, Michael W. Palmer, Ronald E. Masters, and Tania Criner. "Land Use Change Effects on Breeding Bird Community Composition." *Journal of Range Management* 52 (1999): 420–30.

Borenstein, Seth. "U.S. Smothered in Dangerous Smog 32% More in 2002: Auto Emissions, Power Plants Blamed for the Increase." *Milwaukee Journal*, March 21, 2003, A18.

Bosch, Gerhard. "Working Time Reductions, Employment Consequences and Lessons from Europe: Defusing a Quasi-Religious Controversy." In *Working Time: International Trends, Theory and Policy Perspectives*, ed. Lonnie Golden and Deborah M. Figart, 179–95. London: Routledge, 2000.

Bosso, Christopher J. "Environmental Groups and the New Political Landscape." In *Environmental Policy: New Directions for the Twenty-First Century*, ed. Normal J. Vig and Michael E. Kraft, 55–76. Washington, D.C.: CQ Press, 2000.

——. *Pesticides and Politics: The Life Cycle of a Public Issue*. Pittsburgh: University of Pittsburgh Press, 1987.

Botkin, Daniel B., and Robert A. Nisbet. "Projecting the Effects of Climate Change on Biological Diversity in Forests." In *Global Warming and Biological Diversity*, ed. Robert L. Peters and T. E. Lovejoy, 277–93. New Haven, Conn.: Yale University Press, 1992.

Bowles, Samuel, and Herbert Gintis. "Walrasian Economics in Retrospect." *Quarterly Journal of Economics* 115 (2000): 1411–39.

Bright, Chris. *Life Out of Bounds: Bioinvasions in a Borderless World*. New York: W. W. Norton, 1998.

Brittingham M. C., and S. A. Temple. "Have Cowbirds Caused Forest Songbirds to Decline?" *Bioscience* 33 (1983): 31–35.

Brown, Bruce. *Mountain in the Clouds: A Search for the Wild Salmon*. New York: Simon & Schuster, 1982.

Bryner, Gary C. *Blue Skies, Green Politics: The Clean Air Act of 1990 and Its Implementation*, 2nd ed. Washington, D.C.: CQ Press, 1995.

Brynjolfsson, Erik, and Lorin Hitt. "Beyond Computation: Information Technology, Organizational Transformation and Business Performance." *Journal of Economic Perspectives* 14 (2000): 23–48.

——. "Paradox Lost? Firm-Level Evidence of the Returns to Information Systems Spending." *Management Science* 42 (1996): 541–58.

Burns, Arthur F. *Production Trends in the United States since 1870*. New York: National Bureau of Economic Research, 1934.

Callicott, J. Baird. *Earth's Insights: A Survey of Ecological Ethics from the Mediterranean Basin to the Australian Outback*. Berkeley: University of California Press, 1994.

——. "The Case against Moral Pluralism." *Environmental Ethics* 12, (1990): 99–124.

——. "Intrinsic Value, Quantum Theory, and Environmental Ethics." *Environmental Ethics* 7 (1985): 257–75.

——. "Hume's *Is/Ought* Dichotomy and the Relation of Ecology to Leopold's Land Ethic." *Environmental Ethics* 4, (1982): 163–74.

Canfield, Jodie E., L. Jack Lyon, J. Michael Hillis, and Michael J. Thompson. "Ungulates." In *The Effects of Recreation on Rocky Mountain Wildlife: A Review for Montana*, coord. Gayle Joslin and Heidi Youmans, 6.1–6.25. Committee on Effects of Recreation on Wildlife, Montana Chapter of the Wildlife Society, 1999.

Carson, Rachel. *Silent Spring*. Boston: Houghton Mifflin, 1962.

Case, Karl E., and Ray C. Fair. *Principles of Macroeconomics, Sixth Editions*. Upper Saddle River, N.J.: Prentice-Hall, 2001.

Catalano, Ralph. "The Health Effects of Economic Insecurity." *American Journal of Public Health* 81 (1991): 1148–52.

Catalano, Ralph, David Dooley, Georjeanna Wilson, and Richard Hough. "Job Loss and Alcohol Abuse: A Test Using Data from the Epidemiologic Catchment Area Project." *Journal of Health and Social Behavior* 341 (1993): 215–25.

Chao, Angela, and Juliet B. Schor. "Empirical Tests of Status Consumption: Evidence from Women's Cosmetics." *Journal of Economic Psychology* 19 (1998): 107–31.

Childers, Terry L., and Akshay R. Roa. "The Influence of Familial and Peer-based Reference Groups on Consumer Decisions." *Journal of Consumer Research* 19 (1992): 198–211.

Christenson, Gary A., Ronald J. Faber, Martina de Zwann, Nancy C. Raymond, Sheila M. Specker, Michael D. Ekern, Thomas B. Mackenzie, Ross D. Crosby, Scott J. Crow, Elke D. Eckert, Melissa P. Mussell, and James E. Mitchell. "Compulsive Buying: Descriptive Characteristics and Psychiatric Comorbidity." *Journal of Clinical Psychiatry* 55 (1994): 5–11.

Clark, Andrew E., and Andrew J. Oswald. "Unhappiness and Unemployment." *Economic Journal* 104 (1994): 648–59.

Cline, William R. *The Economics of Global Warming*. Washington, D.C.: Institute for International Economics, 1992.

Coase, Ronald. "The Problem of Social Cost." *Journal of Law and Economics* 3 (1960): 1–44.

Coffin, Barbara, and Lee Pfannmuller. *Minnesota's Endangered Flora and Fauna*. Minneapolis: University of Minnesota Press, 1988.

Cooper, Clare C. "The Role of Railroads in the Settlement of Iowa: A Study in Historical Geography." Unpublished M.A. thesis, University of Nebraska, 1958.

Costain, W. Douglas, and James P. Lester. "The Evolution of Environmentalism." In *Environmental Politics and Policy: Theories and Evidence*, ed. James P. Lester. 15–38. Durham, N.C.: Duke University Press, 1995.

Costanza, Robert, Ralph d'Arge, Rudolf de Groot, Stephen Farber, Monica Grasso, Bruce Hannon, Karin Limburg, Shahid Naeem, Robert V. O'Neill, Jose Paruelo, Rober G. Raskin, Paul Sutton, and Marjan van den Belt. "The Value of the World's Ecosystem Services and Natural Capital." *Nature* 387: 253–60.

Cronon, William. *Nature's Metropolis: Chicago and the Great West*. New York: W. W. Norton, 1991.

Crooks, Kevin R., and Michael E. Soulè. "Mesopredator Release and Avifaunal Extinctions in a Fragmented System." *Nature* 400 (1999): 563–66.

Curtis, John T. *The Vegetation of Wisconsin: An Ordination of Plant Communities*. Madison: University of Wisconsin Press, 1959.

Czech, Brian, Paul R. Krausman, and Patrick K. Devers. "Economic Associations among Causes of Species Endangerment in the United States." *Bioscience* 50 (2000): 593–601.

Daily, Gretchen C., Pamela A. Matson, and Peter M. Vitousek. "Ecosystem Services Supplied by Soil." In *Nature's Services: Societal Dependence on Natural Ecosystems*, ed. Gretchen C. Daily, 113–32. Washington, D.C.: Island Press, 1997.

Daly, Herman E. *Beyond Growth: The Economics of Sustainable Development.* Boston: Beacon Press, 1996.

———. *Steady-State Economics: Second Edition with New Essays.* Washington, D.C.: Island Press, 1991.

Davis, Bob, and David Wessel. *Prosperity: The Coming Twenty-Year Boom and What it Means to You.* New York: Random House, 1998.

Davis Margaret B., and Catherine Zabinski. "Changes in Geographical Range Resulting from Greenhouse Warming: Effects on Biodiversity in Forests." In *Global Warming and Biological Diversity,* ed. Robert L. Peters and T. E. Lovejoy, 297–308. New Haven, Conn.: Yale University Press, 1992.

Dewey, Scott Hamilton. *Don't Breathe the Air: Air Pollution and U.S. Environmental Politics, 1945–1970.* College Station, Tex.: Texas A&M University Press, 2000.

Diener, Ed, and Shigehiro Oishi. "Money and Happiness: Income and Subjective Well-Being across Nations." In *Culture and Subjective Well-being,* ed. Ed Diener and Eunkook M. Suh, 185–218. Cambridge, Mass.: The MIT Press, 2000.

Diener, Ed, Ed Sandvik, Larry Seidlitz, and Marissa Diener. "The Relationship Between Income and Subjective Well-Being: Relative or Absolute?" *Social Indicators Research* 28 (1993): 195–223.

Dowie, Mark. *Losing Ground: American Environmentalism at the Close of the Twentieth Century.* Cambridge, Mass.: MIT Press, 1995.

Downs, Anthony. *New Visions for Metropolitan America.* Washington, D.C.: The Brookings Institution, 1994.

———. "Up and Down with Ecology—The 'Issue-Attention Cycle.'" *The Public Interest* 28 (1972): 38–50.

———. *An Economic Theory of Democracy.* New York: Harper Row, 1957.

Doyle, Jack. *Taken for a Ride: Detroit's Big Three and the Politics of Pollution.* New York: Four Walls Eight Windows, 2000.

Dreger, Christian, Olaf Fuchs, and Jurgen Kolb. "The Effection of a Reduction in Working Hours on Employment: Empirical Evidence for West-Germany." *Journal of Economics* 27 (2001): 69–81.

Dukes, Jeffrey S., and Harold A. Mooney. "Does Global Change Increase the Success of Biological Invaders?" *Trends in Ecology and Evolution* 14 (1999): 135–39.

Dunlap, Riley E. "Public Opinion and Environmental Policy." In *Environmental Politics and Policy: Theories and Evidence,* ed. James P. Lester, 87–93. Durham, N.C.: Duke University Press, 1995.

———. "Trends in Public Opinion toward Environmental Issues: 1965–1990." *Society and Natural Resources* 4 (1991): 285–312.

Dunlap, Riley E., and Kent D. Van Liere. "The 'New Environmental Paradigm' A Proposed Measuring Instrument and Results." *Journal of Environmental Education* 9 (1978): 10–19.

Easterlin, Richard A. "Will Raising the Incomes of All Increase the Happiness of All?" *Journal of Economic Behavior and Organization* 27 (1995): 35–47.

Ehrlich, Paul R. "The Loss of Diversity: Causes and Consequences." In *Biodiversity,* ed. Edward O. Wilson, 21–27. Washington, D.C.: National Academy Press, 1988.

Elster, Jon. *Strong Feelings: Emotion, Addiction, and Human Behavior.* Cambridge, Mass.: MIT Press, 1999.

Faber, Ronald J. "Money Changes Everything: Compulsive Buying from a Biopsy-chological Perspective." *American Behavioral Scientist* 35 (1992): 809–19.

Faber, Ronald J., and Gary A. Christenson. "In the Mood to Buy: Differences in Mood States Experienced by Compulsive Buyers and Other Consumers." *Psychology and Marketing* 13 (1996): 803–19.

Faber, Ronald J., Gary A. Christenson, Martina de Zwaan, and James Mitchell. "Two Forms of Compulsive Consumption: Comorbidity of Compulsive Buying and Binge Eating." *Journal of Consumer Research* 22 (1995): 296–304.

Farrow, Cherry. "Communicating about Climate Change: An NGO View." In *The Daily Globe: Environmental Change, the Public and the Media*, ed. Joe Smith, 189–97. London: Earthscan, 2000.

Ferguson, Charles H., and Charles R. Morris. *Computer Wars: How the West Can Win in a Post-IBM World*. New York: Random House, 1993.

Fey, Bruno S. and Alois Stutzer. *Happiness and Economics: How the Economy and Institutions Affect Well-being*. Princeton, N.J.: Princeton University Press, 2002.

Fishlow, Albert. *American Railroads and the Transformation of the Ante-Bellum Economy*. Cambridge, Mass.: Harvard University Press, 1965.

Francois, Patrick, and Huw Lloyd-Ellis. "Animal Spirits through Creative Destruction." *American Economic Review* 93 (2003): 530–50.

Frank, Robert H. *Luxury Fever: Money and Happiness in an Era of Excess*. Princeton, N.J.: Princeton University Press, 1999.

———. *Choosing the Right Pond: Human Behavior and the Quest for Status*. New York: Oxford University Press, 1985.

Franklin, J. F., K. Cromach, Jr., W. Denison, A. McKee, C. Maser, F. Sedell, F. Swanson, and G. Juday. *Ecological Characteristics of Old-Growth Douglas-Fir Forests*. Portland, Ore.: USDA Forest Service, GTR, PNW-8, 1981.

Franklin, J. F., H. H. Shugart, and M. E. Harmon. "Tree Death as an Ecological Process: the Causes, Consequences, and Variability of Tree Mortality." *BioScience* 37 (1987): 550–56.

Franklin, Jerry F., Frederick J. Swanson, Mark E. Harmon, David A. Perry, Thomas A. Spies, Virginia H. Dale, Arthur McKee, William K. Ferrell, Joseph E. Means, V. Gregory Stanley, John D. Lattin, Timothy D. Schowalter, and David Larsen, "Effects of Global Climatic Change on Forests in Northwestern North America." In *Global Warming and Biological Diversity*, ed. Robert L. Peters and T. E. Lovejoy, 244–57. New Haven, Conn.: Yale University Press, 1992.

Frey, Bruno S., and Alois Stutzer. *Happiness and Economics: How the Economy and Institutions Affect Well-being*. Princeton, N.J.: Princeton University Press, 2002.

Fuguitt, Glenn V., and Calvin L. Beale. "Recent Trends in Nonmetropolitan Migration: Toward a New Turnaround?" *Growth and Change* 27 (1996): 156–74.

Gallatin County Planning Board. *Zoning District Model*. Bozeman, Mont.: Gallatin County, 1996.

Gallatin County Planning Department. *Springhill Planning and Zoning District*. Bozeman, Mont., 1992.

Gallman, Robert E. "Commodity Output, 1839–1899." In *Trends in the American Economy in the Nineteenth Century*, National Bureau of Economic Research. Princeton, N.J.: Princeton University Press, 1960.

Garreau, Joel. *Edge City: Life on the New Frontier*. New York: Doubleday, 1991.

Georgescu-Roegen, Nicholas. *The Entropy Law and the Economic Process.* Cambridge, Mass.: Harvard University Press, 1971.

Ger, Guliz, and Russell W. Belk. "Cross-cultural Differences in Materialism." *Journal of Economic Psychology* 17 (1996): 55–77.

Goldman, Robert. *Reading Ads Socially.* London: Routledge, 1992.

Goldstein, Avram. *Addiction: From Biology to Drug Policy.* New York: W. H. Freeman, 1994.

Gottlieb, Robert. *Forcing the Spring: The Transformation of the American Environmental Movement.* Washington, D.C.: Island Press, 1993.

Gould, Roy. *Going Sour: Science and Politics of Acid Rain.* Boston: Birkhauser, 1985.

Graetz, Brian. "Health Consequences of Employment and Unemployment: Longitudinal Evidence for Young Men and Women." *Social Science and Medicine* 36 (1993): 715–24.

Grossman, Gene M., and Alan B. Krueger, "Economic Growth and the Environment." *Quarterly Journal of Economics* 110 (1995): 353–77.

Gustanski, Julie A., and Roderick H. Squires. *Protecting the Land: Conservation Easements Past, Present, and Future.* Washington, D.C.: Island Press, 2000.

Habermas, Jürgen. *The Structural Transformation of the Public Sphere: An Inquiry into a Category of Bourgeois Society.* Trans. Thomas Berger with the assistance of Frederick Lawrence. Cambridge, Mass.: MIT Press, 1991.

——. *Moral Consciousness and Communicative Action.* Trans. Christian Lenhardt and Shierry Weber Nicholsen. Cambridge, Mass.: MIT Press, 1990.

——. *The Theory of Communicative Action: Volume 1, Reason and Rationalization of Society.* Trans. Thomas McCarthy. Boston: Beacon Press, 1984.

——. *The Theory of Communicative Action: Volume 2, Lifeworld and System: A Critique of Functionalist Reason.* Boston: Beacon Press, 1984.

Hamburg, James F. *The Influence of Railroads upon the Processes and Patterns of Settlement in South Dakota.* New York: Arno Press, 1981.

Hammarstrom, Anne. "Health Consequences of Youth Unemployment—Review from a Gender Perspective." *Social Science and Medicine* 38 (1994): 699–709.

Hansen, Andrew J., Ray Rasker, Bruce Maxwell, Jay J. Rotella, Jerry D. Johnson, Andrea Wright Parmenter, Ute Langer, Warren B. Cohen, Rick L. Lawrence, and Matthew P. V. Kraska. "Ecological Causes and Consequences of Demographic Change in the New West." *BioScience* 52 (2002): 151–62.

Hansen, Andrew J., and Jay J. Rotella. "Biophysical Factors, Land Use, and Species Viability in and around Nature Reserves." *Conservation Biology* 16 (2002): 1112–22.

Harmon, Mark E., and Jerry F. Franklin. "Tree Seedlings on Logs in *Picea-Tsuga* Forests of Oregon and Washington." *Ecology* 70 (1989): 45–59.

Harrabin, Roger. "Reporting Sustainable Development: A Broadcast Journalist's View." In *The Daily Globe: Environmental Change, the Public and the Media,* ed. Joe Smith, 49–63. London: Earthscan, 2000.

Harris, Larry D., and Wendell P. Cropper, Jr. "Between the Devil and the Deep Blue Sea: Implications of Climate Change for Florida's Fauna." In *Global Warming and Biological Diversity,* ed. Robert L. Peters and T. E. Lovejoy, 309–24. New Haven, Conn.: Yale University Press, 1992.

Harrison, Robert L. "A Comparison of Gray Fox Ecology between Residential and Undeveloped Rural Landscapes." *Journal of Wildlife Management* 61 (1997): 112–22.

Hays, Samuel P. *Beauty, Health, and Permanence: Environmental Politics in the United States, 1955–1985*. Cambridge: Cambridge University Press, 1987.

Heerink, Nico, Abay Mulatu, and Erwin Bulte. "Income Inequality and the Environment: Aggregation Bias in Environmental Kuznets Curves." *Ecological Economics* 38 (2001): 359–67.

Herman, Edward S. *Triumph of the Market: Essays on Economics, Politics, and the Media*. Boston: South End Press, 1995.

Herring, Hal. "Strangling the Last Best River." *High Country News* 31–37 (April 12, 1999): 6.

Hilsenrath, Jon E. "Economy Is Falling Short of Potential, Economists Believe." *Wall Street Journal*, August 31, 2001, A2.

Hirschhorn, Joel S. "Natural Amenities and Locational Choice in the New Economy." In *Conservation in the Internet Age: Threats and Opportunities*, ed. James N. Levitt, 269–85. Washington, D.C.: Island Press, 2002.

Hirschman, Elizabeth C. "The Consciousness of Addiction: Toward a General Theory of Compulsive Consumption." *Journal of Consumer Research* 19 (1992): 155–79.

Hobbs, Richard J. "Land-Use Changes and Invasions." In *Invasive Species in a Changing World*, ed. Harold A. Mooney and Richard J. Hobbs, 55–64. Washington, D.C.: Island Press, 2000.

Honda Motor Company Ltd. "Honda Starts Experiments with Hydrogen Production and Fueling for Fuel Cell Vehicles at New Station in California (U.S.)." *Honda Corporate News*, July 10, 2001, http://world.honda.com/news/2001/c010710.html.

Howe, Jim, Ed McMahon, and Luther Propst. *Balancing Nature and Commerce in Gateway Communities*. Washington, D.C.: Island Press, 1997.

Ichbiah, Daniel, and Susan L. Knepper. *The Making of Microsoft: How Bill Gates and His Team Created the World's Most Successful Software Company*. Rocklin, Calif.: Prima Publishing, 1991.

Ingram, Helen M., David H. Colnic, and Dean E. Mann. "Interest Groups and Environmental Policy." In *Environmental Politics and Policy: Theories and Evidence*, ed. James P. Lester, 115–45. Durham, N.C.: Duke University Press, 1995.

Intergovernmental Panel on Climate Change. "Climate Change and Biodiversity." *IPCC Technical Paper* V, 2002.

——. *Climate Change 2001—Impacts, Adaptations and Vulnerability*. Cambridge: Cambridge University Press, 2001.

——. *Climate Change 2001: Mitigation*. Cambridge: Cambridge University Press, 2001.

——. *Climate Change 2001: The Scientific Basis*. Cambridge, U.K.: Cambridge University Press, 2001.

——. *Climate Change 1995—Impacts, Adaptations and Mitigation of Climate Change: Scientific-Technical Analyses*. Cambridge: Cambridge University Press, 1996.

Ip, Greg. "Jobless Rate Rose to 5.8% in December." *Wall Street Journal*, January 7, 2002, A2.

———. "It's Official: Economy Is in a Recession." *Wall Street Journal.* November 27, 2001, A2.

Ip, Greg, and Jacob M. Schlesinger. "Great Expectations: Did Greenspan Push High-Tech Optimism on Growth Too Far?" *Wall Street Journal,* December 28, 2001, A1.

Jackson, Kenneth T. *Crabgrass Frontier: The Suburbanization of the United States.* New York: Oxford University Press, 1985.

Jackson, Thomas Penfield. *United States v. Microsoft Corporation: Findings of Fact.* Washington, D.C.: United States District Court for the District of Columbia, 1999, http://usvms.gpo.gov/findings_index.html.

Jacobs, Jane. *The Death and Life of Great American Cities.* New York: Vintage Books, 1961.

Jacobs Jerry A., and Kathleen Gerson. "Who Are the Overworked Americans?" In *Working Time: International Trends, Theory and Policy Perspectives,* ed. Lonnie Golden and Deborah M. Figart, 89–105. London: Routledge, 2000.

Jamison, Michael. "Whitfish-Area Growth May be Funneling Grizzlies into Town." *Missoulian,* November 23, 1999, A1; A7.

Johnson, Kenneth M. "The Rural Rebound of the 1990s and Beyond." In *Conservation in the Internet Age: Threats and Opportunities,* ed. James N. Levitt, 63–82. Washington, D.C.: Island Press, 2002.

Johnson, Lawrence E. "Toward the Moral Considerability of Species and Ecosystems." *Environmental Ethics* 14 (1992): 145–57.

Johnson, Vanessa. *Rural Residential Development Trends in the Greater Yellowstone Ecosystem since the Listing of the Grizzly Bear.* Bozeman, Mont.: Sierra Club Grizzly Bear Ecosystem Project, 2000.

Kahneman, Daniel. "Objective Happiness." In *Well-Being: The Foundations of Hedonic Psychology,* ed. Daniel Kahneman, Ed Diener, and Norbert Schwartz, 3–25. New York: Russell Sage Foundation, 1999.

Kapp, Karl W. "Environmental Disruption and Social Costs: A Challenge to Economics." *Kyklos* 23 (1970): 833–47.

Katz, Michael L., and Carl Shapiro. "Antitrust in Software Markets." In *Competition, Innovation and the Microsoft Monopoly: Antitrust in the Digital Marketplace,* ed. Jeffrey A. Eisenach and Thomas M. Lenard, 29–81. Boston: Kluwer Academic Publishers, 1999.

Kempton, Willett, James S. Boster, and Jennifer A. Hartley. *Environmental Values in American Culture.* Cambridge, Mass.: MIT Press, 1995.

Knopf, Fritz L. "Prairie Legacies—Birds." In *Prairie Conservation: Preserving North America's Most Endangered Ecosystem,* ed. Fred B. Samson and Fritz L. Knopf, 135–48. Washington, D.C.: Island Press, 1996.

Kolar, Cynthia S., and David M. Lodge. "Freshwater Nonindigenous Species: Interactions with Other Global Changes." In *Invasive Species in a Changing World,* ed. Harold A. Mooney and Richard J. Hobbs, 3–30. Washington, D.C.: Island Press, 2000.

Kraft, Michael E. "Environmental Policy in Congress: From Consensus to Gridlock." In *Environmental Policy: New Directions for the Twenty-First Century,* ed. Normal J. Vig and Michael E. Kraft, 128–40. Washington, D.C.: CQ Press, 2000.

Kraft, Michael E., and Dana Wuertz. "Environmental Advocacy in the Corridors of Government." In *The Symbolic Earth: Discourse and Our Creation of the Environment,* ed. James G. Cantrill and Christine L. Oravec, 95–122. Lexington: University Press of Kentucky, 1996.

La Trobe, Helen L., and Tim G. Acott. "A Modified NEP/DSP Environmental Attitudes Scale." *Journal of Environmental Education* 32 (2000): 12–20.

Leach Mark K., and Thomas J. Givnish. "Ecological Determinants of Species Loss in Remnant Prairies." *Science* 273: 1555–58.

Lekakis, Joseph N. "Environment and Development in a Southern European Country: Which Environmental Kuznets Curves?" *Journal of Environmental Planning and Management* 43 (2000): 139–53.

Lekakis, Joseph, and Maria Kousis. "Demand for and Supply of Environmental Quality in the Environmental Kuznets Curve Hypothesis." *Applied Economic Letters* 8 (2001): 169–72.

Leopold, Aldo. *A Sand County Almanac: With Essays on Conversatin from Round River.* New York: Ballantine Books, 1970.

Lester, James P. "Introduction." In *Environmental Politics and Policy: Theories and Evidence,* ed. James P. Lester, 1–14. Durham, N.C.: Duke University Press, 1995.

Levitt, James N. "Networks and Nature in the American Experience." In *Conservation in the Internet Age: Threats and Opportunities,* ed. James N. Levitt, 11–49. Washington, D.C.: Island Press, 2002.

Levitt, James N. and John R. Pitkin. "Internet Use in a High-Growth Amenity-Rich Region." In *Conservation in the Internet Age: Threats and Opportunities,* ed. James N. Levitt, 99–122. Washington, D.C.: Island Press, 2002.

MacArthur, Robert H., and Edward O. Wilson. *The Theory of Island Biogeography.* Princeton, N.J.: Princeton University Press, 1967.

Mace, Richard D., and John S. Waller. "Demography and Population Trend of Grizzly Bears in the Swan Mountains, Montana." *Conservation Biology* 12 (1998): 1005–16.

Madson, John. *Where the Sky Began: Land of the Tallgrass Prairie.* Boston: Houghton Mifflin, 1982.

Mannan, R. William, Charles E. Meslow, and Howard M. Wight. "Use of Snags by Birds in Douglas-Fir Forests, Western Oregon." *Journal of Wildlife Management* 44 (1980): 787–97.

Marland, G., T. A. Boden, and R. J. Andres. *Trends Online: A Compendium of Data on Global Change.* Oak Ridge, Tenn.: Oak Ridge National Laboratory, Carbon Dioxide Information Analysis Center, 2003, http://cdiac.esd.ornl.gov/trends/trends.htm.

Marti, Michael. "Substitution between Working hours and Employment: An Empirical Analysis for Switzerland." *Journal of Economics and Statistics* 136 (2000): 397–415.

Maser, Chris, Zane Maser, Joseph W. Witt, and Gary Hunt. "The Northern Flying Squirrel: A Mycophagist in Southwestern Oregon." *Canadian Journal of Zoology* 64 (1986): 2086–89.

Maser, Chris, and James M. Trappe. *The Seen and Unseen World of the Fallen Tree.* Portland, Ore.: USDA Forest Service, Pacific Northwest Forest and Range and Experiment Station, GTR PNW-164, 1984.

Maser, Chris, James M. Trappe, and Ronald A. Nussbaum. "Fungal-Small Mammal Interrelationships with Emphasis on Oregon Coniferous Forests." *Ecology* 59 (1978): 799–809.

McHarg, Ian L. "The Place of Nature in the City of Man." In *Western Man and Environmental Ethics: Attitudes toward Nature and Technology*, ed. Ian G. Barbour, 171–86. Reading, Mass.: Addison-Wesley Publishing Company, 1973.

———. *Design With Nature*. Garden City, N.Y.: Natural History Press, 1969.

McSpadden, Lettie. "The Courts and Environmental Policy." In *Environmental Politics and Policy: Theories and Evidence*, ed. James P. Lester, 242–74. Durham, N.C.: Duke University Press, 1995.

Melnick, R. Shep. *Regulation and the Courts: The Case of the Clean Air Act*. Washington, D.C.: The Brookings Institution, 1983.

Meyer, Laurence H. "Comparative Central Banking and the Politics of Monetary Policy." *Business Economics* 36 (2001): 43–49.

Mills, Edwin S., and Bruce W. Hamilton. *Urban Economics*, 5th ed. New York: HarperCollins, 1994.

Ministry of the Environment Finland. *Housing Statistics in the European Union*. Helsinki: Ministry of the Environment Finland, 2001, http://www.euhousing.org.

Minter, Ben A., and Robert E. Manning. "Pragmatism in Environmental Ethics: Democracy, Pluralism, and the Management of Nature." *Environmental Ethics* 21 (1999): 191–207.

Mitchell, Robert C., Angela G. Mertig, and Riley E. Dunlap. "Twenty Years of Environmental Mobilization: Trends among National Environmental Organizations." *Society and Natural Resources* 4 (1991): 219–34.

Mitchell, William J. "The Internet, New Urban Patterns, and Conservation." In *Conservation in the Internet Age: Threats and Opportunities*, ed. James N. Levitt, 50–62. Washington, D.C.: Island Press, 2002.

Morris, Barry Alan. "Wall Street to Main Street: A Narrative Approach to Organization Crisis." In *Corporate Advocacy: Rhetoric in the Information Age*, ed. Judith D. Hoover, 131–47. Westport, Conn.: Quorum Books, 1997.

Murray, Shailagn, and John D. Mckinnon. "Consensus Builds to Help the Economy." *Wall Street Journal*, September 27, 2001, A2.

Myers, J. P., and Robert T. Lester. "Double Jeopardy for Migrating Animals: Multiple Hist and Resource Asynchrony." In *Global Warming and Biological Diversity*, ed. Robert L. Peters and T. E. Lovejoy, 193–200. New Haven, Conn.: Yale University Press, 1992.

Myers, Norman. "Biodiversity's Genetic Library." In *Nature's Services: Societal Dependence on Natural Ecosystems*, ed. Gretchen C. Daily, 255–73. Washington, D.C.: Island Press, 1997.

———. "The World's Forests and Their Ecosystem Services." In *Nature's Services: Societal Dependence on Natural Ecosystems*, ed. Gretchen C. Daily, 215–35. Washington, D.C.: Island Press, 1997.

———. "Tropical Forests and Their Species: Going, Going, . . . ?" In *Biodiversity*, ed. Edward O. Wilson, 28–35. Washington, D.C.: National Academy Press, 1988.

Naidoo, Robin, and Wiktor L. Adamowicz. "Effects of Economic Prosperity on Numbers of Threatened Species." *Conservation Biology* 15 (2001): 1021–29.

Nakamura, Leonard I. "Economics and the New Economy: The Invisible Hand Meets Creative Destruction." Federal Reserve Bank of Philadelphia, *Business Review* (July/August 2000):15–30.

Nell, Edward J. *Prosperity and Public Spending: Transformational Growth and the Role of Public Spending*. Boston: Unwin Hyman, 1988.

Nelson, Robert H. "Mythology Instead of Analysis: The Story of Public Forest Management." In *Forest Lands: Public and Private*, ed. Robert T. Deacon and M. Bruce
Johnson, 23–76. San Francisco: Pacific Institute, 1985.

Neumark, David, and Andrew Postlewaite. "Relative Income Concerns and the
Rise in Married Women's Employment." *Journal of Public Economics* 70 (1998):
157–83.

Neuzil, Mark, and William Kovarik. *Mass Media and Environmental Conflict: America's Green Crusades*. Thousand Oaks, Calif.: Sage Publications, 1996.

Newman, Peter, and Jeffrey Kenworthy. *Sustainability and Cities: Overcoming Automobile Dependence*. Washington, D.C.: Island Press, 1999.

Nordenmark, Mikael, and Mattias Strandh. "Towards a Sociological Understanding of Mental Well-Being among the Unemployed: The Role of Economic and
Psychosocial Factors." *Sociology* 33 (1999): 577–97.

Nordhaus, William D., and Joseph Boyer. *Warming the World: Economic Models of
Global Warming*. Cambridge, Mass.: MIT Press, 2000.

North, Douglass C. *Growth and Welfare in the American Past: A New Economic History*, 2nd ed. Englewood Cliffs, N.J.: Prentice-Hall, 1974.

Norton, Bryan G. "Why I Am Not a Nonanthropocentrist: Callicott and the Failure of Monistic Inherentism." *Environmental Ethics* 17 (1995): 341–58.

——. *Toward Unity among Environmentalists*. New York: Oxford University Press,
1991.

Noss, Reed F., and Allen Y. Cooperrider. *Saving Nature's Legacy: Protecting and
Restoring Biodiversity*. Washington, D.C.: Island Press, 1994.

Noss, Reed F., Michael A. O'Connell, and Dennis D. Murphy. *The Science of Conservation Planning: Habitat Conservation under the Endangered Species Act*. Washington, D.C.: Island Press, 1997.

Nozick, Robert. *Anarchy, State, and Utopia*. New York: Basic Books, 1974.

Odell, Eric A., and Richard L. Knight. "Songbird and Medium-Sized Mammal
Community Associated with Exurban Development in Pitkin County, Colorado." *Conservation Biology* 15 (2001): 1143–50.

O'Guinn, Thomas C., and Ronald J. Faber. "Compulsive Buying: A Phenomenological Exploration." *Journal of Consumer Research* 16 (1989): 147–57.

Olson, Mancur, Jr. *The Logic of Collective Action: Public Goods and the Theory of
Groups*. New York: Schocken Books, 1971.

Orford, Jim. *Excessive Appetites: A Psychological View of Addictions*. Chichester: John
Wiley and Sons, 1985.

Paystrup, Patricia. "Plastics as a 'Natural Resource': Perspective by Incongruity
for an Industry in Crisis." In *The Symbolic Earth: Discourse and Our Creation of the
Environment*, ed. James G. Cantrill and Christine L. Oravec, 176–97. Lexington:
University Press of Kentucky, 1996.

Peele, Stanton. *The Meaning of Addiction: Compulsive Experience and Its Interpretation*. Lexington, Mass.: Lexington Books, 1985.

Peters, Robert L. "Conservation of Biological Diversity in the Face of Climate
Change." In *Global Warming and Biological Diversity*, ed. Robert L. Peters and
T. E. Lovejoy, 15–30. New Haven, Conn.: Yale University Press, 1992.

——. "Effects of Global Warming on Biodiversity." In *The Challenge of Global Warming*, ed. Dean Edwin Abrahamson, 82–95. Washington, D.C.: Island Press, 1989.

Petts, G. E. *Impounded Rivers: Perspectives for Ecological Management.* New York: John Wiley and Sons, 1984.

Pimentel, David, Lori Lach, Rodolfo Zuniga, and Doug Morrison. "Environmental and Economic Costs of Nonindigenous Species in the United States." *Bioscience* 50 (2000): 53–65.

Postel, Sandra, and Stephen Carpenter. "Freshwater Ecosystem Services." In *Nature's Services: Societal Dependence on Natural Ecosystems,* ed. Gretchen C. Daily, 195–214. Washington, D.C.: Island Press, 1997.

Prachowny, Martin F. J. *The Kennedy-Johnson Tax Cut: A Revisionist History.* Cheltenham, U.K.: Edward Elgar, 2000.

Prenteau, Patrick A. "The Exemption Process and the 'God Squad.'" In *Endangered Species Act: Law, Policy, and Perspectives,* ed. Donald C. Baur and Wm. Robert Irvin, 131–54. Chicago: American Bar Association, 2002.

Preston, Christopher J. "Epistemology and Intrinsic Values: Norton and Callicott's Critiques of Rolston." *Environmental Ethics* 20 (1998): 409–28.

Rasker, Ray, and Andrew Hansen. "Natural Amenities and Population Growth in the Greater Yellowstone Region." *Human Ecology Review* 7 (2000): 30–40.

Rawls, John. *Political Liberalism.* New York: Columbia University Press, 1993.

———. *A Theory of Justice.* Cambridge: Belknap Press, 1971.

———. *Justice as Fairness: A Restatement,* ed. Erin Kelly. Cambridge: Belknap Press, 2001.

Reisner, Marc. *Cadillac Desert: The American West and Its Disappearing Water.* New York: Penguin Books, 1987.

Rindfleisch, Aric, James E. Burroughs, and Frank Denton. "Family Structure, Materialism, and Compulsive Consumption." *Journal of Consumer Research* 23 (1997): 312–25.

Risser, Paul G. *The True Prairie Ecosystem.* Stroudsburg, Pa.: Hutchinson Ross Publishing Company, 1981.

Roche, William K., Brian Fynes, and Terri Morrissey. "Working Time and Employment: A Review of International Evidence." *International Labour Review* 135 (1996): 129–57.

Rolston, Holmes, III. *Genes, Genesis, and God: Values and Their Origins in Natural and Human History.* Cambridge: Cambridge University Press, 1999.

———. "Are Values in Nature Subjective or Objective." *Environmental Ethics* 4 (1982): 125–51.

———. "Values in Nature." *Environmental Ethics* 3 (1981): 113–28.

Romme W. H., and M. G. Turner. "Implications of Global Climate Change for Biogeographic Patterns in the Greater Yellowstone Ecosystem." *Conservation Biology* 5 (1991): 373–86.

Rosenbaum, Walter A. "The Bureaucracy and Environmental Policy." In *Environmental Politics and Policy: Theories and Evidence,* ed. James P. Lester, 206–41. Durham, N.C.: Duke University Press, 1995.

Ross, Catherine E., and John Mirowsky. "Does Employment Affect Health?" *Journal of Health and Social Behavior* 36 (1995): 230–43.

Rothman, Dale S. "Environmental Kuznets Curves—Real Progress or Passing the Buck? A Case for Consumption-Based Approaches." *Ecological Economics* 25 (1998): 177–94.

Rothman, Dale S., and Sander M. de Bruyn. "Probing into the Environmental Kuznets Curve Hypothesis." *Ecological Economics* 25 (1998): 143–45.

Rubey, Thomas C. "Profile of Computer Owners in the 1990s." *Monthly Labor Review* 122 (1999): 41–42.

Sachsman, David B. "The Mass Media 'Discover' the Environment: Influences on Environmental Reporting in the First Twenty Years." In *The Symbolic Earth: Discourse and Our Creation of the Environment*, ed. James G. Cantrill and Christine L. Oravec, 241–56. Lexington: University Press of Kentucky, 1996.

Sahu, Anandi Prasad, and Ronald L. Tracy. *The Economic Legacy of the Reagan Years.* New York: Praeger, 1991.

Scherhorn, Gerhard. "The Addictive Trait in Buying Behavior." *Journal of Consumer Policy* 13 (1990): 33–51.

Schor, Juliet B. "Working Hours and Time Pressure: The Controversy about Trends in Time Use." In *Working Time: International Trends, Theory and Policy Perspectives*, ed. Lonnie Golden and Deborah M. Figart, 73–86. London: Routledge, 2000.

———. *The Overspent American: Upscaling, Downshifting, and the New Consumer.* New York: Basic Books, 1998.

———. *The Overworked American: The Unexpected Decline of Leisure.* New York: Basic Books, 1991.

Schorger, A. W. "Extinct and Endangered Mammals and Birds of the Upper Great Lakes Region." *Transactions of the Wisconsin Academy of Sciences, Arts and Letters* 34 (1942): 23–44.

Schumpeter, Joseph A. *Capitalism, Socialism, and Democracy.* 3rd ed. New York: Harper and Brothers Publishers, 1950.

Scitovsky, Tibor. *The Joyless Economy: An Inquiry into Human Satisfaction and Consumer Dissatisfaction.* New York: Oxford University Press, 1976.

Searle, John R. *The Construction of Social Reality.* New York: Free Press, 1995.

Selden, Thomas M., and Daqing Song. "Environmental Quality and Development: Is There a Kuznets Curve for Air Pollution Emissions?" *Journal of Environmental Economics and Management* 27 (1994): 147–62.

Shafik, Nemat. "Economic Development and Environmental Quality: An Econometric Analysis." *Oxford Economic Papers* 46 (1994): 757–73.

Sierra Club. "Sierra Club Yearly Election Results." http://www.susps.org/info/election_results.html.

Solins, P., C. C. Grier, F. M. McCorison, K. Cromack Jr., and R. Fogel. "The Internal Element Cycles of an Old-Growth Douglas-Fir Ecosystem in Western Oregon." *Ecological Monographs* 50 (1980): 261–85.

Solnick, Sara J., and David Hemenway. "Is More Always Better?: A Survey on Positional Concerns." *Journal of Economic Behavior and Organization* 37 (1998): 373–83.

Spash, Clive L. *Greenhouse Economics: Values and Ethics.* London: Routledge, 2002.

———. "Ethics and Environmental Attitudes with Implications for Economic Valuation." *Journal of Environmental Management* 50: 191–208.

———. "Ecosystems, Contingent Valuation and Ethics: The Case of Wetland Recreation." *Ecological Economics* 34 (2000): 195–215.

Spash, Clive L., and Nick Hanley. "Preferences, Information and Biodiversity Preservation." *Ecological Economics* 12 (1995): 191–208.

Spies, Thomas A., and Jerry F. Franklin. "Coarse Woody Debris in Douglas-Fir Forests of Western Oregon and Washington." *Ecology* 69 (1988): 1689–1702.

——. "Old Growth and Forest Dynamics in the Douglas-Fir Region of Western Oregon and Washington." *Natural Areas Journal* 8 (1988): 190–201.

Spithoven, A. H. G. M. "The Third Way: The Dutch Experience." *Economy and Society* 31 (2002): 333–68.

Steinauer, Ernest M., and Scott L. Collins. "Prairie Ecology—The Tallgrass Prairie." In *Prairie Conservation: Preserving North America's Most Endangered Ecosystem,* ed. Fred B. Samson and Fritz L. Knopf, 39–52. Washington, D.C.: Island Press, 1996.

Sugameli, Glenn P. "The ESA and Takings of Private Property." In *Endangered Species Act: Law, Policy, and Perspectives,* ed. Donald C. Baur and Wm. Robert Irvin, 441–58. Chicago: American Bar Association, 2002).

Sullins, Martha J., David T. Theobold, Jeff R. Jones, and Leah M. Burgess. "Lay of the Land: Ranch Land and Ranching." In *Ranching West of the 100th Meridian,* ed. Richard L. Knight, Wendell C. Gilgert, and Ed Marston, 25–32. Washington, D.C.: Island Press, 2002.

Sullivan, Teresa A., Elizabeth Warren, and Jay Lawrence Westbrook. *The Fragile Middle Class: Americans in Debt.* New Haven, Conn.: Yale University Press, 2000.

Suri, Vivek, and Duane Chapman. "Economic Growth, Trade and Energy: Implications of the Environmental Kuznets Curve." *Ecological Economics* 25 (1998): 195–208.

Taylor, Paul W. "The Ethics of Respect for Nature." *Environmental Ethics* 3 (1981): 197–218.

The Nature Conservancy, Northern Tallgrass Prairie Ecoregional Planning Team. *Ecoregional Planning in the Northern Tallgrass Prairie Ecoregion.* Minneapolis, Minn.: The Nature Conservancy, Midwest Regional Office, 1998.

——. *Priorities for Conservation: 1996 Annual Report Card for U.S. Plant and Animal Species* Arlington, Va.: The Nature Conservancy, 1996.

Thompson, Jana. "A Refutation of Environmental Ethics." *Environmental Ethics* 12 (1990): 147–60.

Tietenberg, Tom. *Environmental and Natural Resource Economics,* 5th ed. Reading, Pa.: Addison Wesley Longman, 2000.

——. *Environmental Economics and Policy.* New York: HarperCollins, 1994.

Tiner, Ralph W., Jr. *Wetlands of the United States: Current Status and Recent Trends.* Washington, D.C.: U.S. Department of the Interior, Fish and Wildlife Service, 1984.

Titus, James G. "The Causes and Effects of Sea Level Rise." In *Policy Implications of Greenhouse Warming: Mitigation, Adaption, and the Science Base,* 584–91. National Academy of Sciences, National Academy of Engineering, Institute of Medicine. Washington, D.C.: National Academy Press, 1992.

——. "The Causes and Effects of Sea Level Rise." In *The Challenge of Global Warming.* ed. Dean Edwin Abrahamson, 161–95. Washington, D.C.: Island Press, 1989.

Torras, Mariano, and James K. Boyce. "Income, Inequality, and Pollution: A Reassessment of the Environmental Kuznets Curve." *Ecological Economics* 25 (1998): 147–60.

Torres, Steven G., Terry M. Mansfield, Janet E. Foley, Thomas Lupo, and Amy Brinkhaus. "Mountain Lion and Human Activity in California: Testing Speculations." *Wildlife Society Bulletin* 24 (1996):451–60.

Turner, J. Blake. "Economic Context and Health Effects of Unemployment." *Journal of Health and Social Behavior* 36 (1995): 213–29.

Twitchell, James B. *Lead Us into Temptation: The Triumph of American Materialism.* New York: Columbia University Press, 1999.

U.S. Bureau of the Census, "American FactFinder." Washington, D.C.: U.S. Bureau of the Census, 2000, http://factfinder.census.gov.

——. "American FactFinder." Urban and Rural, Census 2000 Summary File 3 (SF 3), P5. http://factfinder.census.gov (accessed October 18, 2002).

——. *American Housing Survey for the United States: 1999.* Washington, D.C.: U.S. Government Printing Office, 2003, http://www.census.gov/hhes/www/housing/ahs/ahs99/tab1a3.html.

——. "Income Inequality—Table 2," http://www.census.gov/hhes/income/incineq/p60tb2.html.

——. *Statistical Abstract of the United States: 2000.* Washington, D.C.: U.S. Government Printing Office, 2000.

U.S. Congress, Office of Technology Assessment. *Harmful Non-Indigenous Species in the United States.* OTA-F-565. Washington, D.C.: U.S. Government Printing Office, 1993.

USDA Natural Resource Conservation Service. "Summary Report, 1997 National Resources Inventory." http://www.nhq.nrcs.usda.gov/NRI/1997/summary_report/original/table5.html, revised, December 2000.

U.S. Department of Commerce, Bureau of the Census. *Historical Statistics of the United States: Colonial Times to 1970.* Washington, D.C.: U.S. Government Printing Office, 1975.

U.S. Department of Commerce, Economics and Statistics Administration, Bureau of Economic Analysis. *Regional Economic Information System 1969–1997.* Washington, D.C.: U.S. Department of Commerce, CD-ROM, 1999.

U.S. EPA. "EPA Global Warming Site: Impacts—Birds." http://yosemite.epa.gov/OAR/globalwarming.nsf/content/ImpactsBirds.html (accessed October 14, 2002).

——. *Inventory of U.S. Greenhouse Gas Emissions and Sinks: 1990–2000.* Washington, D.C.: U.S. Environmental Protection Agency, 2002.

——. *Latest Findings on National Air Quality: 2001 Status and Trends.* Research Triangle Park, N.C.: Office of Air Quality Planning and Standards, Environmental Protection Agency, September, 2002.

——. *Latest Findings on National Air Quality: 1999 Status and Trends.* Research Triangle Park, N.C.: Office of Air Quality Planning and Standards, August 2000.

——. *National Emissions (1970–1998).* Research Triangle Park, N.C.: Office of Air Quality Planning and Standards, March 2000.

U.S. Executive Office of the President, Council of Economic Advisors. *Economic Report of the President: Transmitted to the Congress, February 2002.* Washington, D.C.: U.S. Government Printing Office, 2002.

Valence, Gilles, Alain d'Astous, and Louis Fortier. "Compulsive Buying: Concept and Measurement." *Journal of Consumer Policy* 11 (1988): 419–33.

Van Driesche, Jason, and Roy Van Driesche. *Nature Out Place: Biological Invasions in the Global Age.* Washington, D.C.: Island Press, 2000.

van Duijn, J. J. *The Long Wave in Economic Life.* London: George Allen & Unwin, 1983.

Veblen, Thorstein. *The Theory of the Leisure Class: An Economic Study of Institutions.* New York: Mentor Books, 1953.

Vig, Normal J. "Presidential Leadership and the Environment: From Reagan to Clinton." In *Environmental Policy: New Directions for the Twenty-First Century,* ed. Normal J. Vig and Michael E. Kraft, 107–15. Washington, D.C.: CQ Press, 2000.

Vileisis, Ann. *Discovering the Unknown Landscape: A History of America's Wetlands.* Washington, D.C.: Island Press, 1997.

Vitousek, Peter M., Carla M. D'Antonio, Lloyd L. Loope, and Randy Westbrooks. "Biological Invasions as Global Environmental Change." *American Scientist* 84 (1996): 468–78.

Vitousek, Peter M., Harold A. Mooney, Jane Lubchenco, and Jerry M. Melillo. "Human Domination of Earth's Ecosystems." *Science* 277 (1997): 494–99.

Vogel, William O. "Response of Deer to Density and Distribution of Housing in Montana." *Wildlife Society Bulletin* 17 (1989): 406–13.

von Reichert, Christiane, and Gundar Rudzitis. "Multinomial Logistic Models Explaining Income Changes of Migrants to High-Amenity Counties." *The Review of Regional Studies* 22 (1992): 25–42.

Wall, Brian R. *Log Production in Washington and Oregon: An Historical Perspective.* Portland, Ore.: USDA Forest Service, Resource Bulletin, PNW-42, 1972.

Wallace, James, and Jim Erickson. *Hard Drive: Bill Gates and the Making of the Microsoft Empire.* New York: John Wiley and Sons, 1992.

Waller, Donald M. "Getting Back to the Right Nature: A Reply to Cronon's 'The Trouble with Wilderness.'" In *The Great New Wilderness Debate,* ed. J. Baird Callicott and Michael P. Nelson, 541–67. Athens: University of Georgia Press, 1998).

Waring, R. H., and J. F. Franklin. "Evergreen Coniferous Forests of the Pacific Northwest." *Science* 204 (1979): 1380–85.

Warner, Sam B., Jr. *Street Car Suburbs: The Process of Growth in Boston, 1870–1900.* New York: Atheneum, 1974.

Welch, E. B., and T. Lindell. *Ecological Effects of Wastewater: Applied Limnology and Pollutant Effects.* London: Chapman & Hall, 1992.

Wenz, Peter S. "Minimal, Moderate, and Extreme Moral Pluralism." *Environmental Ethics* 15 (1993): 61–74.

——. *Environmental Justice.* Albany: State University of New York, 1988.

Williams, Barry L. "Conservation Genetics, Extinction, and Taxonomic Status: A Case History of the Regal Fritillary." *Conservation Biology* 16 (2002): 148–57.

Wilson, Edward O. "The Current State of Biological Diversity." In *Biodiversity,* ed. Edward O. Wilson, 3–18. Washington, D.C.: National Academy Press, 1988.

Wittfogel, Karl. *Oriental Despotism: A Comparative Study of Total Power.* New Haven, Conn.: Yale University Press, 1957.

World Commission on Environment and Development. *Our Common Future.* Oxford: Oxford University Press, 1987.

World Resources Institute. *World Resources: 1998–99.* Oxford University Press, 1998.

Worster, Donald. *Rivers of Empire: Water, Aridity, and the Growth of the American West.* New York: Pantheon Books, 1985.

Zweibel, Ken. *Harnessing Solar Power: The Photovoltaics Challenge.* New York: Plenum Press, 1990.

Index

Index

About the Author

Douglas E. Booth lives in Milwaukee, Wisconsin, with his wife, Carol Brill, and his younger son, Jeremy. His older son, Edward, is off to college. After teaching for twenty-six years at Marquette University, he retired recently to spend more time working with the land trust movement and writing. While at Marquette he taught macroeconomics, environmental and natural resource economics, and a variety of other courses, and he coordinated an interdisciplinary undergraduate major and minor in urban and environmental affairs. Booth is the author of *Searching for Paradise: Economic Development and Environmental Change in the Mountain West, The Environmental Consequences of Growth: Steady-State Economics as an Alternative to Ecological Decline, Valuing Nature: The Decline and Preservation of Old-Growth Forests,* and *Regional Long Waves, Uneven Growth, and the Cooperative Alternative,* as well as numerous articles. He is also a founding board member of the Driftless Area Land Conservancy, a land trust located in southwestern Wisconsin. In his spare time, Booth loves to backpack, hike, and botanize.